# New forms of work organisation

## *Can Europe realise its potential?*

**Results of a survey
of direct employee
participation in Europe**

# New forms of work organisation

## *Can Europe realise its potential?*

**Results of a survey
of direct employee
participation in Europe**

*Prepared by the EPOC Research Group*

**EUROPEAN FOUNDATION**

**for the Improvement of Living and Working Conditions**

Wyattville Road, Loughlinstown, Co. Dublin, Ireland
Tel: +353 1 204 3100  Fax: +353 1 282 6456/282 4209
E-mail: postmaster@eurofound.ie.

The paper used in this book is chlorine-free and comes from managed forests in Northern Europe. For every tree felled, at least one new tree is planted.

Cataloguing data can be found at the end of this publication
Luxembourg: Office for Official Publications of the European Communities, 1997

ISBN 92-828-1888-8

Printed in Ireland.

# Foreword

In recent years there has been a growing interest in new forms of organising work which would make European enterprises more competitive on the global markets. As part of this new interest in organisational efficiency, direct participation arrangements, such as total quality management, quality circles, team work and re-engineering, have gained in popularity. The indications are that this new direct approach to employee involvement is of benefit, not only to the organisation, but also to the workforce. For enterprises there is the increased efficient use of the human resource and for workers the possibility of more meaningful jobs and a greater input into the workplace issues which directly effect their working lives. Unions and employers in Europe, in showing a greater interest in direct participation, are seeking to develop a social model which is unique to Europe and in contrast to the emergence of workplace models in other trading blocks.

In order to address these developments, the European Foundation for the Improvement of Living and Working Conditions initiated the EPOC Project (**E**mployee direct **P**articipation in **O**rganisational **C**hange). The objective of this project is to research the trend towards more direct participation in European enterprises, to provide information which would feed into the debate, between the social partners and the European Union institutions, on the most appropriate form of work organisation for Europe.

So far the Foundation has produced four publications as part of this ongoing research project. The first report presented the conceptual framework of the EPOC Project. The second publication was based on an analysis of research into the attitudes and understanding of the social partners, in EU Member States, and the extent to which the application of direct participation can influence the humanisation of work while, at the same time, increase profitability.

The third report reviewed empirical research into direct participation in Europe, the United States and Japan and gives an overview of the existing knowledge on the topic. It examines the extent of the Japanese 'Toyota' model and contrasts it with the Scandinavian 'Volvo' model of work organisation and has the most extensive literature review on this subject yet published in Europe.

Having carried out these research projects the Foundation paused to take stock and a summary of the results so far was published in a booklet in 1996, which drew together all the knowledge EPOC had contributed to the debate. However, many questions were still un- answered and knowledge gaps remained, so the fill these gaps the Foundation carried out a survey of management, in ten Member States, as to the extent and nature of direct participation within their establishments. The responses to this survey have provided a wealth of information and this publication is the first report of the analysis of these results.

This report comes at an opportune time in the debate on work organisation within the European Union. In April, 1997, the European Commission published a Green (discussion) Paper entitled *Partnership for a New Organisation of Work*. This publication is a significant contribution by the European policy makers to the debate on new forms of work organisation. of work. It sets as one of its main objectives improvement in the competitiveness of European enterprises by considering the challenge facing management to reconcile security for workers with the flexibility which enterprises requires in the modern business world.

It includes a recognition that there is a need for a 'replacement of hierarchical and rigid structures by more innovative and flexible structures' and that there is a role of direct participation in 'the scope for improving employment and competitiveness through a better organisation of work at the workplace, based on high skill, high trust and high quality'. In effect, organisational change has to be based on partnership and trust.

The Green Paper raises a number of policy options, for discussion, which would 'support rather than hinder, fundamental organisational renewal and how to strike a productive balance between the interests of business and the interests of workers, thereby facilitating the modernisation of working life'.

This EPOC report is a significant input into the discussion now focused on the policy debate by the Green Paper. It provides, for the first time, among the results, detailed information on the extent of the different types of direct participation, its economic and social impact, the attitudes of European management to it as a process for the efficient organisation of work and the results of involving workers and their representatives in the process of change. As a further step in the analysis of the results of this survey the Foundation will, in the future, examine what constitutes a participative enterprise in the context of the emerging European social model.

| | |
|---|---|
| Clive Purkiss | Eric Verborgh |
| Director | Deputy Director |

# Contributors

Keith Sisson (Editor)
*IRRU, Warwick Business School*

Alain Chouraqui
*LEST-CNRS, Aix-en-Provence*

Dieter Fröhlich
*ISO-Institut, Cologne*

Adelheid Hege
*IRES, Paris*

Fred Huijgen
*Nijmegen Business School*

Hubert Krieger
*European Foundation for the Improvement of Living and Working Conditions*

Kevin O'Kelly
*European Foundation for the Improvement of Living and Working Conditions*

Ulrich Pekruhl
*Institut Arbeit und Technik, Gelsenkirchen*

Georges Spyropoulos
*formerly of the ILO*

# Preface

Mindful of the growing debate about the importance of direct participation, in 1992 the European Foundation for the Improvement of Living and Working Conditions launched a major investigation into its nature and extent and its role in organisational change. Details of the objectives of investigation, known as the EPOC project, together with the names of the researchers involved, will be found in Appendix 1.

Activities in the first phase included:

- work on the concept of direct participation to make it more accessible to empirical research;

- a study of the attitudes and approaches of the Social Partners throughout Europe in 1993-94 involving around 200 interviews with senior representatives of the peak organisations and employers' organisations and trade unions in two main sectors, i.e. engineering and banking;

- an appraisal of available research in the USA and Japan as well as EU member countries to establish the current state of knowledge and understanding of direct participation; and

- round-tables and conferences of Social Partner and national government representatives in Dublin in February 1995, Lisbon in June 1996, Dublin in October 1996 and Amsterdam in April 1997 to discuss the general issues and a number of case studies;

The major activity in the second phase, which is reported on here, has been the design, implementation and analysis of a representative postal survey of workplaces in ten EU countries with the objective of helping to fill the information gap identified in the Social Partner and literature studies.

Many people helped to make the survey possible. Especially important were members of the EPOC Advisory Committee (i.e. representatives of the ETUC, UNICE and national governments nominated by the European Foundation's Advisory Board). Their guidance and support was invaluable at every stage - winning the necessary funds, designing the questionnaire and writing up the results. Warm thanks are also due to the nearly 5,800 managers who took the time to compete the questionnaire; but for them there would be nothing to report.

EPOC Research Group

# Contents

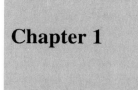

# Chapter 1 Introducing the EPOC survey

This report presents the preliminary results of the EPOC survey into direct employee participation in the EU. It is an interim report in the sense that it is intended to be the first rather than the last word on the subject; the EPOC survey is an immensely rich data source and more detailed studies will follow. The survey, which was commissioned by the European Foundation for the Improvement of Living and Working Conditions, is the most comprehensive review of its kind. A standard questionnaire, translated with the help of industrial relations 'experts', was posted to a representative sample of workplaces in ten EU member countries. Altogether, some 5,800 managers, from manufacturing and services, and the public and the private sector, responded. The size threshold was 20 or 50 employees depending on country. The respondent was either the general manager or the person he or she felt was the most appropriate. The main subject of the questions was the largest occupational group.

## 1.1 The significance of direct participation

The survey, along with the other work of EPOC described in Appendix 1, has its origins in the debate on work organisation, which saw a strong revival throughout the industrialised world in the 1980s and 1990s. New ideas and practices came to prominence. *Human Resource Management* (HRM), *Total Quality Management* (TQM), *lean production*, *flexible organisation* and *empowerment* are just some of the terms that have become part of today's language of industrial relations.

The key process at the heart of many of these developments is the direct participation of employees. Direct participation, to use the short-hand, has a long history in Europe. Trade unions have campaigned for decades for greater industrial democracy in the workplace – including, at times, demands for full workers' control or self-management – as well as improved working conditions. Such campaigns, particularly pronounced in the 1970s, have played an important role in raising awareness of quality of working life (QWL) issues. In the 1950s and 1960s, acclaimed management-inspired experiments in the Scandinavian countries, including the introduction of group work at Volvo and Saab in Sweden, sought to overcome problems of turnover and absenteeism by encouraging greater employee involvement in the organisation of work. Significant government initiatives to promote this employee involvement include the *Humanisierung der Arbeit* in Germany in the mid 1970s and similar national programmes in France and the Scandinavian countries. At the international level, bodies such as the International Labour Organisation have also been very active to the same end.

As the executive summary reporting the first phase results of the EPOC project emphasised (Sisson, 1996:3), however, the novelty is the unprecedented widespread management interest in using direct participation to improve business performance. In the words of one commentator (Osterman, 1994:173), the need for direct participation in the organisation of work has become a 'new conventional wisdom'. Severe economic pressures confronting EU member states in recent years lie behind the present interest. Lack of stable markets, coupled with the continuous erosion of competitive positions in key sectors, has set the context. In particular, the speed with which Japanese enterprises have successfully penetrated world markets for motor vehicles and electronics using direct participation, simultaneously, to improve quality and reduce costs has led to a fundamental re-appraisal of traditional work organisation.

So-called 'Taylorist' or 'Fordist' work organisations are deemed to be incompatible with the market needs of quality production and flexible specialisation. Hierarchical structures are inefficient in separating decision making from doing and extremely expensive in adding several tiers of managers who add little value. Specialisation, in which tasks, jobs and functions are defined as narrowly as possible, produces inflexibility rather than the flexibility increasingly required. Bureaucracy, with its emphasis on rules and procedures, promotes control and compliance at the expense of the commitment and co-operation essential to continuous improvement. In Peters' (1987:302-3) uncompromising words, 'the only possible implementers' of a strategy of quality production are 'committed, flexible, multi-skilled, constantly re-trained people, joined together in self-managed teams'.

In the circumstances, it is perhaps not surprising that for policy makers direct participation has begun to assume a fundamental significance. The European Commission's Green Paper *Partnership for a new organisation of work* published in April 1997 reminds us that the 1993 White Paper on *Growth, Competitiveness and Employment* highlighted organisational capacity as one of the key components of a firm's competitiveness; while the European Council meeting in Essen in 1994 stressed the need to increase the employment intensity of growth, in particular by a 'more flexible organisation of work in a way which fulfils both the wishes of employees and the requirements of competition' (p.1).

The Green Paper itself marks a most important step in policy makers' recognition of the significance of direct participation. In its own words,

> It is about the scope for improving employment and competitiveness through a better organisation of work at the workplace, based on high skill, high trust and high quality. It is about the will and ability of management and workers to take initiatives, to improve the quality of goods and services, to make innovations and to develop the production process and consumer relations.

> The purpose ... is to stimulate a European debate on new forms of organisation of work to release this potential.

It notes that:

> There are already a number of case studies demonstrating the potential for productivity and prosperity of a new organisation of work. However, the great majority of firms – and public authorities – are still in the traditional form of organisation. The diffusion of new practices seems to be slow.

The Green Paper raises a number of policy challenges to which the final chapter of this report returns. Significant, too, is the choice of the principal means to deal with them: the building of a partnership for a new organisation of work involving the social partners and public authorities.

> The Green Paper invites the social partners and public authorities to seek to build a partnership for the development of a new framework for the modernisation of work. Such a partnership could make a significant contribution to achieving the objective of a productive, learning and participative organisation of work.

> The word "framework" should be given a broad interpretation. It could include everything from the creation of a common understanding of the importance of new forms of work organisation, through joint declarations, to binding contractual or legal initiatives (Executive Summary).

The Green Paper's objective might be interpreted as the development of a 'European social model'. As well as involving a high degree of social partnership, such a model offers the opportunity to exploit sources of competitive advantage, such as the education and skills of the workforce, to produce high quality goods and services at the same time as satisfying employees' long-standing demands for more challenging and rewarding jobs, together with on-going training and development opportunities. Ideologically, as well as practically, it has come to be regarded as the only realistic alternative to the model of a highly deregulated labour market combined with a low-wage employment growth associated with the USA. In the European context, this would mean lowering wages and living standards to socially and politically unacceptable levels (see also Lange, 1992).

The significance of direct participation is widely recognised by the social partners as EPOC's study of their views (Regalia, 1995) and the reports of the direct participation European Round Tables sponsored by the European Foundation confirm. There was a measure of consensus about the objectives of direct participation, as well as widespread understanding of what was involved, even though different labels were used and concerns expressed that there was sometimes a down-side in the form of work intensification, stress and self-exploitation. Employer representatives often emphasised the social, as well as the economic, benefits of direct participation, while their trade union counterparts did not limit their expectations to improving working conditions, but also mentioned improved economic performance. This suggests, at the very least, a shared industrial relations culture and, in some cases, increasing co-operation between the social partners. Some employer representatives even agreed with their trade union colleagues that the definition of direct participation used in the EPOC Project was overly 'management oriented'.

## 1.2   Defining direct participation

Direct participation is a term often used but rarely clearly defined. In keeping with the conceptual framework developed in its early days (for further details, see Geary and Sisson, 1994), the focus of the EPOC project has been on the two main forms of *direct participation*, which for the purposes of empirical enquiry can be defined as follows:

> *consultative participation* – management encourages employees to make their views known on work-related matters, but retains the right to take action or not.

> *delegative participation* – management gives employees increased discretion and responsibility to organise and do their jobs without reference back.

The essence of direct participation can be better understood by contrasting it with the other main forms of involvement and participation listed in Figure 1.1.

**Figure 1.1  Types of involvement and participation**

| information disclosure |

| financial participation |

*profit sharing*
*share ownership*

| direct participation |

*consultative*
*delegative*

| indirect or representative participation |

*joint consultation*
*co-determination*
*collective bargaining*
*worker directors*

In the contrast with information disclosure, i.e. through team briefing or company bulletin, and financial participation, i.e. profit-sharing and share ownership, the key distinguishing features are consultation and delegation. These approaches may be an integral feature of a participative strategy, but do not necessarily involve consultation or delegation. In the contrast with indirect or representative participation, the word *direct* is key; whereas *indirect* participation takes place through the intermediary of employee representative bodies, such as works councils or trade unions, direct participation involves employees themselves.

Both *consultative* and *delegative participation* can involve individual employees or groups of employees. The two forms of consultative participation can be further subdivided. Individual consultation can be 'face-to-face' or 'arms-length'; group consultation can involve temporary or permanent groups. This gives us six main forms of direct participation regardless of the particular label applied. The six forms are set out in Figure 1.2, together with examples of relevant practices from EPOC's research review (Fröhlich and Pekruhl, 1996) and round-table discussions. It is around these types that the EPOC survey's questions were structured.

**Figure 1.2  The main forms of direct participation**

- individual consultation

  *'face-to-face'*: arrangements involving discussions between individual employee and immediate manager, such as regular performance reviews, regular training and development reviews and '360 degree' appraisal;

  *'arms-length'*: arrangements which allow individual employees to express their views through a 'third party', such as a 'speak-up' scheme with 'counsellor' or 'ombudsman', or through attitude surveys and suggestion schemes

- group consultation

  *'temporary' groups*: groups of employees who come together for a specific purpose and for a limited period of time, e.g. 'project groups' or 'task forces'

  *'permanent' groups*: groups of employees that discuss various work related topics on an ongoing basis, such as quality circles

- individual delegation

  individual employees are granted extended rights and responsibilities to carry out their work without constant reference back to managers – sometimes known as 'job enrichment'

- group delegation

  rights and responsibilities are granted to groups of employees to carry out their common tasks without constant reference back to managers – most often known as 'group work'.

## 1.3  The rationale for the EPOC survey

Surprising as it may seem, the debate about the significance of direct participation has taken place in something of a vacuum. As EPOC's social partner and literature studies clearly demonstrated, it was not just that there is a great deal of conceptual ambiguity – different commentators using different labels to describe the same phenomenon; a myriad of definitions of what is essentially the same practice. The data currently available do not allow us to establish the nature and extent of what has been happening, let alone compare and contrast the experience of different countries. There have been relatively few surveys providing data even on the incidence of the practices associated with direct participation. Moreover, most of these have been country-specific and concerned with manufacturing only; very few have included the service sector, either private or public, where the majority of the workforce is now employed. The survey results are also hardly comparable, such has been the extreme diversity in substance and methods as well as depth of measurement and analysis. It was to help fill this vacuum that the EPOC questionnaire survey, reproduced in Appendix 2, was designed and implemented.

Of course, no questionnaire survey can answer all the questions on a topic. It is virtually impossible with a questionnaire survey, for example, to get any impression of the process, especially the historical process, involved in an activity as complex as direct participation A postal questionnaire also has major weaknesses compared with an interview survey: it cannot be too long otherwise people will not bother to return it; and it cannot respond to the interviewee's need to clarify a question or take into account the complexity of an answer. A postal questionnaire is, nonetheless, a practical way of getting representative data from a large population and, more to the immediate point, it can help to improve our knowledge and understanding in many of the areas identified in the balance sheet drawn up in the executive summary of the first phase results of the EPOC project, viz.

- **The nature and extent of direct participation.** What is the incidence of direct participation – which workplaces practice which forms? What is the coverage of direct participation – how many employees are involved? What is the scope of direct participation – how extensive is the range of issues on which employees are consulted or given rights to make decisions? how much autonomy do groups have to decide their members and the issues they discuss and/decide? Do the incidence, coverage and scope of direct participation vary by sector, size and country? Does direct participation have generalised application or is it associated with organisations in particular markets using particular technology? Which form of direct participation do managers think is most important?

- **Motives.** What are managers' main motives for introducing direct participation? What weight do managers put on direct participation to improve business performance, on the one hand, and enhance the quality of working life, on the other? How important in the introduction of direct participation are the demands of employees and employee organisations? How important in the introduction of direct participation are the requirements of collective agreements and legislation?

- **The links with organisational strategies.** What are the links between the practice of direct participation and the organisational strategies being pursued by the workplaces in the EPOC survey? What is the extent of the other initiatives, apart from direct participation, which managers are taking in the light of the changing environment? Is competition the driving force behind the introduction of direct participation? Are multinational companies at the forefront of the introduction of direct participation?

- **The effects of direct participation.** What do managers think are the effects of direct participation on key business performance indicators such as output, costs and quality? Do they think that direct participation has had an effect on sickness and absenteeism? Do they think it has had an effect on the numbers of employees and the number of managers? Are some forms of direct participation regarded as more effective than others? Is the application of multiple forms of direct participation seen to be more effective than that of individual forms?

- **The regulation of direct participation.** To what extent are employees and/or their representatives involved in the introduction of direct participation? With which representative body does any negotiation take place – a works council or a trade union? To what extent does this involvement influence the design and implementation of direct participation? How do managers value this involvement?

- **Qualification and training.** What is the relationship between the qualification of employees and direct participation? Is the scope of direct participation related to the qualification of employees? Does qualification make for more effective direct participation? How important is the training of employees for direct participation? How important is the training of managers for direct participation?

- **Remuneration systems.** What is the relationship between the remuneration system and direct participation? Is the scope of direct participation related to particular types of remuneration system? Do some types of remuneration system make for more effective direct participation than others?

## 1.4   The plan of the report

The next chapter describes the methodology of the survey and chapter 3 gives brief details of the respondents' workplaces and their activities. Each of the seven chapters which follow presents the results of the EPOC survey in the areas discussed above. Chapter 4 deals with the nature and extent of direct participation. Chapter 5 considers management's motives for introducing direct participation. Chapter 6 discusses the links between direct participation and the organisation's wider strategy. Chapter 7 reports management's views on the effects of direct participation. Chapter 8 focuses on the regulation of direct participation. Chapter 9 investigates the significance of qualification and training, while Chapter 10 does the same for remuneration systems. Chapter 11 offers our first thoughts on some of the implications of the results.

In the interests of keeping the results digestible, key points are highlighted in boxes at the beginning of the relevant sections. Also a number of the more detailed tables referred to in the text will be found in Appendix 3 and most of the percentages here and elsewhere have been rounded up or down to the nearest whole number. References have been kept to a minimum as well.

## References

European Commission. 1997. Green Paper, *Partnership for a new organisation of work.*

Fröhlich, D. and U. Pekruhl. 1996: *Direct Participation and Organisational Change – Fashionable but Misunderstood? An analysis of recent research in Europe, Japan and the USA.* EF/96/38/EN. Luxembourg: Office for the Official Publications of the European Communities.

Geary, J. and K. Sisson. 1994: *Conceptualising Direct Participation in Organisational Change. The EPOC Project.* EF/94/23/EN. Luxembourg: Office for the Official Publications of the European Communities.

Lange, P. 1992. 'The politics of the social dimension' in A. Sbragia (ed) *Euro-Politics: institutions and policy making in the 'new' European Community.* Washington: The Brookings Institute.

Osterman, P. 1994. 'How Common is Workplace Transformation and How can we explain who adopts it: Results from a National Survey?' *Industrial and Labor Relations Review,* Vol. 47, No. 2, 173-88.

Peters, T. 1987. *Thriving on Chaos: Handbook for a Management Revolution.* London: Macmillan.

Regalia, I. 1995. *Humanise Work and Increase Profitability? Direct participation in organisational change viewed by the social partners in Europe.* EF/95/21/EN. Luxembourg: Office for the Official Publications of the European Communities.

Sisson, K. 1996. *Closing the Gap – Ideas and Practice. Direct Participation in Organisational Change.* EF/96/15/EN. Luxembourg: Office for the Official Publications of the European Communities.

# Chapter 2　Methodology

## 2.1　The Respondents

The survey was planned to be representative of workplaces in as many countries as the budget would reasonably allow taking into account a range of different populations and geographical positions. The ten countries finally chosen were: Denmark, France, Germany, Ireland, Italy, the Netherlands, Portugal, Spain, Sweden and the UK. The choice of the workplace as the level and the general manager as the immediate target is explained by the overall aim of the survey – which was to gather as much data as possible about what was happening in practice. A survey directed at higher levels in the organisation was unlikely to have produced such information and there was some concern that small workplaces in particular might not have a personnel manager. In any event, the general manager was invited to complete the questionnaire him/herself or to pass it on to the manager most capable of doing so.

In targeting managers only, and not employees or their representatives as well, the EPOC survey is open to the criticism that its results are one-sided. Much as the EPOC Research Group would like to have included employee representatives especially in the survey, the costs of doing so proved to be prohibitive. In many workplaces it would have been necessary to get a response from more than one employee representative and in some countries there would have also been enormous complexity in identifying the most appropriate respondent(s).

The omission of employee respondents is perhaps not as much of a weakness as it might at first appear, however. The main objective of the EPOC survey was to establish the nature and extent of direct participation. The experience of the European Foundation's survey on *Workplace Involvement in Technological Innovation in the European Community* (Fröhlich, Gill and Krieger 1993), which involved responses from almost 4,000 employee representatives as well as from an identical number of managers, showed a high consensus about factual issues between both groups of workplace respondents. Also a unique feature of the EPOC survey was that it did not simply ask about the incidence of direct participation, which managers might have been tempted to exaggerate. Questions designed to estimate the coverage, scope and intensity of the processes involved, as Chapter 4 will demonstrate, helped to ensure a balanced picture.

## Key points:

- ten countries were involved in the EPOC survey: Denmark, France, Germany, Ireland, Italy, the Netherlands, Portugal, Spain, Sweden and the UK

- respondents were workplace general managers or the manager he/she felt was the most appropriate

- the focus was the workplace's largest occupational group

- the size threshold was 25 employees in the case of the smaller countries and 50 in the case of the larger

- the total number of respondents was almost 5,800

- the overall response rate for the ten countries was almost 18 per cent – with a range between 9 per cent (Spain) and 39 per cent (Ireland)

The survey, it must also be remembered, comprises only one strand of the EPOC project. Readers who would like information on the reaction to and experience of employees of direct participation are reminded that the EPOC literature review (Fröhlich and Pekruhl, 1996) contains such information not only for European countries but also Japan and the USA; while an analysis of the views of trade union representatives in the 15 EU member countries will be found in EPOC's social partners study (Regalia, 1995).

## 2.2   The organisation of the survey

The questionnaire, which is reproduced in full in Appendix 2, was initially drawn up in English by members of the research group, with the help of a team from the Industrial Relations Research Unit at the University of Warwick, and translated by themselves and trusted experts into the other languages. Tenders to administer it were invited in the Official Journal of the European Union in September 1995. In December 1995, INTOMART, representing GfK Europe, and based in Hilversum (the Netherlands), was commissioned to do the job. With INTOMART's help , the questionnaire was pre-tested in the ten countries in the winter of 1995 and the spring of 1996.

The pre-test questionnaire which, like the main questionnaire, was directed to the general manager, had two objectives: to test the validity of the questions through 50 face-to-face interviews (five in each country): and to test the appropriateness of the mailing procedure through about 1,000 mailed questionnaires (around 100 in each country). In the first instance, the specific questions were:

•   Did the respondents think the questionnaire properly covered direct participation strategies and practices within the workplace?

•   Did respondents find the questions clear and unambiguous?

In the second, the questions were:

•   To what extent was the mailing procedure likely to generate the expected return rate per country?

•   Was the general manager the 'right' person to target?

The results of the pre-test suggested that the mailing procedure was likely to achieve the hoped-for response and that the general manager was the most appropriate recipient. Some respondents found several of the original questions ambiguous, however, and so the questionnaire was changed and adapted in April and May 1996. The covering letter was also changed to make the questionnaire more attractive for organisations that did not practice direct participation and, to give the survey more authority, the EU Social Affairs Commissioner, Padraig Flynn, kindly agreed to contribute an accompanying letter emphasising its importance.

## 2.3   Details of the main survey

The gross sample of workplaces, drawn up by the national GfK members, differed for the ten countries according to population size, the number of employees in industry and services, and the number of workplaces with 20 or more employees (for the smaller and medium-sized countries) and 50 or more employees (for the larger ones). For the larger countries (France, Germany, Italy, Spain, the UK) the gross sample was 5,000 workplaces; for the medium countries (Denmark, the Netherlands and Sweden) 2,500 and for the smaller countries (Ireland and Portugal) 1,000.

The mailing was carried out in two full waves, including the questionnaire and the accompanying letter, followed by one additional reminder letter. The first questionnaires were mailed in the beginning of June 1996. Because of the varying times of summer holidays, an additional mailing was carried out in certain countries with a lower response rate in October 1996, focusing on particular sectors. The additional mailing used the original representative sample.

Each of the national GfK member institutions drew up the final gross samples for their respective countries. Table 2.1 holds the final gross sample figures, the net samples (gross sample minus 'return to sender'), the number of returned questionnaires and the response rate per country. The response rate in column 4 is based on columns 2 and 3.

**Table 2.1  Sample sizes and questionnaire returns**

|  | gross sample | net sample | questionnaire returns | response |
|---|---|---|---|---|
|  | absolute nos | absolute nos | absolute nos | % |
| Denmark | 2,600 | 2,535 | 674 | 26.6 |
| France | 5,028 | 4,870 | 598 | 12.3 |
| Germany | 4,954 | 4,887 | 826 | 16.9 |
| Ireland | 1,000 | 984 | 382 | 38.8 |
| Italy | 3,949 | 3,849 | 499 | 13.0 |
| Netherlands | 2,386 | 2,303 | 505 | 21.9 |
| Portugal | 1,000 | 996 | 298 | 29.9 |
| Spain | 5,062 | 4,872 | 460 | 9.4 |
| Sweden | 2,448 | 2,401 | 732 | 30.5 |
| United Kingdom | 5,000 | 4,881 | 812 | 16.6 |
| Total | 33,427 | 32,582 | 5,786 | 17.8 |

From the gross-sample of 33,427 questionnaires, 845 (2.5 per cent) were returned to sender by the different postal services either because the address was wrong or unknown, or the addressee had moved to an unknown address, or the company had ceased to exist altogether. By 15 November 1996, 5,786 questionnaires had been returned and it was on the basis of these that the data analysis took place.

In data analysis, the remaining sample distortions regarding sector and size of the workplace were weighted for each sector/size cell to reflect the original research universe. The sample distortions between countries were corrected by a weighting factor that accounted for the number of employees represented in the data set for each country and the overall size of the workforce in that country.

Figure 2.1: EPOC and Price-Waterhouse-Cranfield survey response rates

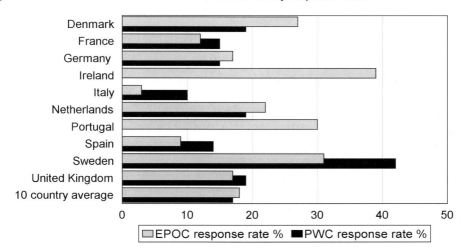

Note: PWC response rate for Ireland and Portugal not available:
(Price-Waterhouse-Cranfield: Switzerland 16%, Norway 28%)

## 2.4 Assessment of the response

The number of explicit refusals was very low: only about 400 potential respondents indicated that they were not willing to co-operate. On the basis of remarks made by respondents either on the telephone or in the questionnaire, direct participation was regarded as a subject of some importance. In addition, a large number of respondents (47 per cent) responded positively to the question asking if they would like to receive a summary of the results.

An overall return rate of 18 per cent was not as high as the Research Group hoped for. It is not out of line, however, with the only comparable cross-national survey of Price-Waterhouse-Cranfield (PWC) carried out in 1991 at company level. Like the EPOC survey, this was a postal survey. Its overall return rate of usable questionnaires was 17.1 per cent, which is almost identical to the EPOC response rate. Figure 2.1 compares the results of the two surveys in detail.

It will be seen that the EPOC response rates for France, Spain, Sweden and the United Kingdom were below the PWC equivalents. Setting aside Ireland and Portugal, which were not included in the PWC study, the return rates of the remaining countries were higher in the EPOC survey.

Additional information from similar national surveys is also instructive:

- a **German** national postal survey on the same topic in the production sector had an identical response rate to that of the EPOC survey: 18 per cent (cf. ISI 1996).

- an earlier **Dutch** national postal survey on a similar topic (Muffels, Heinen and van Mil 1982) had a return rate of 28 per cent which is higher than that of the EPOC survey (22 per cent).

- the EPOC survey's response rate for **Portugal** (30 per cent) is very high. A similar postal survey carried out by Kovacs, Cerdeira and Moniz (1992) had a return rate of 12 per cent.

- high return rates seem to be the norm in **Sweden**. The EPOC rate for this country (31 per cent) is below that of the PWC survey (42 per cent), but it approaches the figure (34 per cent) of a recent national postal survey on flexible organisations (NUTEK 1996).

Thus, with the exception of Portugal, the return rates for Germany, the Netherlands and Sweden data were not out of line with what appears to be the norm for these countries. Taking the PWC study in addition, the rates for France, the United Kingdom and Spain in particular seem to be somewhat below expectations.

Comparable though it may be, an 18 percent overall return rate raises the question of how far the estimated parameters of interest suffer from a probability bias. In other words, are the workplaces with direct participation under-represented or over-represented in the EPOC results? Are the data negatively or positively biased? This issue was investigated recently in a project, undertaken by NUTEK, dealing with the spread and functioning of 'flexible organisations' in Sweden in preparation for the G7-summit in France in early summer 1996. The representative survey had a response rate of 34 per cent, which is very close to that of the EPOC survey for Sweden. To evaluate the representativity of the data, telephone follow-ups were made to try to establish the degree of flexibility in non-respondent organisations. The verdict was that, 'The non-response sample seems to have a larger proportion of workplaces defined as a flexible work organisation' as compared to the respondents (NUTEK, 1996, p.195, cf. also p.198). In other words, the survey results underestimated the extent of flexible organisations in Sweden.

It does not necessarily follow that the same is true of the EPOC results. It simply suggests that under-representation is a possibility as is over-representation. There is no reason to believe that the EPOC results are biased one way or the other.

## 2.5 Statistical techniques

In this interim report, the results have been presented largely in descriptive form in the interests of speedy and digestible presentation. Refined statistical techniques have not been used. They will be employed in subsequent and more detailed analyses of the results.

### References

Fröhlich, D., C. Gill and H. Krieger 1993: *Workplace Involvement in Technological Innovation in the European Community*, volume I: *Roads to Participation*, Luxembourg.

Fröhlich, D., and U. Pekruhl. 1996: *Direct Participation and Organisational Change – Fashionable but Misunderstood? An analysis of recent research in Europe, Japan and the USA.* Luxembourg.

G. Lay, C. Dreher, and S. Kinkel 1996: *Neue Produktionskonzepte leisten einen Beitrag zur Sicherung des Standorts Deutschland. Mitteilungen aus der Produktionsinnovationserhebung*, Fraunhofer Institut Systemtechnik und Innovationsforschung, Karlsruhe, Juli 1966.

Muffels, R., T. Heinen and G. van Mil 1982: *Werkoverleg en werkstructurering en de subsidieregeling arbeidsplaatsverbetering: En onderzoek bij bedrijven met meer dan 100 personeelsleden*, IVA, Tilburg.

Kovacs, I., C. Cerdeira and A. Brandao Moniz 1992: *Technological and Work Organisational Change in the Portuguese Industry*, Lisbon: G.G.I, G.G.T.p.e.Ceso I&D, Programme PEDIP.

NUTEK 1996: *Towards Flexible Organisations*, Stockholm.

THE PRICE WATERHOUSE CRANFIELD PROJECT on International Strategic Human Resource Management, Report 1991, Cranfield.

Regalia, I., 1995. *Humanise Work and Increase Profitability? Direct participation in organisational change viewed by the social partners in Europe.* EF/95/21/EN. Luxembourg: Office for the Official Publications of the European Communities.

# Chapter 3

# The workplaces and their activities

This chapter gives an overview of the basic characteristics of the workplaces in the EPOC survey. In doing so, it focuses on the contrasts between the workplaces *with* and *without* direct participation. It describes both groups in terms of their sector and size. It typifies their workforces and their tasks. It compares their competitive situation. It investigates the implications of their ownership. A final section offers a preliminary breakdown of some of the results by country.

The reference point for the contrast is the incidence of *any* of the forms of direct participation introduced in Chapter 1. Data on the incidence of the *various* forms, along with their coverage, scope and intensity, are left for Chapter 4. Detailed analysis of the topics raised in this chapter is dealt with in the following chapters.

## 3.1 Sector and size

Most of our knowledge about direct participation derives from the paramount interest of public commentators and social scientists alike in industry and, in particular, metal working and automotives. The EPOC survey data in Table 3.1 are important in reminding us that the centre of employment in all developed countries has moved away from industry and is now concentrated in services. Across the 10 countries, industry accounted for only 36 per cent of all workplaces and construction for another 7 per cent. Services, by contrast, had no fewer than 57 per cent or nearly six out of ten.

Table 3.1 shows, too, that the share of workplaces practising direct participation was comparatively lower in industry and construction than in most service sectors. This was particularly true of wholesale, banking and insurance, professional services and public administration, health and social welfare, which had comparatively high shares of direct participation. Only in hotels and catering, public utilities and culture, recreation and leisure was the pattern more similar to industry. Chapter 4 discusses the breakdown by sector in greater detail.

**Table 3.1  The workplaces by sector**

|  | *all* workplaces | workplaces *with* direct participation | workplaces *without* direct participation |
|---|---|---|---|
|  | % | % | % |
| mining | 0.4 | 0.4 | 0.3 |
| manufacturing industry | 30.3 | 29.5 | 33.6 |
| process industry | 5.9 | 5.6 | 7.2 |
| construction and installation | 6.9 | 5.9 | 11.3 |
| wholesale | 9.1 | 9.6 | 7.1 |
| retail trade | 11.4 | 11.6 | 10.5 |
| catering, hotels | 1.7 | 1.7 | 2.0 |
| banking and insurance | 1.7 | 1.8 | 1.3 |
| professional services | 6.7 | 6.9 | 5.6 |
| public utilities | 2.7 | 2.5 | 3.3 |
| public administration | 7.2 | 7.5 | 6.1 |
| (public) health and social welfare | 6.2 | 7.1 | 2.6 |
| education | 4.3 | 4.8 | 2.3 |
| culture and recreation, leisure | 1.3 | 1.3 | 1.4 |
| total % | 100.0 | 100.0 | 100.0 |
| **total no** | **5,786** | **4,696** | **1,090** |

## Key findings:

• services accounted for the greater proportion of workplaces in the EPOC survey (57 per cent), industry for 36 per cent and construction for 7 per cent

• the share of workplaces with direct participation was greater in services, notably public services, than in industry or construction

• about a quarter of the workplaces had less than 50 employees, 35 per cent had between 50-99, 24 per cent between 100-199 and 19 per cent between 200 and 499; only 5.5 per cent had more than 500

• there was little variation in the incidence of direct participation by size of workplace

As for the size of the workplaces (measured in terms of the total number of employees), Figure 3.1 shows that about a quarter had less than 50 employees, the size ranges 50-99 and 100-199 accounted for a further 35 and 24 per cent respectively, while larger workplaces with more than 500 employees contributed only 5.5 per cent.

Overall, there is little variation in the incidence of direct participation by size. The medium size workplaces apply measures of direct workforce participation slightly more often than very large and particularly very small workplaces. In the case of the small workplaces, this lower figure is most likely explained by the lack of detailed bureaucratic structures and the higher degree of informality among social actors which such organisations permit.

Figure 3.1: The size of workplaces

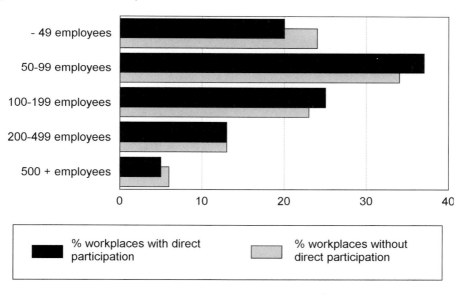

## 3.2 The workforces and their tasks

The sector variations in the incidence of direct participation raise a number of questions: Why is it that industry lags behind, despite the identification of 'Taylorist' work organisation as the bottleneck for successful (international) competition? Why has the service sector attracted so little interest, although new organisational structures seem to be more prominent?

A possible explanation involves the specific traits of the workforces, their skill structure and the nature of their tasks: under certain conditions, there might be more need or greater opportunity to involve employees. Certainly, the EPOC survey data in Figure 3.2 show that it was not workplaces relying on a manual workforce that were the leader in practising direct participation, but those with predominantly white-collar employees.

Our respondents were also asked to designate their largest number of non-managerial employees (according to given categories). Although these categories, reproduced in Figure 3.2, are not completely, unambiguous there is a clear trend: where workplaces relied mainly on production, operational and transport personnel, direct participation was (comparatively) less likely. The balance towards more participation shifts where a workplace relied mainly on higher skilled maintenance and technical personnel; when the largest occupational group was composed of white collar employees(commercial, sales, marketing) or professionals (medical, educational, administrative), such workplaces tended to engage their workforce to a comparatively large degree.

## Key findings:

- around half the employees in the largest occupational group were involved in production/ operations/transport, about 40 per cent were in commercial/ administrative/professional jobs, and the remainder in technical ones

- the largest occupational group was made up of men only in just under one in four workplaces; women were a minority in a further 43 per cent and the majority in the remaining 35 per cent

- the distribution of workplaces *with* and *without* direct participation was more or less the same for men and women

- task complexity characterised the work situation of most workplaces

- around half the workplaces were involved in a team activity

- a majority of workplaces reported the need for 'high' qualification *and* internal training of new recruits

- direct participation was more likely in workplaces with 'white collar' occupations, task complexity, team activity, high qualification and internal training

In terms of gender, the largest occupational group was made up of men only in just under one in four workplaces. Women were a minority in a further 43 per cent and the majority in the remaining 35 per cent. It also seems that, at this level of aggregation, the distribution of workplaces *with* and *without* direct participation is

Figure 3.2: Job categories of the largest occupational group - men and women

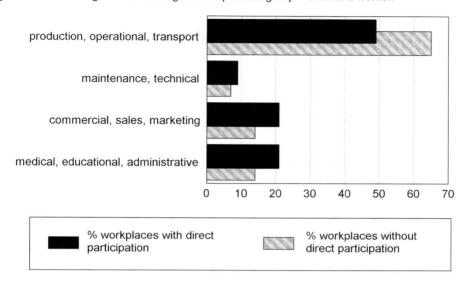

Figure 3.3: Job categories of the largest occupational group - women only

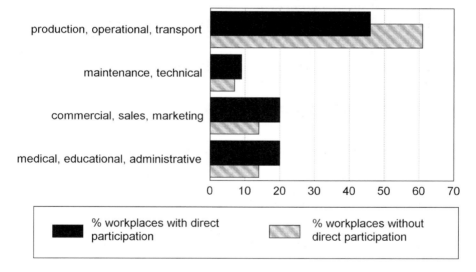

more or less the same for men and women by largest occupational group, confirming the importance of sector and occupation (see Figure 3.3).

Further support for this finding comes from the details of the task complexity of the largest occupational group and their involvement in team-based processes in Figures 3.4 and 3.5. Overall, Figure 3.4 suggests, task complexity was dominant;

repetitive work was in a clear minority position. Yet there are distinct differences between workplaces *with* and *without* direct participation. The share of 'complex' workplaces *with* (72 per cent) was distinctly higher than that of 'repetitive' ones (60 per cent). The share of 'repetitive' workplaces *without* (21 per cent) was almost double that of those *with*.

One might argue that the higher share of complex work was the result, rather than the cause, of direct participation: that these workplaces started out with more repetitive and less complex work and increased task complexity through direct participation. To test this argument, Figure 3.4 includes the data for workplaces introducing direct participation only recently (within the last two years). The data show that theses workplaces have slightly less complex and slightly more repetitive work, which supports the idea that direct participation has the potential to alter task complexities. This is only part of the story, however. It seems much more likely that workplaces with higher work complexity ventured into direct participation more often than workplaces with less complex and more repetitive work. Thus, task complexity might necessitate and enable the adoption of direct participation practices at the same time. It seems equally clear from Figure 3.5 that direct participation was practised more often in workplaces where work was essentially team-based. In both workplaces *with* and *without* direct participation, work was seen as a team rather than individual activity. Team-based work was more

Figure 3.4: The task complexity of the largest occupational group

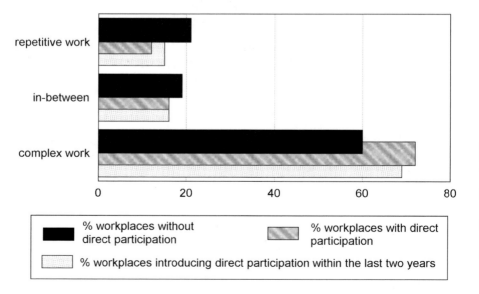

Figure 3.5: The work organisation of the largest occupational group - individual or team activity?

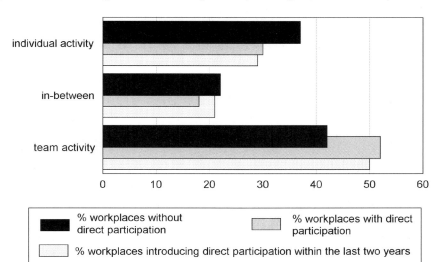

Figure 3.6: Level of qualification of the largest occupational group

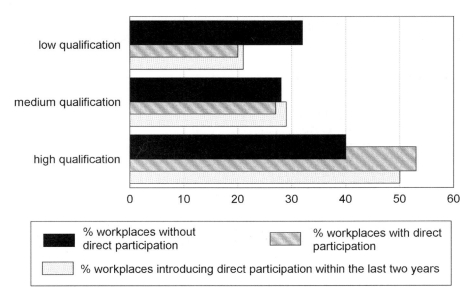

pronounced in workplaces *with* direct participation than *without*, however. Only to a minor extent, too, did team-based work seem to be the result of direct participation. Rather workplaces with team-based work were more ready to venture into direct participation, thus enforcing an already existing trend.

Figure 3.7: External and internal training of recruits to the largest occupational group

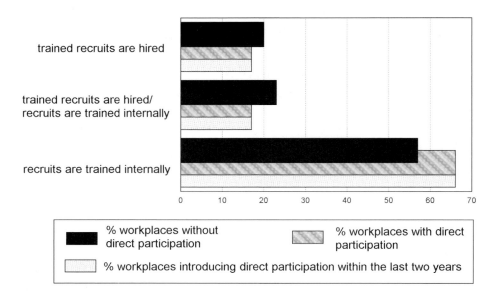

Finally, in this section, Figure 3.6 gives details of the qualification requirements for the largest occupational group. Again, it will be seen that in both workplaces *with* and *without* direct participation, the qualification requirements lean towards the high side. But, whereas only 40 per cent of those *without* typified their qualification needs as 'high', 53 per cent of those *with* did so.

Higher task complexity, more team-based work and higher qualification needs in workplaces *with* direct participation tie in with the analysis of workforce characteristics above. Both the workforce and task characteristics contribute to the fact that the service sector is leading in the adoption of direct participation policies. Certain occupations, tasks and processes seem to be more open to direct participation or need more involvement of this kind than others.

The public and scientific debate overwhelmingly indicates a need for new qualifications and continuous learning. The talk is of the *learning organisation* and *employability*. Traditional patterns of knowledge and organisational behaviour, it is argued, have become increasingly obsolete. Open communications, trust and workforce engagement and flexibility are what are required. Such organisation-specific attributes are difficult to hire on the external labour market, however. The external labour market can provide high professional qualification, but it is the internal market that has to meet the training needs of flexibility.

The EPOC survey data in Figure 3.7 offer some support for these views. Workplaces *with* direct employee participation depended on the internal training of new personnel more (66 per cent) than those *without* (57 per cent). Chapter 9 investigates the issue of qualification and training in more detail.

## 3.3 The competitive environment

It is now a commonplace to argue that increased consumer demands for high quality products and services and growing domestic, intra-European and global competition require more flexible organisation structures to survive in the competitive race and secure and increase market share. Direct participation is seen as one means to gain such organisational flexibility. Conventional wisdom, which received widespread support from EPOC's social partner and studies, would lead us to expect organisations *with* direct participation to operate under greater pressure on the price, quality, variety and service of their activities than organisations *without*.

### Key findings:

- the most important factors for competitive success were almost identical for workplaces *with* and *without* direct participation: quality (87 per cent), service (80 per cent) and variety (47 per cent); those *with* were slightly less likely to compete on the basis of price, however

- most workplaces operated under conditions of both domestic and foreign competition (40 per cent) or only domestic competition (29 per cent)

- a majority of workplaces reported competition had increased either significantly (around a half) or slightly (around a quarter)

At the level of the simple incidence of direct participation, the EPOC survey results reveal that the most important factors for competitive success were almost identical for workplaces *with* and *without* direct participation. 87 per cent of workplaces nominated 'quality' as very important, followed by 'service' (80 per cent) and 'variety of product or service' (47 per cent). Only in regard to price competitiveness is there a difference: workplaces *without* direct participation were competing on price to a larger extent (79 per cent) than those *with* (69 per cent).

As Figure 3.8 confirms, most workplaces in the EPOC survey were operating under conditions of both domestic and foreign competition (40 per cent). Given the Single European Market, this result is not surprising. More surprising is the fact that the shares of both types of workplaces in this situation, the ones *with* and *without* direct participation, differ only minimally. The same – minimal or no difference – holds true for the two other forms of competitive situation and for 'no competition'.

Figure 3.8: The competitive situation of workplaces

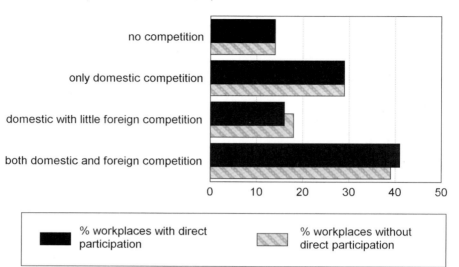

Figure 3.9: Changes in the competitive situation of workplaces

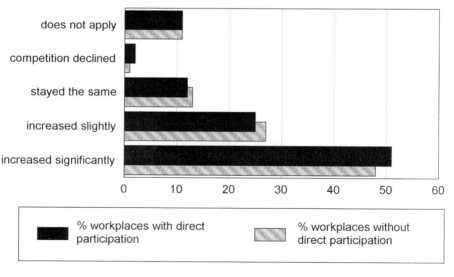

Also contrary to expectations, as Figure 3.9 confirms, the intensity of competition was very similar regardless of whether workplaces had or did not have direct participation. Most workplaces, it seems, were experiencing more competition: around a half reported competition had increased 'significantly' and a quarter 'slightly'.

Figure 3.10: Changes in e mployment and significantly increased competition

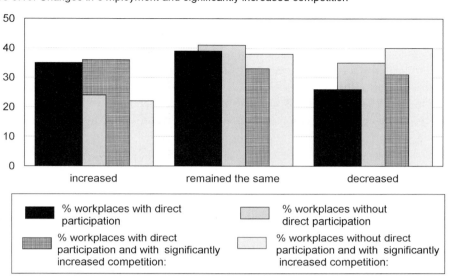

This 'non-result' is difficult to explain and will be discussed in more detail in Chapter 6. Growing competition, especially international, supposedly pushes organisations to adapt to an increasingly demanding situation by involving employees. Yet a sizeable minority – roughly 20 per cent – do not. Questions arise such as how do they cope? Do they adopt other strategies?

A partial answer comes from looking at the employment situation and its development during the last three years in Figure 3.10. The data show that in two out of five workplaces the workforce was stable over this period, regardless of whether they practised direct participation. But the workplaces differed in regard to workforce growth and decrease: 35 per cent of the workplaces *with* direct participation increased their personnel during the last three years and 26 per cent reported a reduction – a positive balance of 9 per cent. In workplaces *without* direct participation, by contrast, there was a negative balance of 11 per cent: 35 per cent reduced their workforce and only 24 per cent increased it.

One approach to dealing with increased competition seems to be a policy of cost rationalisation by workforce reduction and work intensification. This becomes particularly apparent when looking at the figures for workplaces reporting 'significantly increased competition' in Figure 3.10 showing: the positive employment balance for workplaces *with* direct participation is reduced but is still + 5 per cent. Under the same conditions, workplaces *without* direct participation make distinctly more use of workforce reductions, with a negative employment balance of 18 per cent.

The picture is more complicated than this, however. Not all workplaces *without* direct participation have a negative balance of employment. The data show, too, that many of these workplaces thrive quite well with their type of work organisation and are able to expand and increase their workforces. Chapter 7 discusses the effects of direct participation in greater detail and pays particular attention to the employment issue.

## 3.4   Ownership and the 'greenfield' issue

Our attention now turns to the ownership of the workplaces in the EPOC survey. The majority (about 53 per cent) were legally independent entities. Another third were subsidiaries of domestically-owned companies. Of particular interest in this case are foreign-owned workplaces, where the parent may be EU or non-EU-based, which amounted to about 16 per cent of the total sample. It is the subsidiaries of multinational companies (MNCs) that have attracted much of the public and scientific attention in the debate over work organisation: it is they which, supposedly, have been at the forefront of many of the changes taking place including direct participation. There is also a widespread assumption that the subsidiaries of MNCs are more likely to be 'greenfield' operations, which enhances the opportunity to make such changes.

Figure 3.11: Legal status

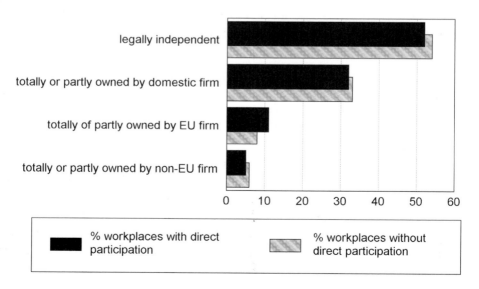

Figure 3.12: Stability and change in ownership

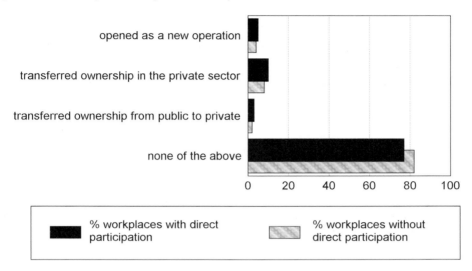

The EPOC survey data reported in Figure 3.11 support these conventional wisdoms only up to a point. In the case of EU owned subsidiaries, workplaces *with* direct participation (11 per cent) exceed those *without* (8 %). But the trend is reversed in case of workplaces owned by non-European companies (5 per cent *with* direct participation and 6 per cent *without*. The implication would seem to be that some MNCs may be influenced by other considerations, such as product markets and relative labour costs, in their choice of location rather than the potential for direct participation. A later section elaborates this point and Chapter 6 discusses the multinational company effect in more detail.

Changes in ownership might also offer opportunities for organisational change. Figure 3.12 tells us that during the previous three years the majority of workplaces – 78 per. cent across the ten countries – did not experience any change of ownership. Of those that did, there seems to be a slight trend for direct participation to be more prevalent: workplaces *with* direct participation included more of those newly created, subject to changed ownership within the private sector or privatised. The proportion of so-called 'greenfield' workplaces within the EPOC sample (around 5 per cent) shown in Figure 3.12 is clearly very small. The data do suggest one significant conclusion, however. Patently, and contrary to received wisdom, not all 'greenfield' workplaces took advantage of their new operations to introduce direct participation. Indeed, it seems that they were almost as likely not to introduce it.

**Key findings:**

- workplaces which were EU-owned subsidiaries were slightly more likely to practise direct participation, whereas those owned by non-European companies were slightly less likely to

- there was a slight trend for direct participation to be more prevalent in workplaces which had changed ownership

- not all 'greenfield' workplaces took advantage of their new operations to introduce direct participation; indeed, they were almost as likely not to introduce it

## 3.5   The ten countries in perspective

Our focus so far has been on the ten countries together. Space does not permit us to repeat the presentation of the data by country much of which, in any event, mirrors the general picture.

There are nonetheless a number of the data by country which do merit attention, either because they are intrinsically interesting or because they have a bearing on the analysis in later chapters. The first of these is the issue of qualification. As the full details in Figure 3.13 show, for high workforce qualification requirements, Denmark and Italy lead the way (71 and 67 per cent), followed by Germany, Sweden and the Netherlands (between 59 and 57 per cent). With shares between 40 and 45 per cent, Spain, Ireland and France range distinctly below the ten-country average of 53 per cent. It is the UK which stands out, however: only 29 per cent of managers indicated high qualification needs for their largest occupational group.

With one exception, too, Figure 3.13 also confirms that high qualification needs go together with the presence of direct participation. This is above all true of the Netherlands, Spain, France and Italy with differences of more than 20 per cent points between the workplaces *with* and *without* direct participation. The country which, again, stands out is the UK. In this case, the situation is reversed: 39 per cent of workplaces *without* direct participation claim the need for high workforce qualification, compared with only 27 per cent of workplaces *with*.

So far, we were unable to identify structural traits that could help us explain country differences. The competitive situation in these countries is no exception to the rule (Figure 3.14). The data tell us that in some  countries 'significantly increased competition' goes together with the practice of direct participation whereas in other countries it does not. Increased competition is distinctly (positively) related to the

Figure 3.13: High qualification requirements for the largest occupational group by country

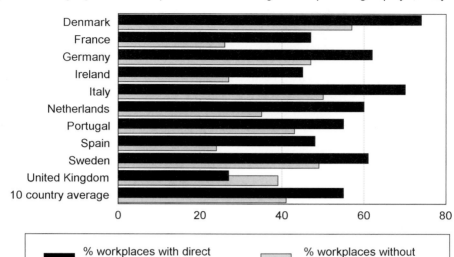

Figure 3.14: Significantly increased competition by country

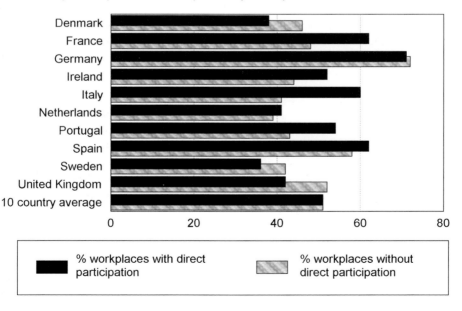

adoption of direct participation in France, Ireland, Italy and Portugal. But in Denmark, Sweden and the UK, more workplaces *without* direct participation report significantly increased competition than those *with*.

The EPOC survey data (see Tables 3.2a and 3.2b) also show that the countries differ considerably in the balance between domestically-owned and foreign-owned workplaces. Against a ten-country average of 14 per cent, Spain hosted the highest proportion of foreign-owned workplaces (24 per cent), followed by Ireland and the UK (19 per cent each). Germany, Portugal and Sweden are the countries with the lowest shares (9 per cent each).

Distinguishing between foreign-owned workplaces in regard to direct participation runs into the problem of small numbers. In most countries, the absolute numbers of such workplaces *without* direct participation was below 20; in the case of Germany, Italy and Portugal, the numbers were between 4 and 6.

These methodological constraints permit only tentative conclusions and need careful interpretation. One is that, on average, foreign-owned workplaces do not differ from domestically-owned ones in the incidence of direct participation: just as in the overall sample, 82 per cent of such workplaces had it, 18 per cent did not.

## Key findings:

- the UK had by far the smallest proportion of workplaces (29 per cent) indicating that the largest occupational group needed high qualification; the UK was also unique in that more respondents said high qualification was need in workplaces *without* direct participation than *with*

- in three countries, Denmark, Sweden and the UK, more respondents *without* direct participation reported significantly increased competition than those *with*

- against a ten-country average of 14 per cent, Spain (24 per cent) hosted the largest proportion of foreign-owned workplaces, followed by Ireland and the UK (19 per cent each); Germany, Portugal and Sweden had the lowest (9 per cent each)

- foreign-owned workplaces in Italy, the Netherlands and Sweden were more likely to practise direct participation than domestically-owned ones (93 against 87 per cent); Spain and Portugal had the highest shares of foreign-owned workplaces without direct participation followed by France and the UK

There are nonetheless distinct country differences. In Germany, Italy, the Netherlands and Sweden, the proportion of foreign owned workplaces *with* direct participation was above average (between 93 and 87 per cent). Spain and Portugal had the highest shares of foreign-owned workplaces *without* direct participation, followed by France and the UK – suggesting that relatively lower labour costs may have been an important consideration in the location decision. In any event, our overall conclusion must be that the assumption that foreign-owned workplaces are more likely to practice direct participation needs to be qualified.

## 3.6   Summary

Our initial overview of the practice of direct participation in ten European countries has placed question marks against various commonly accepted notions. The simple incidence of direct participation is wide-spread in the ten countries.

Industry is not the 'leader' in this practice, however: services have the 'pole' position. Direct participation workplaces can be characterised by having a white-collar workforce of higher qualification operating in complex task structures. Their work is strongly team-based; the workplaces' qualification needs are high and training provided for mainly within the workplace.

With the exception of price, the workplaces *with* and *without* direct participation do not differ in regard to competitive success factors such as quality of product and services, variety and service. The competitive situation is very similar too – to some extent confounding the conventional wisdom that competition is the driving force behind the introduction of direct participation. Generally speaking, workplaces *with* direct participation show increases in employment, whereas those *without* show a negative employment balance. There is a sizeable minority of workplaces *without* which have increased employment, however.

The data show, further, that another common assumption, that foreign-owned workplaces, form the spear-head of workforce involvement, is not supported. Ownership changes seem to offer some opportunities for a fresh start, however

Looking at the single countries, the UK is exceptional in that workplaces *without* direct participation have distinctly higher qualification needs than those *with*. There seems to be a trend that organisations in the 'Southern European' countries (and also Ireland) have introduced direct participation more strongly under the impact of increased competition. Elsewhere there is less evidence of the impact of competition. Indeed, in Denmark, Sweden and the UK, workplaces *without* direct participation report more intensive competition than those *with*.

### Table 3.2a  Foreign-owned workplaces by country

|  | number of foreign-owned workplaces in each country | foreign-owned workplaces as % of the total number of workplaces |
|---|---|---|
|  | no | % |
| ten-country average | 828 | 14 |
| Denmark | 101 | 15 |
| France | 91 | 15 |
| Germany | 77 | 9 |
| Ireland | 73 | 19 |
| Italy | 60 | 12 |
| Netherlands | 66 | 13 |
| Portugal | 27 | 9 |
| Spain | 110 | 24 |
| Sweden | 67 | 9 |
| United Kingdom | 156 | 19 |

### Table 3.2b  Foreign-owned workplaces by country

|  | foreign-owned workplaces *with* direct participation | foreign-owned workplaces *without* direct participation |
|---|---|---|
|  | % | % |
| ten-country average | 82 | 18 |
| Denmark | 84 | 16 |
| France | 79 | 21 |
| Germany | 90 | 10 |
| Ireland | 85 | 15 |
| Italy | 93 | 7 |
| Netherlands | 91 | 9 |
| Portugal | 74 | 26 |
| Spain | 73 | 27 |
| Sweden | 87 | 13 |
| United Kingdom | 78 | 22 |

Spain, Ireland and the UK have the largest shares of foreign-owned workplaces. But this does not necessarily mean the equation of direct participation with 'greenfield' operations: foreign-owned workplaces are no more likely to practise direct participation than domestically-owned ones. Moreover, in Portugal, Spain, the UK and France, foreign-owned workplaces were less likely, albeit only slightly, to have direct participation than domestically-owned ones. The following chapters will investigate these and other issues in more detail, beginning with the nature and extent of direct participation.

## References

Fröhlich, D. and U. Pekruhl. 1996. *Direct Participation and Organisational Change – Fashionable but Misunderstood? An analysis of recent research in Europe, Japan and the USA.* EF/96/38/EN. Luxembourg: Office for the Official Publications of the European Communities.

Regalia, I. 1995. *Humanise Work and Increase Profitability? Direct participation in organisational change viewed by the social partners in Europe.* EF/95/21/EN. Luxembourg: Office for the Official Publications of the European Communities.

# Chapter 4

# The nature and extent of direct participation

The EPOC literature study suggested that the delegative forms of direct participation had been prioritised in both the policy and scientific debates. Group work in particular was seen as the 'dominating concept' and the 'core element of new forms of work organisation' (Fröhlich and Pekruhl, 1996:79). Another major implication of the EPOC literature study was that there was a considerable gap between the rhetoric and the reality of direct participation. Direct participation may well have become, in Osterman's (1994:173) words, the 'new conventional wisdom'. Yet the conclusions of the individual surveys reported on pointed to a very different conclusion so far as practice in Europe was concerned: direct participation, it seemed, especially the more advanced forms such as semi-autonomous group working, was very much a minority movement.

The results of the EPOC survey go a long way towards answering the questions raised about the nature and extent of direct participation in Europe. They have given us a unique opportunity to map, for ten EU member countries, the three key dimensions of the forms of direct participation:

- *incidence* – which workplaces practise which forms;

- *coverage* – the proportion of employees in the largest occupational group involved in the form;

- *scope* – a dimension which takes into account the range of issues on which employees are consulted or given rights to make decisions

Additionally, the results have given us an equally unique opportunity to establish the views of our respondent managers on the most important form of direct participation at their workplace.

The EPOC results also allow us to explore in more detail than ever before the patterns of direct participation by sector. Much of the policy debate and scientific focus, it can be argued, has been 'sector-blind' – there has been almost exclusive focus on manufacturing, and within that on the automotive sector, to the neglect of services (public as well as private) where the bulk of the workforce is employed.

There are also many issues to illuminate about the position of the individual countries. For example, an issue which dominated the second EPOC Roundtable on direct participation in Lisbon in 1996, was whether there were distinctly 'Northern' and 'Southern' European patterns. Some of the conference members felt that the extent of direct participation might be expected to be less in Portugal, Spain and (to a lesser extent) Italy, reflecting special features of industrial structure (a proportionately larger number of small family-owned businesses) and a relatively recent and conflictual industrial relations system. Others, equally strongly, denied that this was the case and quoted the presence of some of the most 'advanced' workplaces in Europe in these countries.

It is with these issues that the present chapter is concerned. The chapter begins with an overview of the different dimensions of direct participation – the incidence, coverage, scope and most important forms. It then goes on to examine the results by sector. It concludes with a review of the results by country.

## 4.1   An overview of the dimensions of direct participation

*The incidence of direct participation*

At first sight, direct participation seems to be widely practised by the workplaces in the EPOC survey. Indeed, there was an unexpected high incidence of direct participation suggesting widespread organisational change. Altogether, no fewer than four out of five workplaces (82 per cent, i.e. 4,696) said that they practised at least one of the forms of direct participation. Only one in five said they did not.

### Key findings:

- four out of five workplaces practised at least one form of direct participation

- the incidence of the individual forms of participation was much higher than expected from previous surveys

- the individual and consultation forms were most prevalent – group delegation, the dominant topic of public and social science debate, was less in evidence

- relatively few workplaces appeared to be pursuing an integrated approach – only four per cent had the complete array of six forms

Table 4.1 shows the incidence of the different forms of direct participation. Two points are worthy of note. First, the incidence of the individual forms of participation was much higher than might have been expected from earlier national surveys (cf. EPOC literature study, Chapter 7). Second, it seems that the forms involving individuals and consultation were the most prevalent in our workplaces. Group delegation – the dominant topic of public and social science debate- was less widespread. This is a finding to which the chapter returns.

The figures in Table 4.1 add up to 223 per cent. This tells us that the six forms of direct employee participation were not always applied as isolated measures, but that many managements practised two or more forms at the same time. Multiple use of the different forms of direct participation might be seen as an indicator of integrated approaches such as Total Quality Management.

Although our results cannot confirm the presence of an integrated approach, they do nonetheless enable us to say something about the issue of integration. The data on the practice of multiple forms of direct participation in Table 4.2 tell us that one in four workplaces had just one form. Another quarter had two, and a further 22 per cent had three forms. This means that as many as seven out of ten workplaces had three forms or less. Only four per cent of workplaces had the complete array of six forms. On this basis, the approach to direct participation would appear to be largely partial: there were relatively few workplaces pursuing an integrated approach.

**Table 4.1    The incidence of the main forms of direct participation: ten countries**

|  | Total % |
|---|---|
| individual consultation: *'face-to-face'* | 35 |
| individual consultation: *'arm's length'* | 38 |
| group consultation: *temporary groups* | 32 |
| group consultation: *permanent groups* | 31 |
| individual delegation | 54 |
| group delegation | 33 |
| Total % | 223 |

**Table 4.2    The incidence of multiple forms of direct participation: ten countries**

|  | Total % |
|---|---|
| one form | 23 |
| two forms | 25 |
| three forms | 22 |
| four forms | 16 |
| five forms | 10 |
| six forms | 4 |
| Total % | 100 |

*The coverage of direct participation*

A further dimension which needs to be considered is the coverage of direct participation, i.e. the proportion of the largest occupational group involved in the practice of direct participation. A respondent may have indicated that their workplace practised a particular form, but this could involve only a small handful of employees or embrace the total number.

In the case of individual forms it was neither advisable nor feasible to collect data on coverage. For example, suggestion schemes that are part of 'arm's length' consultation do not easily lend themselves to measurement: these schemes are there for anyone to use, and knowing how many employees took part in attitude surveys is not very informative either.

## Key findings:

- the coverage of the three group forms of direct participation was by no means comprehensive

- in none of the three cases was more than 50 per cent of the largest occupational group involved

In the case of 'face-to-face' consultation and individual delegation, it would have been interesting to know which sections, and how many, of the workforce were involved. But here it was necessary to live with the restrictions of a postal questionnaire: such knowledge would have required a much longer and more complicated questionnaire – and our pre-test interviews had already warned us not to extend our questionnaire further. In the case of the group forms, however, it was much more feasible to ask about coverage and here it made real sense to inquire into this issue. As the EPOC literature review suggested, it is one thing for organisations to have quality circles or group work. Much more important is whether these are just some experimental or isolated applications involving relatively few employees or whether they have widespread application.

Table 4.3 presents the data on the coverage of the three main forms of group activity: the two forms of group consultation – temporary and permanent groups – and group delegation. It will be seen that the number of respondents reporting that the coverage of their temporary consultation groups was more than 50 per cent was around 48 per cent; for permanent consultation groups, it was 48 per cent; and for group delegation about 47 per cent. In short, in none of the three cases did coverage exceed 50 per cent of the largest occupational group.

**Table 4.3 The coverage of the group forms of direct participation: ten countries**

|  | % of workplaces involving 50+ per cent of their largest occupational group |
|---|---|
| group consultation: *temporary groups* | 48 |
| group consultation: *permanent groups* | 48 |
| group delegation | 47 |

*The scope of direct participation*

The EPOC survey was specifically designed to produce data not only on the incidence of direct participation, but also on its scope. Knowing that a workplace practises one of the forms of direct participation only takes us so far. It does not tell us how on many issues employees were consulted or given rights to make decisions, for example.

In the case of the main forms of individual consultation ('face-to-face' and 'arms-length') and of group consultation (temporary and permanent groups), respondents were asked on which of eight issues they consulted with employees and how often they did so ('regularly', 'sometimes and 'never'). The issues were work organisation, working time, health and safety, training and development, quality of product or service, customer relations, changes in technology and changes in investment. These items were reduced to separate indexes to scope with the categories 'low', 'medium' and 'high' for each form of employee consultation.

The measure of scope for individual delegation was based on the number of rights of individual employees to make decisions on how their own work is performed without reference to the immediate management: the rights in this case were scheduling of work, quality of product or service, improving work processes, dealing with 'internal' customers, dealing with external clients, time keeping, attendance and working conditions.

The scope measure for group delegation follows the same logic of individual delegation and was developed from the group's right to their own allocation of work, scheduling of work, quality control, time keeping, attendance and absence control, job rotation, co-ordination of work with other internal groups and improving the work process.

Also a single overall measure of scope was developed to characterise the practice of direct participation. This measure was based on combining the number of issues discussed (in the case of individual and group consultation), the number of rights granted (in case of individual and group delegation) and the number of practices of direct participation applied in a workplace. It is a rough but suitable indicator of the overall intensity of direct participation.

Particularly in the case of group delegation, but also permanent consultation groups such as quality circles, there are additional indicators like choosing the group members and the group leader or group members deciding on the issues to be discussed. These are often cited as important considerations influencing the 'quality' of such forms of participation. These items did not enter the measures of scope at this stage, but are included later when characterising different types of group delegation.

## Key findings:

- while the incidence of direct participation was widespread, the scope in terms of number of issues involved was relatively limited for each of the forms

- the proportion of workplaces with high scores for scope reached double figures in the case of one form only, that of individual delegation

- there is little evidence for the adoption of the 'Scandinavian' model of group work – most cases seem to have been positioned between the 'Scandinavian' and 'Toyota' models with a tendency towards the 'Toyota'

Our measures of scope are open to the criticism that they measure different things. In the case of individual and group consultation, the basis is the number of *issues* on which management ask employees for their advice In the case of individual and group delegation, we are dealing with *rights* given to employees to make their own decisions. Even so, it seemed sensible to have a common term and, as long as it is remembered that the application reflects the specific form, "scope" seemed an appropriate word to describe the range of the practice.

It will be seen from Figure 4.1 that the number of respondents with low scores was more than 50 per cent in the case of three of the forms – both types of individual consultation ('face-to-face' and 'arm's length') and temporary group consultation – and was more than a third in the case of the other three. The highest score for scope, that for permanent group consultation, was only 25 per cent or one in four.

Quite clearly, the picture of extensive direct participation which comes from the figures for incidence begins to take on a different meaning in the light of the results for scope. While the incidence was widespread, the scope in terms of number of issues involved and the number of rights given to employees was relatively limited for most direct participation forms. Moreover, it must also be remembered that the figures for scope in Figure 4.1 involve only those workplaces practising the

Figure 4.1: The scope of the main forms of direct participation: ten countries -
respondents practising direct participation

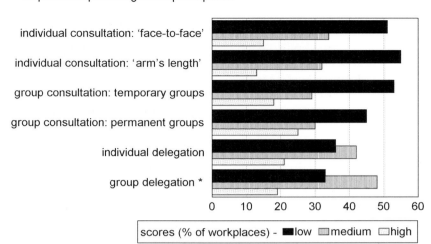

individual consultation: 'face-to-face'

individual consultation: 'arm's length'

group consultation: temporary groups

group consultation: permanent groups

individual delegation

group delegation *

0   10   20   30   40   50   60

scores (% of workplaces) - ■low ▨medium ☐high

* These scores combine those for scope *and* autonomy (see text below)

different forms of direct participation. A much more accurate impression of the current position in the ten countries comes from setting these figures against the total population of workplaces in the survey. This is done in Figure 4.2 and shows the reality in even sharper relief. The proportion of workplaces overall in the ten countries achieving high scores for scope for any of the forms of direct participation fell even further. Indeed, the proportion reached double figures in the case of one form only, that of individual delegation.

Such data also enable us to make a first contribution to the on-going debate about group work and its potential for organisational change. This debate focuses on the difference between the so-called 'Toyota' or 'lean production' model, which is generally applied in Japan and often in European and US-American 'greenfield sites', and the 'Scandinavian' model associated with some of the early experiments involving organisations such as Saab and Volvo. As the ideal-typical expression of them in Figure 4.3 suggests, the two models have very different implications in terms of the relative degree of management control and employee autonomy. The first has been described as 'flexible Taylorism' (Berggren, 1993), while the second equates with the semi-autonomous work group which many European policy makers aspire to. Both models are said to have their strengths and weaknesses. The 'Scandinavian' model is often seen as not sufficiently productive, whereas the 'Toyota' model is considered too rigid and too mean (rather than lean) to employees. The result is that, under the label of ' Japanese Inspired Production

Figure 4.2: The scope of the main forms of direct participation: ten countries - all respondents

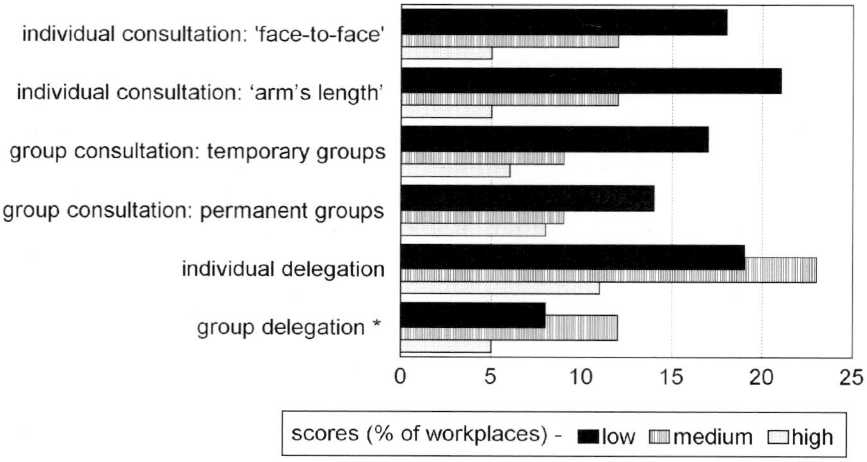

* These scores combine those for scope *and* autonomy (see text below)

## Figure 4.3  Types of group work

| dimensions | Scandinavian | Toyota/lean production |
|---|---|---|
| membership | voluntary | mandatory |
| selection of group members | by the group | by management |
| selection of group leader | by the group | by management |
| qualifications | mixed | generalists |
| reward | skill dependent | uniform (seniority) |
| task | complex | simple |
| technology | independent of pace | dependent on pace |
| autonomy | large | narrow |
| internal division of labour | voluntary | largely prescribed |

Based on Fröhlich and Pekruhl, 1996.

Systems' (JIPS) or 'para-Japanese' approaches (for further details, see Fröhlich and Pekruhl, 1996:89-92), European, US and Japanese companies are currently experimenting with forms combining the strength of both models while avoiding their handicaps.

To assess the group delegation reported in the survey on the dimensions of the continuum set by the extremes of the 'Scandinavian' and 'Toyota' models in Figure

4.3, a measure of intensity was developed. This combined the scores for scope (i.e. the number of rights group members have) with those for autonomy (i.e. the ability of groups to chose their own members and decide the issues they wanted to discuss). It is the scores for intensity which appear in the last line of Figures 4.1 and 4.2.

On the basis of these scores for intensity, it is possible to make the first ever quantitative assessment of some reliability so far as the state of play of the two models of group work and their 'in-between' solutions is concerned. In Figure 4.1, it will be seen that 19 per cent of the cases of group delegation achieved high scores for intensity; around a third (33 per cent) had low scores; and almost a half (48 per cent) fell in between. Again, it must be remembered that the figures for in Figures 4.1 relate only to those workplaces practising group delegation. A much more accurate impression of the current position in the ten countries comes from setting these figures against the total population of workplaces in the survey in Figure 4.2: it will be seen that only 5 per cent of workplaces in the ten countries achieved high scores for the intensity of group delegation, 12 per cent had medium scores and 8 per cent low scores. In other words, the diffusion of the 'Scandinavian-type' group work would appear to extremely limited; most group work seems to have been positioned in between the 'Scandinavian' and the 'Toyota' models with a tendency towards the latter.

*The most important form of direct participation*

As well as providing data on the incidence and scope of direct participation, the EPOC survey allows us to investigate managers' views on the most important form of direct participation. A workplace might practise a number of forms and, for that reason alone, it is valuable to know which form is regarded as the most important. Some forms may carry greater weight in management's approach, whereas others are considered secondary or just supportive. More importantly, such information helps to test some of the prevailing wisdom about the relative weight being attached to the different forms. One is especially dominant: the view that the forms of delegation and especially group work, rather than the consultative forms, are at the leading edge.

## Key findings:

- most respondents (two-thirds) thought the consultative forms were more important than the delegative forms

- even many of the managers practising the delegative forms nonetheless assessed them as of lesser importance than the consultative forms

The results give considerable grounds for reflection. As will be seen from Table 4.4, three-quarters of the managers of the EPOC survey reported that one of the consultative forms was most important, whereas only quarter said that the delegative forms were. The proportion favouring individual consultation was reduced considerably; that of group consultation was roughly in line with the incidence of these forms shown in Table 4.1. The proportion favouring the two forms of delegation, by contrast, was down to a large extent. Whereas 54 per cent of managers said they practised individual delegation, only 11 per cent considered this their most important practice; only 11 per cent considered this their most important practice; 33 per cent indicated the practice of group delegation, but only 13 per cent considered it the most important form. Critically, it seems, and contrary to the conventional wisdom, even many of the managers from workplaces practising the delegative forms nonetheless assessed them as of lesser importance than the consultative forms.

**Table 4.4  The most important form of direct participation: ten countries**

|  | Total % |
|---|---|
| individual consultation: *'face-to-face'* | 11 |
| individual consultation: *'arm's length'* | 22 |
| group consultation: *temporary groups* | 14 |
| group consultation: *permanent groups* | 29 |
| individual delegation | 11 |
| group delegation | 13 |

## 4.2  A manufacturing phenomenon? The significance of sector

Much of the debate about direct participation has focused on the production sector. In the case of group work, it is not unfair to suggest that there has been an exclusive interest with metalworking and, in particular, the automotive sector. Such a narrow focus overlooks the fact that considerably more people are employed in the service sector and that the production sector is shrinking. The great advantage of the EPOC survey is that it included all economic sectors (with the exception of agriculture).

The value of this approach is shown in the results in Table 4.5. The industrial sector, it seems, was not the 'leader' in matters of direct participation. The 'pole' position was occupied by the public services, followed by trading sector. Incidence was lowest in construction.

As for the different forms of direct participation, Table 4.6 suggests that 'face-to-face' consultation was most widespread in the three service sectors (between 37 and 45 per cent), followed by industry (31 per cent). It was rarely used in construction (19 per cent). 'Arm's length' consultation did not vary so much. It was somewhat more applied in industry (40 per cent) and private services (40 per cent). Temporary consultation groups were to be found in almost equal shares in all sectors, with the exception of construction, which rated below the average. There was the same, almost equal, distribution for permanent consultation groups of the quality circle type, again with the exception of construction (20 per cent as against an average of 38 per cent). Individual delegation was most pronounced in public services (63 per cent), whereas its use in industry and construction was below 50 per cent. In the case of group delegation, the variation between the sectors was less. Again, however, it was in the trading sector and public services – and not industry – that group delegation was more likely to be found.

**Table 4.5 The incidence of direct participation by sector: ten countries**

|  | % of workplaces *with* direct participation | number of workplaces *with* direct participation |
|---|---|---|
| ten-country average | 82 | 4,694 |
| manufacturing | 79 | 1,670 |
| construction | 69 | 278 |
| trade | 84 | 994 |
| private services | 81 | 725 |
| public services | 87 | 1,027 |

**Table 4.6  The incidence of the main forms of direct participation by sector: ten countries**

|  | individual consultation: 'face-to-face' | individual consultation: 'arm's length' | group consultation: temporary groups | group consultation: permanent groups | individual delegation | group delegation |
|---|---|---|---|---|---|---|
|  | % | % | % | % | % | % |
| ten-country average | 35 | 38 | 32 | 31 | 54 | 33 |
| industry | 31 | 40 | 34 | 29 | 47 | 29 |
| construction | 19 | 27 | 20 | 15 | 45 | 28 |
| trade | 44 | 42 | 30 | 35 | 56 | 39 |
| private services | 39 | 40 | 31 | 31 | 57 | 31 |
| public service | 37 | 33 | 36 | 36 | 63 | 35 |

## Key findings:

- the industrial sector was not the 'leader' in matters of direct participation

- the incidence, coverage and scope of direct participation was greater in services and, especially, public services,

- direct participation was less likely in construction than the other sectors

Not surprisingly, the pattern of the scope measures is very similar to that for the incidence of direct participation discussed above (Tables not included). Thus, it was not industry that was the 'leader' in the scope of direct participation. Rather it was services and, in particular, public services that had the greater proportion of workplaces with high scores for scope for each of the main forms of direct participation. Significantly, in view of the scientific and policy debate, this was as true of group delegation as it was of the other forms.

At the other end of the spectrum, construction also confirmed its position. Not only was the incidence of the forms of direct participation in this sector less than in the others, but also there were proportionately fewer cases registering high scores for the scope of the practice.

**Table 4.7  The most important form of direct participation by sector: ten countries**

|  | individual consultation: 'face-to-face' | individual consultation: 'arm's length' | group consultation: temporary groups | group consultation: permanent groups | individual delegation | group delegation |
|---|---|---|---|---|---|---|
|  | % | % | % | % | % | % |
| ten-country average | 11 | 22 | 14 | 29 | 11 | 13 |
| industry | 9 | 22 | 16 | 28 | 10 | 15 |
| construction | 16 | 40 | 10 | 8 | 15 | 11 |
| trade | 11 | 20 | 10 | 37 | 7 | 15 |
| private services | 15 | 27 | 14 | 27 | 9 | 8 |
| public service | 9 | 19 | 14 | 30 | 15 | 13 |

A breakdown of the results for the most important form of direct participation suggests that there were not great differences by sector (see Table 4.7). Industry somewhat represented the average, with 'face-to-face' consultation (9 per cent) and group delegation (15 per cent) being deemed to be slightly less and more important respectively. Construction workplaces relied most strongly on both practices of individual consultation, notably 'arm's length' (40 per cent) and on individual delegation (15 per cent). All group forms were below the average. Trading workplaces regarded both forms of group consultation as well as group work as their most important forms. The other private services relied mainly on individual consultation at the expense of both forms of delegation. Public service organisations preferred both forms of group consultation as well showing a strong trend toward individual delegation.

## 4.3 A strong country effect?

So far the analysis has been concerned with the results for the ten countries together. Our task now is to consider the dimensions of direct participation by individual country. Our interest is to see whether there were any significant patterns reflecting well-known differences in economic and industrial relations systems.

As the summary of the key findings in the box confirms, the results do not lend themselves to easy categorisations along geographical lines. It is possible to identify a 'Southern' European pattern embracing Italy and Portugal and Spain. It is much more difficult to do the same for 'Northern' Europe, however. Close neighbours such as Germany and the Netherlands, and Denmark and Sweden, appear to be quite different from each other. Similarly, there does not appear to be any obvious link between the tradition of 'voluntarism' associated with Ireland and the UK and the nature and extent of direct participation. The Auroux laws do appear to have had an impact on the pattern in France, however.

### Key findings:

- there appears to be a strong 'Southern' European pattern – the incidence and scope of direct participation was lower in Italy, Portugal and Spain

- there is no uniform 'Northern' European pattern – the Netherlands vies with Sweden for 'pole' position, but Denmark and Germany are only similar to the ten-country average

- there is no obvious 'voluntarism' effect in Ireland and the UK

- the French pattern seems to be consistent with what might be expected in the light of the Auroux laws

*Italy, Portugal and Spain: evidence of a 'Southern' European pattern?*

With 61 and 65 per cent practising at least one form of direct participation, Portugal and Spain were clearly below the European average of 82 per cent (Table 4.8) Italy, by contrast was above average with 85 per cent. In all aspects, Portuguese managers were way below their European colleagues, but especially so in the case of individual delegation (Table 4.9). Spanish workplaces displayed a similar profile of below-average use of direct participation. Here, the low use of group delegation (10 per cent) stands out as the most distinct deviation from the ten-country average. Italian workplaces were above average for the use of the two group forms of consultation, but appear to have been comparatively hesitant to delegate responsibilities to their employees either as individuals or in groups. In the case of the multiple forms of direct participation (Table 4.10), Portugal (43 per cent) and Spain (31 per cent) had the largest proportions of workplaces relying on just one form. At the other extreme, Spain, Italy and Portugal (in that order) occupied the last three positions for the proportion of workplaces with five or six forms – Spain being especially noteworthy because not a single workplace practised all six measures. Significantly, however, Portugal and Spain (though not Italy) had relatively high levels of coverage of the group forms of direct participation where these were practised (Table 4.11).

The picture is not dissimilar in the case of the scope measures (Figures 4.4 – 4.11 and see also Table 4.12). Overall, taking all respondents into account, Italy, Portugal and Spain had – with rare exceptions – some of the lowest scores for the proportion of workplaces with high scope. And things are not different when only the respondents practising direct participation are the focus – suggesting, again, that where the practice exists, it is likely to be relatively low-profile (Figure 4.11).

Portugal and Spain are especially interesting in another way. Both countries had the lowest shares of workplaces with direct participation (61 and 65 per cent against the average of 82 per cent). Although both countries differed in their shares of foreign-owned establishments – Portugal being one of the lowest (9 per cent) and Spain the highest (24 per cent; cf. Tables 3.2a and b) – they had this in common: their share of foreign-owned workplaces *with* direct participation was the lowest among all ten countries; more than one in four workplaces did not practise direct participation. This seems to indicate that, more than in other countries, lower labour costs may have been an important consideration in the location decision.

## Table 4.8  The incidence of direct participation by country

|  | % of workplaces with direct participation | absolute number of workplaces with direct participation |
|---|---|---|
| ten-country average | 82 | 4,731 |
| Denmark | 81 | 545 |
| France | 87 | 520 |
| Germany | 81 | 674 |
| Italy | 85 | 326 |
| Ireland | 82 | 409 |
| Netherlands | 90 | 454 |
| Portugal | 61 | 182 |
| Spain | 65 | 298 |
| Sweden | 89 | 652 |
| United Kingdom | 83 | 671 |

## Table 4.9  The incidence of the main form of direct participation by country

|  | individual consultation: 'face-to-face' | individual consultation: 'arm's length' | group consultation: temporary groups | group consultation: permanent groups | individual delegation | group delegation |
|---|---|---|---|---|---|---|
|  | % | % | % | % | % | % |
| ten-country average | 35 | 40 | 31 | 30 | 55 | 36 |
| Denmark | 27 | 45 | 30 | 28 | 57 | 30 |
| France | 52 | 33 | 40 | 34 | 54 | 40 |
| Germany | 20 | 38 | 26 | 31 | 64 | 31 |
| Ireland | 39 | 22 | 36 | 28 | 62 | 42 |
| Italy | 32 | 42 | 42 | 21 | 44 | 28 |
| Netherlands | 38 | 73 | 26 | 35 | 59 | 48 |
| Portugal | 25 | 18 | 20 | 25 | 26 | 26 |
| Spain | 30 | 20 | 23 | 23 | 40 | 10 |
| Sweden | 29 | 45 | 34 | 29 | 69 | 56 |
| United Kingdom | 52 | 40 | 33 | 41 | 53 | 37 |

**Table 4.10  The incidence of multiple forms of direct participation by country**

|  | 1 form % | 2 forms % | 3 forms % | 4 forms % | 5 forms % | 6 forms % |
|---|---|---|---|---|---|---|
| ten-country average | 23 | 25 | 22 | 17 | 10 | 4 |
| Denmark | 25 | 27 | 21 | 15 | 11 | 3 |
| France | 21 | 21 | 23 | 21 | 12 | 3 |
| Germany | 27 | 27 | 22 | 14 | 8 | 3 |
| Ireland | 18 | 37 | 20 | 15 | 6 | 4 |
| Italy | 25 | 28 | 26 | 14 | 5 | 2 |
| Netherlands | 14 | 25 | 21 | 24 | 12 | 5 |
| Portugal | 43 | 19 | 19 | 8 | 4 | 6 |
| Spain | 31 | 34 | 21 | 11 | 2 | 0 |
| Sweden | 19 | 20 | 26 | 22 | 10 | 4 |
| United Kingdom | 19 | 23 | 18 | 14 | 17 | 8 |

**Table 4.11  The coverage of the group forms of direct participation**

|  | *% of workplaces involving 50+ per cent of their largest occupational group* | | |
|---|---|---|---|
|  | group consultation: temporary groups % | group consultation: permanent groups % | group delegation: group work % |
| ten country average | 48 | 48 | 47 |
| Denmark | 51 | 50 | 66 |
| France | 50 | 58 | 45 |
| Germany | 23 | 28 | 26 |
| Ireland | 73 | 71 | 58 |
| Italy | 24 | 12 | 12 |
| Netherlands | 59 | 63 | 53 |
| Portugal | 77 | 56 | 58 |
| Spain | 49 | 41 | 56 |
| Sweden | 59 | 66 | 55 |
| United Kingdom | 52 | 42 | 47 |

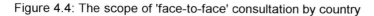

Figure 4.4: The scope of 'face-to-face' consultation by country

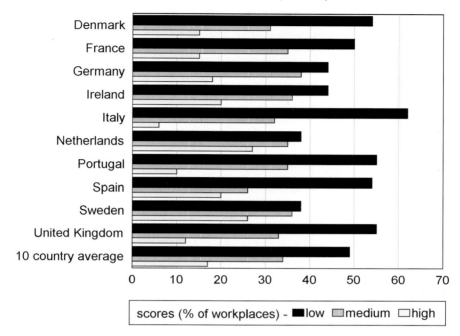

Figure 4.5: The scope of 'arm's-length' consultation by country

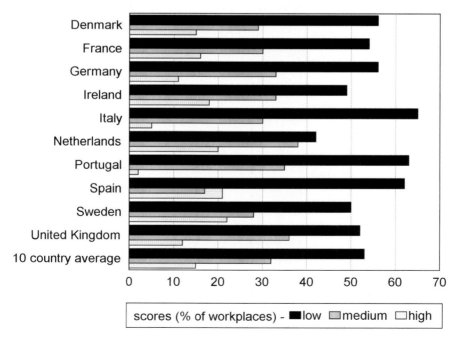

Figure 4.6: The scope of temporary group consultation by country

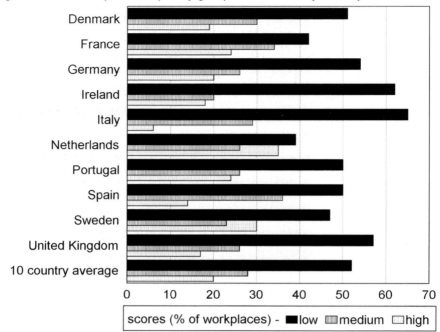

scores (% of workplaces) - ■low ▦medium □high

Figure 4.7: The scope of permanent group consultation by country

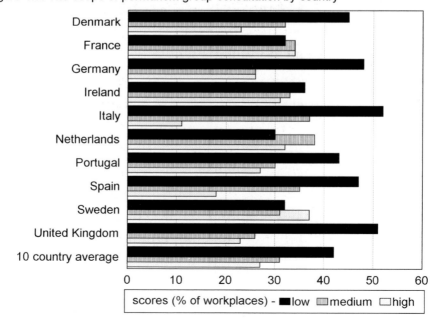

scores (% of workplaces) - ■low ▦medium □high

Figure 4.8: The scope of individual delegation by country

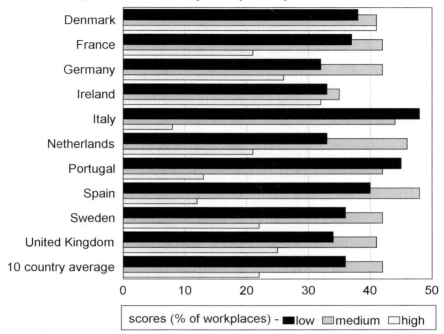

Figure 4.9: The intensity* of group delegation by country

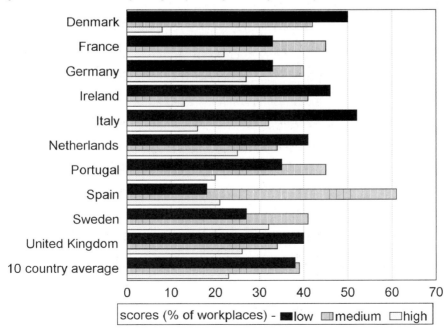

Figure 4.10: Measure of the overall scope of direct participation by country - respondents practising direct participation

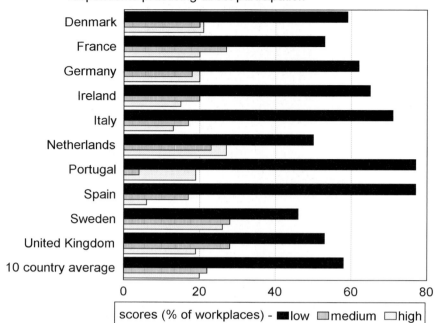

Figure 4.11: Measure of the overall scope of direct participation by country - all respondents

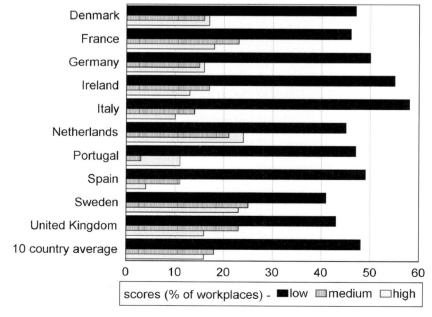

**Table 4.12  % of workplaces achieving high scores for scope for each form of direct participation by country – all respondents**

|  | individual consultation: 'face-to-face' | individual consultation: 'arm's length' | group consultation: temporary groups | group consultation: permanent groups | individual delegation | group delegation |
|---|---|---|---|---|---|---|
|  | % | % | % | % | % | % |
| ten-country average | 6 | 6 | 6 | 8 | 12 | 6 |
| Denmark | 4 | 7 | 8 | 7 | 12 | 7 |
| France | 8 | 5 | 9 | 12 | 11 | 4 |
| Germany | 4 | 4 | 5 | 8 | 17 | 6 |
| Ireland | 8 | 4 | 7 | 9 | 20 | 3 |
| Italy | 2 | 2 | 2 | 2 | 3 | 3 |
| Netherlands | 10 | 15 | 9 | 11 | 12 | 8 |
| Portugal | 2 | 0 | 5 | 7 | 3 | 5 |
| Spain | 6 | 4 | 3 | 4 | 5 | 0 |
| Sweden | 8 | 10 | 10 | 11 | 15 | 15 |
| United Kingdom | 6 | 5 | 6 | 9 | 13 | 5 |

**Table 4.13  The most important form of direct participation by country (% of workplaces)**

|  | individual consultation: face-to-face | individual consultation: at arm's length | group consultation: project groups | group consultation: permanent groups | individual delegation | group delegation |
|---|---|---|---|---|---|---|
|  | % | % | % | %% | % |  |
| ten-country average | 10 | 22 | 13 | 27 | 10 | 17 |
| Denmark | 8 | 30 | 15 | 24 | 12 | 11 |
| France | 21 | 11 | 21 | 31 | 3 | 13 |
| Germany | 5 | 33 | 10 | 23 | 21 | 8 |
| Ireland | 18 | 16 | 11 | 24 | 7 | 24 |
| Italy | 8 | 26 | 28 | 13 | 9 | 16 |
| Netherlands | 3 | 47 | 14 | 23 | 4 | 9 |
| Portugal | 16 | 11 | 11 | 26 | 5 | 31 |
| Spain | 11 | 11 | 11 | 22 | 15 | 30 |
| Sweden | 7 | 14 | 11 | 22 | 14 | 32 |
| United Kingdom | 14 | 16 | 10 | 46 | 5 | 9 |

*The Netherlands and Germany: little evidence of a 'Northern' European pattern?*

If there is a 'Southern' European pattern, it is much less obvious that there is a 'Northern' equivalent. The difficulty of establishing such as pattern is most clearly illustrated by comparing the Netherlands and Germany. Close neighbours, these two countries have not dissimilar industrial relations systems – notably they have works councils with relatively extensive powers. In both countries, too, the level of debate about quality of working life issues has been especially pronounced.

The pattern of direct participation seems to be quite different, however. Overall, the Netherlands vies with Sweden for pole position on a number of dimensions of direct participation. By contrast, and surprisingly, Germany was around the average or below the average for the ten countries on many dimensions. Thus, against a European average of 82 per cent workplaces with at least one form of direct participation, Dutch workplaces showed up most strongly of all (90 per cent), whereas their Germany equivalents were just under the average with 82 per cent. In the case of four out of the six individual forms ('face-to-face', 'arms-length', group consultation and group delegation), the Netherlands was in advance of Germany – in three cases ('face-to-face', 'arms-length' and group delegation) considerably so. Only in the case of individual delegation did the Netherlands cede second place. The proportion of Dutch workplaces with five or six forms, which was second only to the UK, was 5 per cent points up on that of Germany, and the coverage of the three group forms was twice as much as that of Germany. Indeed, the coverage in Germany was among the lowest of the ten countries. The Dutch workplaces also had the higher scores for the scope of direct participation. Indeed, taking all respondents into account, they achieved higher scores for scope for five of the six forms. Intriguingly the one exception is not the group delegation which has been the subject of such interest and debate in Germany but its individual equivalent.

*Denmark and Sweden: a 'Scandinavian' connection?*

Two other close neighbours normally regarded as strong candidates for inclusion in a 'Northern' Europe pattern, Denmark and Sweden, might also have been expected to be similar. The Scandinavian countries in general have long been regarded as pioneers in matters of direct participation – the Saab and Volvo experiments, in particular, attracted considerable interest from around the world. A reliance on collective bargaining, both at the inter-professional and (most relevantly for present purposes) at the workplace levels, is also something that distinguishes them from most other EU member countries.

When the ten countries are compared, Sweden stands out on many counts, whereas the performance of Denmark is more uneven. Against a European average of 82 per cent workplaces with at least one form of direct participation, Swedish workplaces showed up most strongly (89 per cent), whereas Denmark was slightly less than the average with 81 per cent. In the case of the individual forms, incidence was similar for 'face-to-face' and 'arms length' consultation and the two forms of group consultation. A much higher proportion of workplaces in Sweden had individual and group delegation, however, and the latter, in particular, was rated as the most important form by a larger proportion of managers than in any other country (see Table 4.13). In both countries the proportion of workplaces with five or six forms was about the 10-country average. Coverage of group delegation was greater in Denmark, but Sweden had the advantage for the two forms of group consultation. It is when the measures of scope are taken into account that a gap opens, however. Swedish workplaces achieved higher scores for scope for each of the four forms of consultative participation by a significant margin in most cases (see also Table 7.12). Indeed, Denmark was only around the 10 country average in most of these cases. Denmark's strength, it seems, lies in the two forms of delegation. Denmark's score for the intensity of group delegation was the second highest after Sweden; its score for the scope of individual delegation was the highest of the ten countries, including Sweden, by a considerable margin.

*Ireland and the UK: does 'voluntarism' make a difference?*

There are significant differences between Ireland and the UK in terms of size of population and industrial structure. The industrial relations systems have also been pulling away from one another in the last two decades – Ireland has moved closer to the continental European model of social partnership and central agreements, whereas the UK has seen a significant programme of deregulation coupled with a decline in collective bargaining and strong support from the Conservative governments for employee 'involvement'. As well as a common language, (and some trade unions), the two countries nonetheless share the tradition of 'voluntarism' in industrial relations, i.e. there is relatively little legal regulation of industrial relations (for example, there are no statutory forms of workplace representation and collective agreements are 'gentlemen's' agreements rather than legally-enforceable contracts) and the parties are more autonomous than they are in most other EU countries.

In the event, there are no obvious differences which can be put down to the tradition of 'voluntarism'. Any differences between the two countries would seem to reflect industrial structure and recent trends in industrial relations.

Against a European average of 82 per cent workplaces with at least one form of direct participation, Ireland was above – indeed it was third after Sweden, the Netherlands and France with 85 per cent. The profile of Irish workplaces was characterised by a strong reliance on 'face-to-face' consultation contacts plus individual and group delegation. The incidence of either form of group consultation was relatively low as were multiple forms of direct participation. Ireland, along with Portugal and Spain, nonetheless appeared to have relatively high levels of coverage of the group forms of direct participation where these existed – which, like

Portugal, might be explained by the number of greenfield operations in these countries. The picture is not dissimilar in the case of the scope measures. Here perhaps the most intriguing finding is the relatively exceptional score for the scope of individual delegation, which is the highest of all the ten countries. The score for group delegation, by contrast, is the second lowest.

As for the UK, the picture is similar to that which emerged from the most recent Workplace Industrial Relations Survey (Millward et al., 1992). Any expectation that recent developments, notably the decline in collective bargaining, might have lead to above average levels of direct participation does not appear to be substantiated. The UK was only around about the average for the proportion of workplaces with at least one form of direct participation. It is true that it was above average for 'face to face' and permanent group consultation. It is also true that it had the highest proportion practising five or six forms – indeed, the UK was the outstanding country in this regard. Set against this, the UK was only around the average so far as the two forms of delegation are concerned, with the same being true for the coverage of the group activities – the UK may have been above average for the incidence of permanent groups, for example, but the coverage of these groups is one of the lowest of the ten countries. Perhaps the most significant finding, however, relates to the scope measures: the UK was below the ten-country average for the four consultative forms of direct participation and only slightly above for the two forms of delegation. On the face of it, the direct participation that is taking place is relatively limited.

*France: the Auroux laws make a difference?*

France, because of the Auroux laws and groupes d'expression (a form of permanent group consultation), is the one country in which there is explicit legislative support for direct participation and so deserves particular attention. Against a European average of 82 per cent workplaces with at least one form of direct participation, French workplaces showed up most strongly (87 per cent). French managers seemed to favour 'face-to-face' consultation – France was the highest by some margin – at the expense of its 'arms-length' twin (where it was below average). The incidence of the two forms of group consultation was also above average – which might have been expected as a result of the legislative support for groupes d'expression. So too, perhaps more significantly, was the scope of these group forms (the highest and the second highest after Sweden respectively). The coverage of the two forms of group consultation, however, was only slightly above average. Individual and group delegation slightly exceeded its average use in Europe and the scope was around the average. These findings were also mirrored in managers' views about the most important form of direct participation – 'face-to-face' and permanent group consultation, comparatively speaking, were very highly rated. The pattern in France, it seems, is consistent with the impact that might have been expected in an industrial relations context prone to high institutionalisation. Perhaps as a consequence of this, when asserting highly developed consultation practices, our respondents might have in mind institutionalisation *per se* rather than the practical outcomes.

## 4.4  Summary and conclusions

On the basis of the EPOC survey results, there would appear to be a considerable gap between the rhetoric and reality of direct participation. Admittedly, as Chapter 3 has already pointed out, the incidence of direct participation was greater than that suggested by previous studies. Around four out of five workplaces in the ten countries claim to have some form of direct participation. Most, however, might be said to be pursuing a partial approach. Relatively few – around one in seven – had the five or six forms which might have been expected in organisations with an integrated approach. The coverage of group consultation – temporary groups and permanent groups – and of group delegation was also less than 50 per cent of the workplace's largest occupational group in most cases. The scope of much of the direct participation proved to be rather limited as well. Indeed, when the total population of the workplaces in the survey is taken into account, the proportion with high scores for scope reached double figures in the case of one form of direct participation only, that of individual delegation.

Other findings will need further reflection. Some of these, such as the strong country effect, might have been expected, although not necessarily some of the details. The reputation Sweden has acquired as a pioneer in matters of direct participation, especially group work, is confirmed: both the incidence and scope of this forms, as well as the importance with which managers regard it, are relatively greater than in other countries as is the overall measure. The Netherlands too makes a relatively strong showing overall and, in particular, in the area of group consultation. By contrast, expectations in the case of Denmark (because of the 'Scandinavian' connection), Germany (notably because of the intense debate about group work) and the UK (because of the support for employee 'involvement'), hardly seem to be reflected in the data; the incidence and scope of direct participation is only around the ten-country-average or less for some forms of direct participation.

Further light is also shed on the debate which dominated the second EPOC Roundtable on direct participation in Lisbon in 1996 – whether there is a distinctly 'Southern' European pattern, embracing Portugal, Spain and (to a lesser extent Italy), reflecting special features of industrial structure (a proportionately larger number of small family-owned businesses) and a relatively recent or underdeveloped industrial relations system. Overall, it seems, the incidence and the scope of direct participation in these countries do lag behind those elsewhere. In the case of group delegation, however, the picture is somewhat different. The incidence of group delegation is relatively low. Where it is practised, in particular in Portugal and Spain, however, it is regarded as the most important form of direct participation by proportionately more respondents than in other countries. Also in Portugal the scope of group delegation is greater than in most other countries. The presence of a proportionately larger number of greenfield operations with group delegation from the beginning would appear to be the most plausible explanation as it is for some of the findings from Ireland.

Perhaps one of the most surprising findings relates to the group delegation which commentators and researchers alike have tended to put on a pedestal in discussing direct participation. Not only does group delegation appear to be a minority practice in the workplaces in the EPOC survey, which might have been expected. On the basis of the measure of intensity, which explicitly takes into account autonomy and the issues which groups are allowed to decide, there appears to be little evidence for the adoption of semi-autonomous group work associated with the *Scandinavian* model; if there was a tendency, it seemed to be towards the *Toyota* model. Most significantly, the majority of managers – including, it must be remembered, those who practise it – did not regard group delegation as the most important form of direct participation. That position was occupied by group consultation closely followed by individual consultation.

There are three possible interpretations to be put on the finding that it is the consultative rather than the delegative forms of direct participation that are regarded as most important by management. Two are relevant to the overall results of the EPOC survey and are better left until after the presentation of the data in other chapters. The third explanation, which is more particular, is bound up with the all-encompassing nature of the EPOC survey discussed in Chapter 1. The survey, it must be remembered, is the first of its kind to take into account the private and the public services. Practices such as individual delegation and group work have long been practised in many workplaces in these sectors without having the publicity and, indeed, the labels associated with similar arrangements in manufacturing. In some cases, such as hospitals, they are intrinsic to the organisation of work. A hospital manager, for example, is likely to find little that is exceptional about individual delegation or group work – these are likely to be activities in which nurses are engaged all the time. An attitude survey or problem-solving group initiative, on the other hand, may not only be new (and something for which the individual manager may have been responsible for introducing), but also seen as making a significant contribution to the management of change.

# References

Berggren, C. 1993: 'Lean Production – The End of History?' *Work, Employment and Society*, Vol. 7, No. 2, 163-88.

Fröhlich, D., and U. Pekruhl. 1996: *Direct Participation and Organisational Change – Fashionable but Misunderstood? An analysis of recent research in Europe, Japan and the USA*, Luxembourg.

Millward, N., M. Stevens, D. Smart and W.R. Hawes, 1992: *Workplace Industrial Relations in Transition*. The ED/ESRC/ACAS Surveys. Aldershot: Dartmouth.

Osterman, P. 1994: 'How Common is Workplace Transformation and How can we explain who adopts it? Results from a National Survey'. *Industrial and Labor Relations Review*, Vol. 47, No. 2, 173-88.

# Chapter 5

# Management's motives for introducing direct participation

This chapter is concerned with management's motives for introducing direct participation, which is the "why" question in the list of the EPOC project's original objectives. The questions about motives in the EPOC survey were formulated in an identical way for each of the forms and allowed for multiple answers. They were specifically designed to gather information on the significance of the following:

- productivity

    <need to improve quality of product or service>
    <pressure to reduce costs>
    <pressure to reduce throughput times>

- the quality of working life

    <belief that employees have right to participate>
    <desire to improve quality of working life>

- examples elsewhere in the organisation or in other organisations

- demands from employees or employee organisations

- the requirements of legislation or collective agreement

Management's motives have an important bearing on the significance of direct participation discussed in Chapter 1. Analysis of them helps to understand, in particular, the relative weight that managers put on direct participation in improving business performance as opposed to enhancing the quality of working life. Previous EPOC studies suggested contradictory conclusions. In the EPOC report dealing with the conceptualisation of direct participation, it was suggested on the basis of an initial literature review, that, the need to respond to increased competition, cost rationalisation, a demand for greater flexibility, a requirement to adapt to the introduction of new technology, customisation of production and the reform of managerial behaviour. The need to respond to a shift in employees' expectations of work is likely to be less important (Geary and Sisson, 1994:27).

EPOC's social partner study, however, suggested a more complex web of motives. Questioned on their views on direct participation, employers' representatives 'did not necessarily focus their attention solely on economic objectives: rather systematically they emphasised social values as well – at least because an active employee commitment was considered essential to increase efficiency (Regalia, 1995:37).

The main objective in including examples elsewhere in the organisation or in other organisations was to secure data about the sources of management inspiration for introducing direct participation. This is especially important from a policy perspective. Bench-marking has become a widely-popular management tool in recent years and the promotion of publicity about so-called "best practice" examples has been advocated as one of the most important ways of encouraging managers to move in new directions in a range of areas from marketing, through operations management, to human resource management.

Including demands from employees or employee organisations and the requirements of legislation/collective agreements needs little justification. Not only are these considerations intrinsically important. Again, there is the policy perspective to take into account: it is important to know the extent to which managers respond positively, for example, to these requirements in an area such as direct participation.

A second strand of questions to which it was hoped the EPOC survey results on motivation would give answers reflects the great variety of practice described in the previous chapter. Do particular direct participation forms disclose particular patterns of employer motives? In the opinion of our respondents, do economic, or social, concerns as well as outside stimuli play a more important role for some forms of direct participation than for others?

Finally, motives can be expected to vary according to specific workplace contexts. Here the focus is on three of the main sources of possible variation. First, motivation patterns may differ by country. Second, workplaces experiencing severe and increasing competition may stress different sets of motives from their 'protected' neighbours. Third, the presence of employee representatives and the extent of their involvement in the introduction of direct participation may have an impact on the ranking of motives – for example, social concerns may be emphasised and employees' demands for direct participation may be more frequently taken into account where employee representatives are significantly involved.

The chapter begins by reviewing the overall results from answers to these questions. Do managers focus exclusively on the economic goals of the organisational change or do they emphasise social values as well? It then goes on to consider whether particular forms of direct participation were associated with particular patterns of management motives – did economic, or social, concerns as well as outside stimuli play a more important role for some forms of direct participation than for others? Finally, it looks into two of the main sources of possible variations: the nature and extent of competition; and the presence of employee representatives and the extent of their involvement in the introduction of direct participation.

## 5.1 Business concerns ... and more?

Most managers, regardless of country, emphasised productivity concerns in their decision to introduce direct participation. As Figure 5.1 confirms, the lowest proportion was 72 per cent in the case of 'arms-length' consultation; the highest was 81 per cent in the case of permanent group consultation. Sizeable proportions also emphasised the importance of quality of working life concerns. In each case, however, the proportion was lower than that for productivity – the gap in percentage points ranging from seven in the case of 'arms-length' consultation to 21 for individual delegation.

The frequent occurrence of both productivity and quality of working life motives leads to a further observation. Our interviewees tended to explain their behaviour through a combination of motives. As Figure 5.2 shows, a minority only stressed a single motive: the highest was 25 per cent in the case of individual delegation; the lowest was 18 per cent in the case of the two forms of group consultation. By contrast, with the one exception of temporary group consultation (which was 49 per cent and had an above average figure for those not citing a motive), the proportion emphasising two or more motives was over 50 per cent. Sizeable numbers (one in four in the case of the two forms of individual consultation) also quoted three or more reasons for introducing direct participation.

If we concentrate on the two most frequently cited motives – productivity and quality of working life – the image of a strongly interwoven set of motives in a majority of cases is clearly confirmed (see Figure 5.3). In the case of every one of the six forms of direct participation scarcely 20 per cent or one in five of our respondents mentioned productivity concerns only, whereas the majority referred to both productivity and quality of working life motives – the range being from 54 per cent in the case of group delegation to 66 per cent in the case of permanent group consultation. Interestingly, again, managers were more likely to cite both sets of considerations in the case of the consultative forms than the delegative ones.

## Key findings:

- most managers (seven or eight out of ten depending on the form) emphasised productivity motives in their decision to introduce direct participation

- although lower, sizeable proportions emphasised the importance of quality of working life concerns – and a majority mentioned *both* productivity and quality of working life motives

- the proportions citing examples elsewhere in the organisation or in other organisations were relatively low (around one in five) – direct participation appears to be largely 'home-grown'

- the demands of employees/ employee representatives and the requirements of collective agreements/legislation were cited by even fewer managers – direct participation appears to be primarily management-inspired

To return to Figure 5.1 and the sets of motives, it is also surprising that, though the proportions citing examples elsewhere in the organisation or in other organisations were greater than those for the demands of employees/employee representatives and the requirements of collective agreements/legislation, they were still relatively low. Indeed, only in the case of 'face-to-face' consultation did the figures reach 20 per cent or one in five. As indicated above, bench-marking has become a widely-popular management tool in recent years in most countries. It might have been thought that, given the publicity attaching to some of the developments in direct participation, notably quality circles and group work, more respondents would have cited examples elsewhere This is especially so as some developments, such as group work, represent a major departure and, some of the case study evidence suggests, may need the legitimacy of "best practice" examples to persuade uncertain senior managers to go ahead. On the face of it, it looks very much as if direct participation is largely 'home-grown'.

Given the importance attached to the quality of working life, it might have been thought that large numbers of respondents would have quoted demands from employees and their representatives as being important in the introduction of direct participation. In the event, very few did so. As will be seen from Figure 5.1, the proportion was never higher than 19 per cent, which is only one in five, compared to the seven or eight out of ten mentioning productivity.

Figure 5.1: Motives for introducing different forms of direct participation - % of respondents practising direct participation

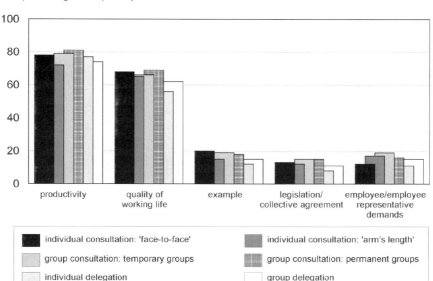

Figure 5.2: Combination of motives: number of motives mentioned - % of respondents practising direct participation

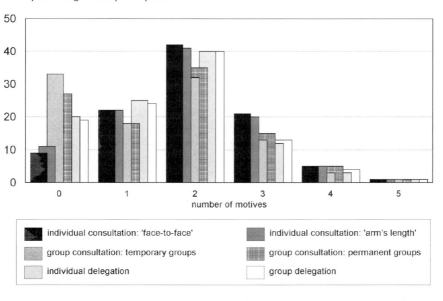

Figure 5.3: Motives: productivity and quality of working life combined - % of respondents practising direct participation

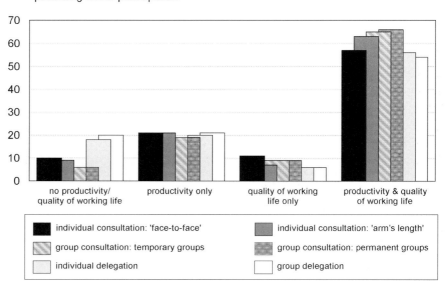

The pattern of responses is very similar for the requirements of legislation and collective agreements. The highest proportions of respondents citing these considerations are to be found in the case of the two forms of group consultation. In neither case, however, do the figures rise above 15 per cent, which is less than one in seven. The figures for the delegative forms are even lower with only one in ten citing them for individual delegation.

In both cases, as a later section will show, the presence of employee representation did make a difference. Managers with some form of employee representation were more than twice as likely to cite demands from employees/employee representatives and the requirements of legislation than those without. Even so, in no case does the proportion exceed 20 per cent.

There is a not dissimilar picture, to anticipate a later section, when the results are broken down by country. As Figure 5A.1 in Appendix 3 shows, there were differences between the countries. Portugal shows the smallest proportion of workplaces citing employee demands, but the highest mentioning the requirements of legislation and collective bargaining. The position is almost the reverse in Sweden. Ireland, Italy and Spain show slightly above average figures for employee demands, with the Netherlands and the UK slightly below. Apart from Portugal, and Spain in the case of 'face-to-face' delegation, no country stands out on account of the requirements of legislation and collective bargaining. It is as if many of the well-known differences between countries and their different traditions did not exist.

It could be, of course, that our respondents were reluctant to acknowledge the demands of employees or employee representatives and the requirements of collective agreements/legislation (along with examples elsewhere) and so underreported the signficance they attached to these considerations. Yet these findings tie in with the answers to other questions on the presence of employee representatives and their involvement in implementing direct participation. Also there is no evidence from the way respondents answered other questions, for example, on the coverage and the scope of direct participation or the implications of direct participation for the need of trade unions, that they were reluctant to give honest answer questions. Moreover, even if the figures were doubled, the proportion of repondents citing the demands of employees/employee representatives and the requirements of collective agreements/legislation would still be in minority. Just as it looks as if direct participation is largely home-grown, so too it appears to be something that is primarily management-inspired.

## 5.2   Similar patterns of motives for different forms of direct participation?

Is the introduction of a particular form of direct participation associated with a particular set of motives? The survey results suggest not. We find on the contrary essentially similar patterns of motives for the six direct participation forms. First of all, productivity and quality of working life considerations appeared to be dominant. Introduction of any direct participation form seems to be far less frequently motivated by examples in other workplaces, legislation and/or employees' demands than by the wish to increase productivity and improve the quality of working life. The first type of motive represents everywhere less than 20 per cent of the answers, whereas the second type systematically got at least 65 per cent of the responses (Figure 5.1).

### Key findings:

- the pattern of motives was very similar for each of the six forms of direct participation

- intriguingly, however, there were more citations for the consultative than the delegative forms regardless of motive

The patterns of response depending on the different forms of direct participation in most cases showed only slight variations, which are difficult to interpret. Concern for quality of working life seemed to be less widespread in the cases of individual and group delegation compared to the other forms; but productivity motives also declined in these groups for which we observe the highest rates of non response. Figure 5.1 shows some 'peaks' which admittedly would need explanation. Quality of working life ranked above productivity for individual 'face-to-face' consultation, whereas productivity predominated elsewhere. The two forms of group consultation reveal the highest frequencies of productivity motives, combined with equally high response rates for quality of working life concerns (> 80 per cent in all cases). Examples in other workplaces seem to have had a not negligible role in the introduction of 'face-to-face' consultation and permanent group consultation (near to 20 per cent of answers, against 15 per cent and less elsewhere).

At this degree of aggregation, no clear hypotheses can be advanced in order to explain these inter-group variations. Although some new questions emerged with the breakdown by country, the image of similarity of motive patterns for the six direct participation forms persisted – despite the national diversities.

One especially intriguing finding deserving comment, however, is that there were more citations for the consultative forms of direct participation than the delegative ones, regardless of the particular motive. In the case of productivity *and* quality of working life motives especially, it might have been thought, on the basis of the conventional wisdom, that the delegative forms would have been cited more. Yet they were not. In the case of examples elsewhere, for which the numbers are admittedly much smaller, it might have been thought that group delegation would have scored relatively highly. In the event, it not only comes after permanent group consultation but also temporary group consultation *and*, especially surprisingly, 'face-to-face' consultation. With one exception, fewer managers also cited the demands of employees/employee representatives and the requirements of collective agreements/legislation in the case of the delegative forms. Intriguing though these results are, they are none the less of a piece with one of the key findings in Chapter 4, namely that our respondents viewed the consultative forms of direct participation as more important than delegative ones.

## 5.3   National hierarchies of motives: variations on a theme

An overview of the EPOC survey results by country strongly reproduces the now familiar features. Productivity and quality of working life concerns were common motives in all countries; in most cases, as Figure 5A.1 in Appendix 3 confirms, more than 60 per cent of our respondents answered positively to both of these questions for most direct participation forms. Economic and social reasons thus are both at work where direct participation is introduced in the workplaces regardless of country; the survey does not reveal any national exceptionalism in this respect. Examples in other workplaces seem to be in most cases, although not systematically, the third motive by frequency. On a country, as well as on a European average level, the demands of employees/employee representatives and the requirements of collective agreements/legislation ranked far behind economic and social motives, even though they are not of negligible weight.

## Key findings:

- productivity and quality of working life concerns far out-ranked other motives in all countries

- productivity motives noticeably ranked above quality of working life concerns in Germany, Italy, Portugal, and Spain, whereas in Denmark, the Netherlands, and Sweden quality of working life was equally often cited

- examples elsewhere were more likely to be cited in Germany, Sweden and the Netherlands

- the demands of employees figured most prominently in Denmark, Italy, Ireland and Sweden

- the requirements of collective agreements/legislation featured most strongly in France and Portugal

Yet cross-country comparison also reveals noticeable variations. Productivity motives noticeably ranked above quality of working life concerns in Germany, Italy, Portugal and Spain. By contrast, quality of working life was the most frequently cited motive in Denmark, the Netherlands, and Sweden (except, in the latter case, for permanent group consultation). French, Irish and UK respondents showed varying priorities according to particular forms of direct participation. But, again, these variations do not reveal very readable patterns. Countries with either productivity or quality of working life priorities also show high frequencies for the second motive (the differences seldom exceeded 10 percentage points for already high response rates – 15 when the first mention gets 85 per cent or more of answers). The three countries alternating between economic and social priorities followed sometimes similar and sometimes contrasting patterns.

Analysis of diversity proved equally difficult in the case of the other motives. Italian respondents declared rather less frequently than their European neighbours that examples (in other workplaces) led to introduction direct participation (<8 per cent of answers, except in the case of permanent group consultation). The same motive systematically scored double figures in Germany, Sweden and the UK, exceeding or coming very close to 20 per cent for 'face-to-face' consultation and both types of group consultation. French employers got over the 20 per cent mark for the two forms of individual consultation and permanent group consultation.

Except for individual 'face-to-face' consultation, neither legislation nor collective bargaining seemed to play a major role in introducing direct participation in Germany, by noticeable contrast – at least for the consultation forms – to France, Ireland and Portugal. Demands from employees or their organisations played a minor role in Portugal, the Netherlands (except temporary group consultation), Germany and the UK (except 'arms-length' consultation in the two latter countries). They were often taken into account in Sweden, Italy, Ireland (consultation forms) and France (except delegation forms).

Finally, country analysis did not make any more understandable, at this stage of analysis, the contrasts between the patterns of motives behind different forms of direct participation. Both in regard to the European average and to national frequency distributions of motives, variations within countries did not seem strong or systematic enough to build up an explanatory framework.

## 5.4    The scope of direct participation, competition and trade union involvement – looking for the motive connection

Our attention now shifts to the differences between the main forms of direct participation. For instance, is the scope of direct participation discussed in Chapter 4 linked to particular combinations of motives? Do the motive patterns alter according to different workplace characteristics? For reasons of space, but also because of the absence of straightforward relationships, the focus is on the most often cited motives, i.e. productivity and the quality of working life. The data in Figures 5.4a and 5.4b suggest that where managers declared themselves 'strongly' motivated by quality of working life concerns (when more than one answer box was ticked), direct participation tended to earn higher scores for scope. Thus, workplaces where group delegation was introduced without the motive of quality of working life being cited mostly achieved low scores for scope. The opposite is the case where a strong belief in improving quality of working life prevailed: this motive had the highest occurrence in workplaces achieving medium scores for scope (one respondent in two) and was frequently cited in workplaces scoring highly (by one in four, against one in 15 for non-respondents). The relationship was less unambiguous, though largely positive, for productivity concerns. Yet 'strong' motives were not the prerogative of workplaces with medium and high scores for the scope of direct participation; they were also where direct participation tended to be relatively limited in scope. No unambiguous relationship can thus be constructed between the strength of motives and the scope of direct participation.

What kind of motives were emphasised by respondents exposed to severe and increasing competition compared to those faced with low and essentially stable competition? Again, as Figure 5.5 confirms, detailed analysis contradicts the idea of any systematic link between high exposure to competitive pressures and strong insistence on productivity motives. Where competitive pressure was high, productivity motives were more often mentioned than in 'protected' situations – the exception being 'face-to-face' consultation. The difference stood out for the other three forms of consultation only, however. In the case of the two forms of delegation, the frequency differences between workplaces faced with low and high competition represented not more than 1 to 4 percentage points for high response rates. On the other hand, competition did not alter the solidarity between economic and social motives. Concern for the quality of working life remained (very) strong in high competition workplaces and seemed to be the natural twin of economic motives.

## Key findings:

* where managers declared themselves 'strongly' motivated by quality of working life concerns, direct participation tended to earn higher scores for scope

* high exposure to competitive pressures wnet hand-in-hand with a strong emphasis on productivity motives

* whereas the presence of employee representatives had no systematic effect on the productivity and quality of working life motives, there were increasing figures for the requirements of collective agreements/legislation and employees' demands

Finally, does trade union presence and employee representative involvement in the introduction of direct participation have any influence on motive patterns? Two types of rough indicators help us to examine this question. Table 5.1 compares the motives in workplaces *with* and *without* employee representation (elected representatives and/or union representatives). Whereas recognition of representatives seems to have had no systematic effect on the productivity and quality of working life motives, there were increasing figures for motives linked to requirements of collective agreements and legislation, and to employees' demands. This is particularly clear in the latter case. Managers declared they took into account employees' demands for introducing permanent group consultation in 5 per cent of workplaces *without*, and in 18 per cent of workplaces *with*, employee representation. Introduction of individual 'face-to-face' consultation was motivated by employees' demands in 8 per cent of non-union workplaces and in 16 per cent of workplaces with collective employee representation.

A second indicator allowed us to compare motivation patterns of management in workplaces where employee representation was or was not strongly involved in the introduction of the most important form of direct participation. In workplaces

Figure 5.4a: Motives by scope of direct participation: productivity and quality of working life - % of respondents practising direct participation

Motive: productivity

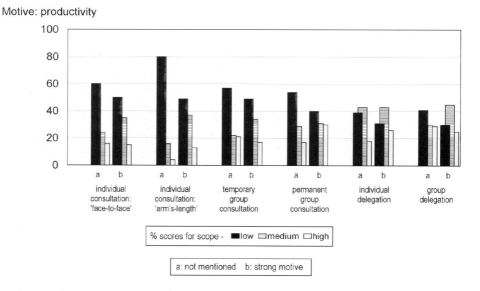

Figure 5.4b: Motives by scope of direct participation: productivity and quality of working life - % of respondents practising direct participation

Motive: quality of working life

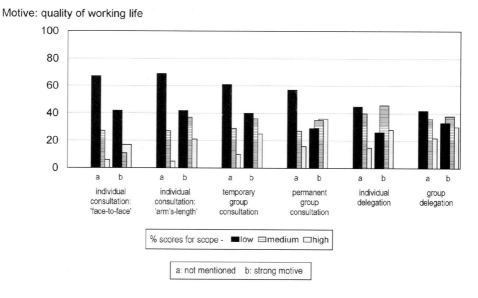

Figure 5.5: Motives by competitive situation - % of respondents practising direct participation

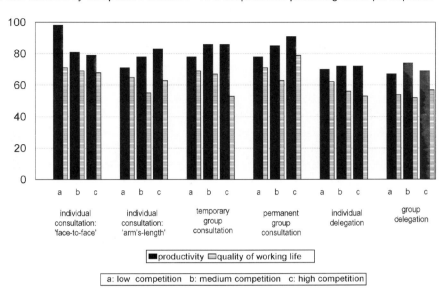

without representative involvement, quality of working life concerns were less frequently cited than in the cases where employee representatives were informed, consulted or involved in negotiations. Neither a similar nor an inverse relationship appeared in the case of productivity motives. Both motives, however, got (very) high frequencies and often exceeded 80 or 90 per cent of the responses.

**Table 5.6  Collective employee representation and motives for introducing direct participation – respondents practising direct participation**

|  | individual consultation: 'face-to-face' | | individual consultation: 'arm's length' | | group consultation: temporary groups | | group consultation: permanent. groups | | individual delegation | | group delegation | |
|---|---|---|---|---|---|---|---|---|---|---|---|---|
|  | no rep | rep | no rep | rep | no rep | rep | no rep | rep | no rep | rep | no rep | rep |
|  | % | | % | | % | | % | | % | | % | |
| productivity | 78 | 78 | 84 | 75 | 82 | 84 | 89 | 83 | 70 | 71 | 79 | 73 |
| quality of working life | 67 | 69 | 64 | 59 | 52 | 63 | 71 | 72 | 55 | 56 | 58 | 56 |
| example | 24 | 19 | 13 | 13 | 8 | 17 | 27 | 19 | 11 | 11 | 16 | 14 |
| requirements of legislation/collective agreement | 9 | 15 | 3 | 10 | 7 | 13 | 8 | 14 | 5 | 9 | 5 | 9 |
| employee/employee representative demands | 8 | 14 | 9 | 16 | 8 | 15 | 5 | 13 | 4 | 9 | 5 | 11 |

## 5.5 Summary and conclusion

Plurality of motives, a focus on productivity and quality of working life concerns rather than the requirements of regulatory frameworks and the demands of employees and their organisations, association of social and economic objectives, little evidence of the influence of other examples: these are the main answers the EPOC survey delivers to our initial questions on management's motives for introducing direct participation. There were no particular clear-cut set of motives behind the different direct participation forms. Neither was it possible to detect strong national motivation patterns. Social and (to a lesser degree) economic motives were most explicit where the scope of direct participation was high. The presence and involvement in the introduction of direct participation of employee representatives seems to have reinforced both managers' concerns about quality of working life and their willingness to take into account employees' demands. On the face of it, however, it looks very much as if direct participation is primarily management-inspired as well as being largely "home-grown".

While these conclusions may reflect the limits of the quantitative approach and of the sample of interviewees, it also tells us more about direct participation. Managers would seem to appreciate the social as well as the economic dimension of direct participation. The economic effects managers hope for seem to impose the parallel focus on the employee dimension. Both economic and social motives, so it seems, converge in the understanding of direct participation. This perhaps is not an unexpected result: at least a part of the story of the success or failure of this approach to organisational change is after all written by employees. There is, of course, an alternative explanation for the rather the standardised pattern of motives – it could indicate that managers do not credit direct participation with as distinctive virtues as the current debate often leads us to believe. Direct participation – possibly part of an answer, but not an answer by itself?

### References

Fröhlich, D. and U. Pekruhl. 1996: *Direct Participation and Organisational Change – Fashionable but Misunderstood? An analysis of recent research in Europe, Japan and the USA.* EF/96/38/EN. Luxembourg: Office for the Official Publications of the European Communities.

Geary, J. and K. Sisson. 1994: *Conceptualising Direct Participation in Organisational Change. The EPOC Project.* EF/94/23/EN. Luxembourg: Office for the Official Publications of the European Communities.

Regalia, I. 1995. *Humanise Work and Increase Profitability? Direct participation in organisational change viewed by the social partners in Europe.* EF/95/21/EN. Luxembourg: Office for the Official Publications of the European Communities.

Sisson, K. 1996. *Closing the Gap – Ideas and Practice. Direct Participation in Organisational Change.* EF/96/15/EN. Luxembourg: Office for the Official Publications of the European Communities.

# Chapter 6

## The links with organisational strategies

Organisations are in a process of permanent change. Be it private companies or public agencies, those who run organisations are constantly having to restructure their internal systems and their relations with the market, clients, suppliers and competitors as well as employees. The necessity for permanent change and renewal follows from the growing dynamics of the environment: clients and employees have fast changing and growing demands; the economic integration of Europe, the 'globalization' of production and services and intensified competition impose ever greater pressure to match world class production and service standards. Meanwhile new information and communication technologies prompt organisations to adapt their systems with far reaching consequences for operations.

During the 1960s, it can be argued, the foremost requirement was efficiency. In the 1970s, quality of products and/or services became more important. During the 1980s, emphasis shifted to flexibility. During the 1990s, more and more organisations have not only had to cope with efficiency, quality and flexibility requirements, but on top of that with an innovation demand as well: the regular and fast introduction of new processes and products/services. As Bolwijn and Kumpe (1991) have argued, it is the accumulation of requirements which marks out the recent past.

Our aim in this chapter is to make an initial attempt at linking the practice of direct participation to the organisational strategies being pursued by the workplaces in the EPOC survey. The first task is to establish the extent of the other initiatives, apart from direct participation, which managers were taking in the light of the changing environment. The important issues here are whether workplaces *with* direct participation differed from those *without* in the extent of other initiatives; whether there was any variation between the extent of initiatives and the scope of direct participation; and whether the extent of activity, of other initiatives *and* direct participation, varied by country.

The second task is to explore some of the underlying considerations which were expected to play a significant role in explaining the diffusion of direct participation discovered in Chapter 4. Two sets of considerations loomed large in EPOC's literature (Fröhlich and Pekruhl, 1996) and social partner (Regalia, 1995) surveys and it is with these that the rest of the chapter is mainly concerned:

*The significance of the competitive environment.* Many commentators and social partner representatives reckoned that it was competition, and in particular international competition, that was the driving force behind the introduction of direct participation, along with other strategic initiatives. For example, there were many references to the vehicle and electronics industries where intense competition from Japanese companies with long-established practice of group work and other forms of direct participation was held to be the critical factor in the presence of a number of significant case studies. This issue is the subject of section 6.2.

*The significance of ownership.* Multinational companies were seen as being in the forefront in the diffusion of direct participation. Key considerations in explaining why such companies might be inclined to see direct participation as a strategic initiative were not only the globally competitive environment, but also the resources to learn from and implement the results of best practice both in a sector and more generally.The question of whether multinationals have taken the lead in the diffusion of direct participation will be addressed in section 6.3.

## 6.1 Active workplaces?

Introducing direct participation is one of a range of possible initiatives which managers may consider in response to the changing environment. Such initiatives may include, for example, strategic alliances, product innovation, pursuing a 'back to core business' approach, outsourcing, relying on the introduction of new information technologies and the automation of processes. Additionally, there are cost minimisation programmes involving downsizing and delayering of management structures. Other measures such as working time flexibility and working time reductions may also be involved.

Subsequent analysis will explore in more detail the linkages between direct participation and the different combinations of these initiatives. At this stage, our aim is the much more modest one of establishing the extent of the activity of workpaces in respect of the initiatives which managers were taking. To this end, the 10 initiatives itemised above were brought together in a simple index to enable us to measure our workplaces' performance on this dimension. In the event, our respondents rarely reported taking more than five initiatives. Accordingly, no initiative or one initiatives was coded as 'low', two and three initiatives as 'medium', and 5 and more initiatives as 'high'.

## Key findings:

- direct participation is generally accompanied by other initiatives

- the greater the number of forms and scope of direct participation, the more initiatives

- most 'active' workplaces are located in Denmark, Germany, the Netherlands and the U K; workplaces in France, Italy, Portugal and Spain, by contrast, are apparently more 'passive'

Table 6.1 presents the data on the extent of management initiatives for workplaces *with* and *without* direct participation. Half of the workplaces *without* direct participation reveal a 'low' level of initiatives and only 15 per cent reported five or more initiatives. By contrast, in workplaces with direct participation, there were only 37 per cent in the 'low' and 42 per cent were in the 'medium' category. At the other extreme, two out of five workplaces were very 'active'. In other words, while other initiatives were to be found in both types of workplaces, they were more likely in those *with* direct participation.

**Table 6.1 The level of management initiatives in workplaces *with* and *without* direct participation: ten countries**

| | workplaces *with* direct participation % | workplaces *without* direct participation % |
|---|---|---|
| *level of initiatives* | | |
| low | 37 | 51 |
| medium | 42 | 34 |
| high | 21 | 15 |
| total % | 100 | 100 |

As Chapter 4 argued, the incidence of direct participation takes us only so far. It is the presence of multiple forms and the scope of application that really counts. The data in both cases revealed a very similar pattern and so only the relationship between the extent of initiatives and the scope of direct participation is documented here. The data, which is presented in Table 6.2, suggest a very clear result. Managers with a low-profile approach to direct participation tend to be relatively inactive when it comes to other initiatives. Only 16 per cent reported five or more initiatives. Managers practising direct participation which was extensive in scope, however, were twice as likely to be taking that number of initiatives.

**Table 6.2  The scope of direct participation and the level of additional management activities: ten countries**

|  | scores for scope | | |
|---|---|---|---|
|  | low | medium | high |
| *level of initiatives* | % | % | % |
| low | 41 | 34 | 28 |
| medium | 43 | 44 | 39 |
| high | 16 | 22 | 33 |
| total % | 100 | 100 | 100 |

In short, a policy of organisational change through direct participation is generally accompanied by other initiatives. Such an accumulation of strategies grows with the practice of multiple forms and the scope of direct participation: the greater the number of forms and the scope of direct participation, the more initiatives managers take at the same time. Those workplaces which practise direct participation more intensively, it seems, are especially 'active'.

The data for the separate countries in Table 6.3 suggests that there are distinct differences between them. Some countries considerably underperform in regard to initiatives in workplaces regardless of whether there is direct participation. Other countries' workplaces distinctly overperform in both cases. Thus, in France, Italy, Portugal and Spain, the approach to organisational change seems rather restricted. Not only did these four countries have the largest shares of workplaces with a low level of change practices (no direct participation and no or only one other initiative), the percentages varying between 55 and 58 per cent against a ten-country average of 49 per cent. These same countries also had the largest shares of workplaces *with* direct participation with a low level of initiatives (between 43 and 63 per cent against a ten-country average of 37 per cent). Portugal is especially noteworthy: the absence of (almost) any initiative was above average (55 per cent), and this absence was even higher in workplaces *with* direct participation (63 per cent). To put this differently, almost two thirds of Portuguese managers relied on direct participation accompanied, at most, by one other initiative.

**Table 6.3  Low and high levels of inititiatives in workplaces *with* and *without* direct participation: individual countries**

|  | workplaces *with* direct participation | | workplaces *without* direct participation | |
|---|---|---|---|---|
|  | low level | high level | low level | high level |
|  | % | % | % | % |
| ten-country average | 37 | 20 | 49 | 13 |
| Denmark | 35 | 26 | 38 | 19 |
| France | 43 | 18 | 56 | 12 |
| Germany | 30 | 22 | 47 | 22 |
| Ireland | 38 | 14 | 32 | 7 |
| Italy | 43 | 14 | 58 | 6 |
| Netherlands | 29 | 21 | 46 | 19 |
| Portugal | 63 | 13 | 55 | 6 |
| Spain | 46 | 16 | 57 | 3 |
| Sweden | 33 | 17 | 51 | 9 |
| United Kingdom | 34 | 29 | 46 | 26 |

Denmark, Germany, the Netherlands and the UK stand out for opposite reasons. Not only did these countries have the largest shares of workplaces *without* direct participation taking other initiatives (19 to 26 per cent high-level initiatives against an average of 13 per cent). At the same time, managers in these four countries were the ones most likely to combine such initiatives with the practice of direct participation. In this group, both Danish and UK managers stand out as the most intensive users of 'stand-alone' change initiatives and the combined application of direct participation and other initiatives.

Thus, in the case of change activities there does appear to be what might be described as a 'North-South' divide. Most 'active' workplaces, it seems, are located in four of the six Northern countries. By contrast, workplaces in France, Italy, Portugual and Spain are more passive.

## 6.2    The significance of the competitive environment

The logic of exploring the links between direct participation and the competitive environment has been spelt out in the introduction to this chapter. Our concern is to establish whether competition has been a major driving force behind the introduction of recent management initiatives; whether workplaces confronted with severe competion were more active in taking initiatives and in introducing direct participation; and whether the level of competition was associated with the scope of direct participation.

Table 6.4 presents an overview of the relations between the level of competition, as perceived by the managers in our survey, on the one hand, and the reported level of initiatives during the last three years, on the other. The measure 'level of competition' is a combination of the answers on questions about the nature and the changes in competition and is considered as a major indication of the dynamics of the environment. 'Weak competition' stands for the combination of 'no' or 'only domestic competition' with 'competition declined, remained the same or increased slightly'. 'Severe competition' combines 'both domestic and foreign competition' and 'competition increased significantly'. The data relates only to workplaces operating in the private sector because, depending on country, competition may not be of relevance for the public sector.

## Key findings:

• workplaces under intense competition were more active strategically: the share of workplaces which practised 5 or more initiatives grows with the level of competition.

• the association between the level of competition and the incidence and scope of direct participation is positive but quite weak

**Table 6.4  Level of competition by level of management initiatives – private sector**

|  | *level of competition* | | |
|---|---|---|---|
|  | weak | medium | severe |
|  | % | % | % |
| *level of initiatives* | | | |
| low | 49 | 35 | 28 |
| medium | 39 | 44 | 43 |
| high | 12 | 21 | 29 |

Table 6.4 shows clear associations between the levels of competition and management initiatives. Half of the workplaces confronted with a low level of competition revealed a low level of initiatives at the same time; only 12 per cent applied many initiatives and so could be conceived of as 'active' workplaces. Only 28 per cent of the workplaces which reported severe competition practised a low level of change initiatives, 43 per cent range in the middle category and almost 30 per cent were high users of additional initiatives. So workplaces under severe competition were more active in taking initiatives.

The data in Table 6.5 gives the beginnings of an answer to the question whether there was a positive relationship between competition and the incidence of direct participation. The share of workplaces practising direct participation was 76 per cent in the case of weak competition and 81 per cent under medium or severe competitive conditions. The level of competition makes a difference, in other words, but the effect is quite small.

**Table 6.5  Level of competition by incidence of direct participation –
private sector**

| | *level of competition* | | |
| | weak | medium | severe |
| | % | % | % |
| *incidence of* | | | |
| *direct participation* | 76 | 81 | 81 |

Does this conclusion also hold for the incidence of the different forms of direct participation? Figure 6.1 gives an overview of the association between level of competition and incidence of the six forms of direct participation and suggests it was very weak: only in the case of temporary group consultation did the data show a clear positive relationship (weak: 32 per cent; severe: 45 per cent). The overall incidence of direct participation (see Table 6.5) and the incidence of most of the separate forms of direct participation hardly varied with the dynamics of the environment, which is an unexpected result.

It was only in the case of the scope of direct participation that the picture was more in line with the expectations of the commentators and social partner representatives referred to in the introduction to this chapter. The data in Figure 6.2 show that the scope of permanent consultation groups, group delegation and, to a lesser extent, 'face-to-face' consultation was higher in the case of severe competition. But the overall scope of direct participation was hardly associated with competition: the figure for high overall scope was 9 per cent in the case of weak competition, and 13 per cent and 11 per cent in the cases of medium and severe competition respectively.

The EPOC survey results do not therefore strongly support the expectation that it was competition, and especially international competition, which is the driving force behind the introduction of direct participation. The association between the level of competition and the incidence and scope of direct participation, on the whole goes in the right direction but is quite weak.

Figure 6.1: Level of competition by the incidence of the main forms of direct participation
- private sector respondents practising direct participation

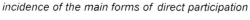

*incidence of the main forms of direct participation*

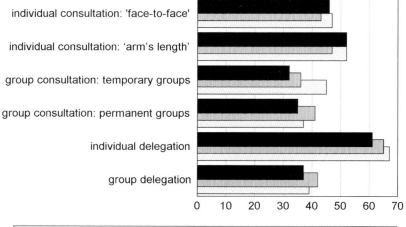

Figure 6.2: Level of competition by scope of the main forms of direct participation
- private sector respondents practising direct participation

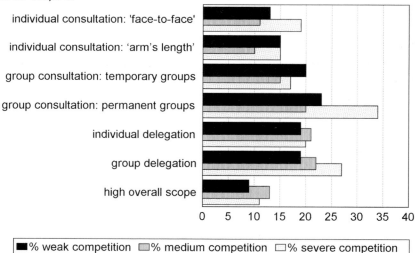

Another interesting result is that workplaces under intense competition were more active: the share of workplaces which practiced 5 or more strategic initiatives increased with the level of competition.

## 6.3 The significance of ownership: a multinational company effect?

In presenting the results of the EPOC survey on the nature and extent of direct participation, Chapter 4 has already touched on the question of ownership. Contrary to conventional wisdom, it found that industry was not the 'leader' so far as the incidence and intensity of direct participation was concerned. The public services, it emerged, were just as likely, if not more likely, to practise direct participation and do so intensively.

### Key findings:

- MNCs were more active in taking other initiatives – especially those operating under severe competition

- MNCs were also more active in the field of direct participation, above all in the case of the incidence (but not the scope) of temporary group consultation and the intensity of group delegation

Within the private sector, nonetheless, multinationals (MNCs) have enjoyed a special position in the debate about direct participation. It is generally felt that they have not only been more active in initiating new strategies but also, in particular, have been at the forefront of the introduction and intensive practice of direct participation. The EPOC survey offered a unique opportunity to see if this was so.

Table 6.6 presents the data on the initiatives of MNCs and other workplaces operating in the private sector. The MNCs in our survey lived up to expectations. They were more 'active, as is demonstrated by the much higher figures for initiatives taken during the last three years compared with those for the category 'other workplaces'.

In part, these results can be explained by the fact that MNCs operated relatively often under intense competition (see Tables 6.7 and 6.9). As Table 6.7 shows, only 8 per cent of the MNCs operated under weak competitive conditions, against 20 per cent of the 'other' workplaces. Also 43 per cent of the MNC respondents perceived their environment to be highly competitive, against 33 per cent of the other workplaces. In Table 6.8 the level of strategic initiatives of MNCs characterized by different levels of competition are compared with those of the other workplaces. MNCs under severe competition again were the most active for strategic initiatives. MNCs confronted with medium competition were also more active than the comparable other workplaces. The same holds for the MNCs under weak competition.

**Table 6.6 Level of management initiatives of MNCs and other private sector respondents practising direct participation**

|                     | MNCs | Others |
|---------------------|------|--------|
|                     | %    | %      |
| *level of initiatives* |      |        |
| low                 | 26   | 40     |
| medium              | 43   | 41     |
| high                | 31   | 19     |

**Table 6.7 Level of competition facing MNC s and other private sector respondents practising direct participation**

|                      | MNCs | Others |
|----------------------|------|--------|
|                      | %    | %      |
| *level of competition* |      |        |
| low                  | 8    | 20     |
| medium               | 49   | 47     |
| high                 | 43   | 33     |

**Table 6.8 MNCs and other private sector respondents practising direct participation by level of competition and level of management initiatives**

|                     | *level of competition* | | | | | |
|---------------------|------|--------|--------|------|--------|--------|
|                     | MNCs | | | Others | | |
|                     | weak | medium | severe | weak | medium | severe |
|                     | %    | %      | %      | %    | %      | %      |
| *level of initiatives* |      |        |        |      |        |        |
| low                 | 49   | 23     | 25     | 49   | 38     | 29     |
| medium              | 24   | 51     | 37     | 40   | 42     | 44     |
| high                | 27   | 26     | 38     | 11   | 20     | 27     |

Chapter 3 suggested that MNCs were not so exceptional so far as the simple incidence of direct participation was concerned. Table 6.9 shows that MNCs under severe competition were more likely to have direct participation, although the difference with the other types of workplaces was not as large as might have been expected: 86 per cent of these workplaces practised direct participation, compared to 80 per cent of the other types of workplaces confronted with severe competition. Much more remarkable is that only 61 per cent of the MNCs under weak competitive conditions reported practising direct participation, against 77 per cent of the comparable group of other workplaces. It is not immediately obvious why this should be so and further analysis of this result will be needed.

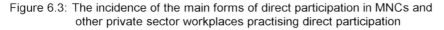

Figure 6.3: The incidence of the main forms of direct participation in MNCs and other private sector workplaces practising direct participation

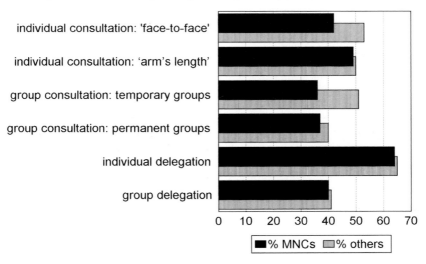

Table 6.9  MNCs and other private sector respondents practising direct participation by level of competition and incidence of direct participation

| | level of competition | | | | | |
|---|---|---|---|---|---|---|
| | MNCs | | | Others | | |
| | weak | medium | severe | weak | medium | severe |
| | % | % | % | % | % | % |
| *direct participation* | 61 | 81 | 86 | 77 | 81 | 80 |

MNCs did not stand out either so far as the individual forms of direct participation are concerned. Indeed, as Figure 6.3 shows, the incidence of 'face-to-face' consultation and temporary group consultation was significanly higher in the workplace of other companies.

The scope of the different forms did appear to be wider in MNCs workplaces, however. Figure 6.4 shows that 15 per cent of the MNCs reported a high overall scope of direct participation against 10 per cent of the other workplaces; 55 per cent of the MNC workplaces were characterised by a low level of overall scope, whereas the comparable figure for the other workplaces was 67 per cent. Admittedly, the differences for some of the individual forms were quite small and, in some cases,

Figure 6.4: The scope of the main forms of direct participation in MNCs and other private sector workplaces with direct participation

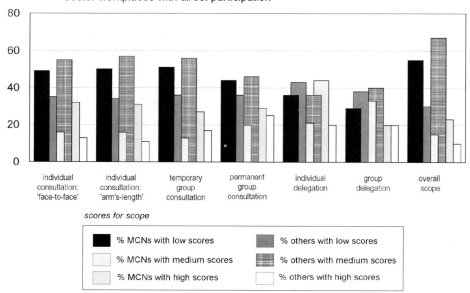

go in favour of the other workplaces. It is perhaps significant however, that in one third of MNC workplaces with group delegation the practice was very intensive, whereas only one fifth of other workplaces with this form could be characterised in the same way.

## 6.4  Summary and conclusions

A policy of organisational change through direct participation is generally accompanied by a range of additional management initiatives. The greater the scope of direct participation, it seems, the more initiatives are being undertaken. The fundamental difference is not so much between the organisations practicising or not practising direct participation. Rather it is between organisations which are active and inactive in the face of the challenges confronting them.

Other findings confirm the complexity of the issues being dealt with. Competition, it seems, helps to account for the diffusion of direct participation, but only up to a point. The same is true of ownership and, in particular ownership by multinational company. MNCs tended to practise direct participation more intensively, as well as taking other initiatives, especially where the competition they were facing was intense, but the difference was not as great as might have been expected.

# References

Bolwijn, P.T. en T. Kumpe (1991): *Marktgericht ondernemen. Management van continuiteit en vernieuwing*. Assen/Maastricht: Van Gorcum.

Fröhlich, D. and U. Pekruhl. 1996: *Direct Participation and Organisational Change – Fashionable but Misunderstood? An analysis of recent research in Europe, Japan and the USA*. EF/96/38/EN. Luxembourg: Office for the Official Publications of the European Communities.

Regalia, I. 1995. *Humanise Work and Increase Profitability? Direct participation in organisational change viewed by the social partners in Europe*. EF/95/21/EN. Luxembourg: Office for the Official Publications of the European Communities.

# Chapter 7

# The effects of direct participation

This chapter analyses the views of management on the effects of direct participation. These effects proved to be one of the main imponderables in both the interviews with the social partner representatives (Regalia, 1995) and the literature review (Fröhlich and Pekruhl, 1996) in the first phase of the EPOC project. There was a particular lack of information about the relationship between the practice of direct participation, on the one hand, and economic performance and employment, on the other.

In the case of economic performance, EPOC's literature review confirmed that there had been no serious attempt to link practices such as those involved in direct performance with outcomes. It was not surprising either. Even management in organisations practising direct participation, though mostly convinced that direct participation has positive effects, rarely attempted to quantify the outcome. Such quantification was difficult and time-consuming and, to some extent, pointless as well – attempting to isolate the effects of one particular change or set of changes was virtually impossible given the wide range of developments their organisations were more or less continuously experiencing.

In the case of the employment effects, EPOC's social partner and literature reviews revealed, as well as concerns about the internal division of labour, there were two main anxieties expressed by trade union representatives: that direct participation would lead to a reduction in the number of employees in general and managers in particular. The implicit starting point for many was the core message of 'half of everything' of Womack and his colleagues in *The machine that changed the world*, which applied as much to personnel as it did to time-to-market, inventory, scrap and so on. Even if the drive for greater flexibility already discussed in Chapter 6 does not necessarily involve a reduction in the number of employees overall – some jobs may go to sub-contractors, for example – it does imply a reduction in the organisation's own commitments compared to what they were under more traditional ways of working. By definition, too, delayering involves a reduction in the number of existing managerial posts – a reduction in overheads is, after all, one of the main reasons for changing existing work organisation.

Most studies of lean production and flattening of hierarchies, EPOC's literature review suggested, implied that these initiatives result in a reduction in the size of the workforce and, above all, the number of middle managers. However, there was no comparable information available on the employment effects of direct participation. Critically, there was rarely any information available what would have happened had the changes not taken place. Again, the implication of a number of studies was that operations might have closed down altogether with the loss of many more employees. Also, and perhaps even fundamentally, there was no comparable information available on employment developments in organisations *with* and *without* direct participation. Any reduction in employment may be greater in organisations *without* direct participation. Certainly, as Chapter 3 has already shown, this was true of the workplaces in the EPOC survey.

The significance of the issues has not been lost on policy makers. If they are to be successful in promoting new forms of work organisation as the means to the end of the 'European social model' discussed in Chapter 1, they have to be able to convince the social partners that direct participation and similar initiatives represent a positive sum game. It is in this connection that the likelihood of a reduction, in particular, in the number of employees as a result of the introduction of direct participation takes on a special significance. In the very diplomatic language of the European Commission's 1997 Green Paper, *Partnership for a new organisation of work*, the main challenge to policy makers is seen as

> ... how to develop or adapt policies which support, rather than hinder, fundamental organisational renewal and how to strike a productive balance between the interests of business and the interests of workers, thereby facilitating the modernisation of working life. An essential objective is to achieve such a balance between flexibility and security throughout Europe (Executive summary).

It is against this background that the present chapter explores the results of the EPOC survey on the effects of direct participation on economic performance and employment. Three sets of indicators form the basis of the analysis. The *first* covers indicators of economic performance:

- cost reduction;

- reduction of throughput time;

- improvement of quality of product or service;

- increase in output.

The *second* includes two indicators of indirect labour cost variables which featured strongly in the debate on direct participation in the 1960s and 1970s:

- decrease in sickness;

- decrease in absenteeism.

The *third* embraces two possible negative labour market indicators resulting from the introduction of direct participation:

- reduction in number of employees;

- reduction in number of managers.

The data have their limitations, of course. First, the indicators are qualitative rather than quantitative. For example, 'reduction of employment', gives no information about how many employees have been laid off, nor does it provide any information as to whether additional labour has been taken on. Likewise, 'cost reduction', gives no indication by how much costs have been introduced in what period of time. Experience in the pilot survey suggested that to have asked for such quantitative information would have reduced the response rate considerably. Second, many workplaces applied multiple forms of direct participation and some interviewees might have found it difficult to attribute a particular effect to a particular form, despite the clear guidance in the questionnaire. It may be that the combination of activities is more significant for the exact attribution of specific effects of direct participation. Third, it might be expected that our respondents would exaggerate the effects of direct participation, especially if they had been associated with its introduction – although this should not have affected their relative judgements.

A further methodological limitation is the low response rate for the indicators measuring the different direct effects of the introduction of direct participation. It varies between 63 per cent (improvement of quality) to 38 per cent (reduction in number of managers). Altogether 43 per cent of respondents did not answer the question on the indicators measuring the effects of direct participation – itself probably a reflection of the difficulties even managers themselves have in coming to a judgement.

This low response rate was tested for systematic bias against three structural variables (country, sector and size of workplace) and against the 6 different forms of direct participation. On the country level, the refusal rate ranges between 31 per cent (the Netherlands) and 65 per cent (Portugal). In only one more country was the refusal rate above 50 per cent (Ireland, 52 per cent). As for sector and workplace size, there was no systematic bias. A similar pattern of no systematic bias emerged between the 6 different forms of direct participation. In short, the low response rate on all 8 indicators has to be considered in the interpretation of the empirical results, but control for systematic bias reveals only minor distortions in respect of two countries (Portugal and the Netherlands).

Even with these limitations, the data provide a valuable insight into the effects of direct participation. Patterns emerged which allowed us to draw two main conclusions with some confidence: our respondents did discriminate between the effects of direct participation on different indicators; and stronger effects were consistently associated with some forms of direct participation than with others. In the eyes of their sponsors, at least, some forms of direct participation were more effective than others.

The remainder of this chapter develops these conclusions in greater detail. The second section presents an overview of the effects of the incidence of the main forms of direct participation. The third considers the effects of the application of multiple forms of direct participation. The fourth presents an in-depth analysis of the effects of scope and intensity of different forms of direct participation. Section 5 focuses particularly on the employment effects of direct participation and section 6 bench marks the different scope and intensity of the various forms of direct participation. The chapter finishes with a brief country comparison.

## 7.1　An overview of the effects of direct participation

Table 7.1 shows the overall relationship between the six types of direct participation and the indicators of performance. All forms of direct participation had, first of all, a strong economic impact in the perception of management. Not surprisingly, the strongest impact was on quality, where between 92 per and 95 per cent of managers saw a positive impact of different direct participation measures. Not as strong, but also with a clear majority, management saw positive effects on throughput time (between 62-70 per cent), cost reduction (between 56-66 per cent) and increased output (between 44-58 per cent). The maximum impact varied between the indicators: group delegation was related to the strongest output increase; suggestion schemes and other measures of 'arm's length' consultation showed the highest cost reduction. Quality improvement was consistent over all six measures of direct participation. From a policy perspective the perceived economic performance of direct participation is impressive and covers not only group delegation, but also the other forms of direct participation.

## Key findings:

- all forms of direct participation were reckoned to have a strong impact on economic performance -nine out of ten respondents in the case of quality reported so

- around a third of respondents reported a reduction in absenteeism and sickness

- the introduction of direct participation was accompanied by a reduction in the number of employees and managers in around a third of cases

The overall effect on the indirect labour cost variables was lower than on the economic performance indicators. This can be exemplified by comparing the results for group delegation in Table 7.1. Around one third of workplaces with group delegation, experienced a reduction in absenteeism (37 per cent) and in sickness (32 per cent), whereas an observed increase in quality was three times stronger and increased output is nearly double (58 per cent). These results concur with the public debate on management expectations of direct participation. In the past, managers focused more on absenteeism, sickness rate and turnover than on economic performance; direct participation has become an organisational development tool used to influence output, throughput time and quality.

Table 7.1 also provides results on the employment impact of direct participation. The introduction of group consultation, for example through quality circles, led in one quarter of workplaces with this form of direct participation, to a reduction of employment. The introduction of group delegation resulted in even stronger negative employment effects (30 per cent). However, the strongest negative employment effects were associated with 'arms length' consultation, such as suggestion schemes, employee surveys and 'speak-up' schemes (37 per cent).

In several workplaces the overall reduction of employees was accompanied by a process of delayering the internal hierarchies and, as a consequence, a reduction of the number of managers. The highest reduction of middle managers was in workplaces which had introduced group delegation (31 per cent). The lowest was in workplaces with quality circles (22 per cent). For the policy debate, one has to conclude that significant negative employment effects are also present as a result of the introduction of direct participation and particularly of individual 'arm's length' consultation and group delegation. Consequently, the fears of many trade unions, in regard of direct participation, seem to be justified. However, the results give no indication about the exact extent of reduction nor about what would have happened to the workplace, if organisational change had not taken place. Due to its political sensitivity and based on additional information in the questionnaire, a more detailed analysis of the employment effects is given in a later section.

**Table 7.1  The effects of the different forms of direct participation –
% of those responding 'Yes'**

|  | individual consultation: 'face-to-face' | individual consultation: 'arms-length' | group consultation: temporary groups | group consultation: permanent groups | individual delegation | group delegation |
|---|---|---|---|---|---|---|
| reduction of costs | 61 | 66 | 64 | 61 | 60 | 56 |
| reduction of throughput time | 64 | 66 | 66 | 62 | 69 | 66 |
| improvement in quality | 94 | 92 | 95 | 94 | 93 | 94 |
| increase in total output | 52 | 47 | 48 | 53 | 44 | 58 |
| decrease in sickness | 39 | 40 | 31 | 37 | 22 | 32 |
| decrease in absenteeism | 42 | 39 | 39 | 39 | 28 | 37 |
| reduction in nos. of employees | 27 | 37 | 30 | 26 | 26 | 30 |
| reduction in nos. of managers | 26 | 25 | 23 | 22 | 28 | 31 |

This summary of the interrelation of the six different forms of direct participation with the performance indicators shows, in general, no significant variation. The expectation that newer forms of direct participation, like group work, would systematically out-perform more traditional forms, such as task forces or suggestion schemes, is not confirmed. This surprising result, however, has to be tested in more detailed analysis of the effects of direct participation.

## 7.2   The effects of multiple forms of direct participation

As has been suggested above, many organisations apply several forms of direct participation simultaneously and, therefore, it is difficult to isolate the effects of the single forms of direct participation in such circumstances. Typically, for example, multiple forms will be involved in such integrated approaches as total quality management. After the analysis of all individual types of direct participation, Figure 7.1 presents the data on the relation between a multiple direct participation application and its effect on economic performance, indirect labour costs and employment. The combined effect is measured as an index from 1 to 6, where the value 6 indicates a parallel use of all six forms of direct participation. In order to reduce the complexity of the data, three overall categories of parallel use have been created: 1-2 forms; 3-4 forms; and 5-6 forms.

## Key findings:

- the more forms of direct participation were used, the greater the reported effects

- respondents with five or six forms consistently reported greater effects than those with one or two forms

Concerning the economic effects, the figures show a clear positive relationship between the multiple use of different measures of direct participation, and all four economic performance measures. The strongest difference between a low and high use of direct participation was on output. If workplaces used only 1 or 2 forms of direct participation, 43 per cent of managers saw an increase in output. However, if workplaces applied 5-6 forms the figure increased to 73 per cent (a difference in percentage points of +30). The other three economic indicators showed a weaker but also significant interrelation. The difference in percentage points between single

Figure7.1: The effects of multiple forms of direct participation - % of those responding 'yes'

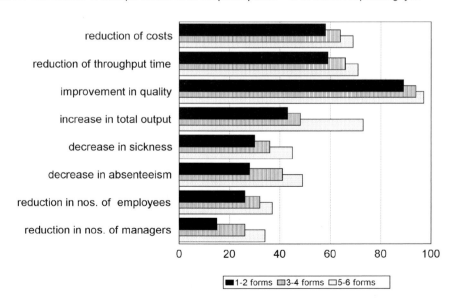

and multiple user workplaces for quality was + 8; for cost reduction, +11; and for throughput time, +12.

Multiple forms of direct participation also had a strong influence on indirect labour costs. In those workplaces with 5-6 forms, 49 per cent of managers attributed a reduction of absenteeism and 45 per cent a decrease in sickness rates to direct participation. This compares to a 28 per cent reduction of absenteeism in workplaces which applied 1-2 forms. The figure for reduced sickness rate was 30 per cent, i.e. the difference in percentage points for absenteeism was +21 and for decrease in sickness, +15.

The strongest employment effect through a simultaneous application of direct participation activities was on management levels, as 34 per cent of workplaces reduced the number of management under these circumstances. This is a difference of +19 percentage points in comparison to workplaces with a single use of direct participation. The employment impact, however, was weaker (+11).

Nearly all results become even stronger, when we examine the small group of workplaces which apply all six forms in parallel and compares those with the workplaces with 1 or 2 forms of direct participation. The difference in percentage points was particularly high on:

- cost reduction        +18
- output increase       +35
- lay offs              +14
- reduction of managers +28

In conclusion, these results confirm conventional wisdom that multiple forms of direct participation are more effective than the isolated measures. Economic performance goes up and direct labour costs go down. The downside of this trend is a negative impact on employment. Multiple forms have a significant impact on the reduction of the workforce in general and the delayering of managers in particular.

## 7.3    The effects of the scope and intensity of direct participation

*Individual consultation*

The previous section presented an analysis of the general and combined effects of direct participation on business performance and employment. The analysis will now focus on the relation between the scope of 'face-to-face' and 'arm's length' consultation and the effect on business performance. Scope, it will be remembered from Chapter 4, is measured by the addition of relevant issues, which were included in review meetings ('face to face') or which were covered through suggestion schemes, attitude surveys or 'speak-up' schemes ('arm's length'). The following issues have been included in the index.

- work organisation
- working time
- health and safety
- training
- quality of product and service
- customer relations
- changes in technology
- changes in investment

## Key findings:

- stronger application of the more traditional forms of 'arms-length' consultation, such as suggestion schemes, had greater effects than equivalent forms of 'face-to-face' consultation

- more developed forms of temporary group consultation had greater effects than equivalent forms of permanent group consultation (e.g. quality circles)

- especially important in the case of individual delegation was the room of manoeuvre for individuals to manage customer relations (external and internal) and a stronger control of time keeping/attendance and scheduling of work

- the scope and intensity of group delegation were of particular importance for economic performance; the coverage had direct effects for absenteeism and sickness and indirect effects for economic performance

The results in Figure 7.2 show no linear relationship between the scope of 'face-to-face' consultation and the performance and labour market effects. The number of relevant issues discussed in the different review meetings had no immediate performance effect.

What of of 'arm's length' consultation? To begin with the economic performance variables, in workplaces with high scores for scope of 'this form there was a strong impact on cost reduction where the value increases from 56 per cent (low) to 81 per cent (high). These traditional measures of individual consultation also reduced

Figure 7.2: The effects of the scope of 'face-to-face' consultation - % of those responding 'yes'

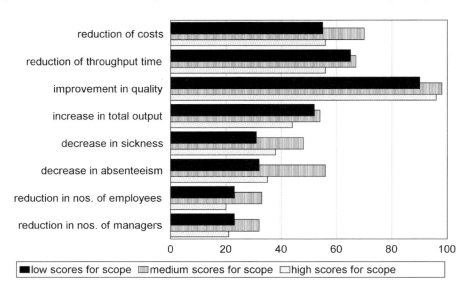

Figure 7.3: The effects of the scope of 'arm's-length' consultation - % of those responding 'yes'

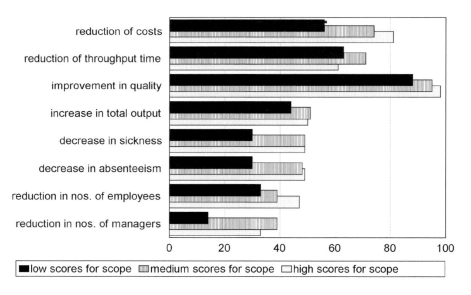

indirect personnel costs significantly, if the consultation covered a wide range of issues. In Figure 7.3, 30 per cent of workplaces with low scores reduced their sickness rate and showed a decrease in absenteeism. A full use of the potential of 'arm's length' direct participation, covering a wide range of issues, increased these figures to 49 per cent, a difference of +19 percentage points.

Figure 7.4: The effects of the scope of consultation with temporary groups - % of those responding 'yes'

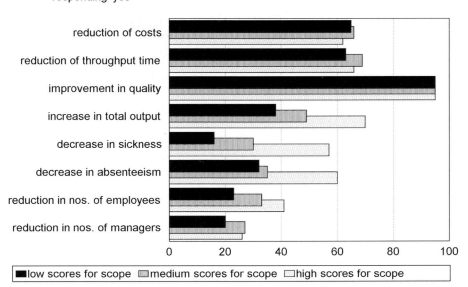

The impact on overall employment was also significant. Half of workplaces with high scores for the scope of 'arm's length' consultation reduced employment, whereas the average of workplaces with low scope was 33 per cent.

Further analysis shows that 'arm's length' consultation was particularly effective if it covered strategic aspects, such as investment or new technology. Proposals made through suggestion schemes, for example, on strategic topics, led to a significant reduction of costs (+26) and increase in quality (+10). It also has a strong effect on the reduction of indirect labour costs (+25 and +34).

Comparing the effects of stronger applications of the more traditional forms of individual consultation, such as suggestion schemes, with stronger forms of 'face-to-face' consultation, one has to conclude the former approach has a stronger economic performance and indirect cost reduction effect than the latter.

*Group consultation*

Table 7.1 suggests that the incidence of temporary consultation groups had a significant effect on the economic performance. Figure 7.4 focuses on the scope of this form. Scope is defined here as the number of issues the group was consulted on.

Figure 7.5: The effects of the scope of consultation with permanent groups - % of those responding 'yes'

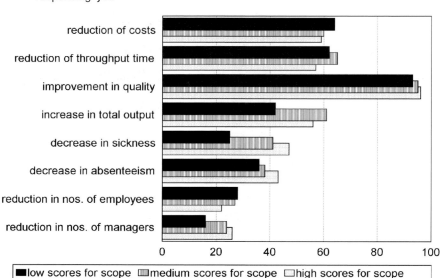

Within this definition, the effect of temporary consultative groups on the economic performance of direct participation workplaces was limited. First, there was a significant increase of output, with a difference of +32 percentage points between workplaces with low and high scores for scope. A background analysis shows that this increase was explained by temporary groups dealing particularly with customer and strategic issues. Second, there was also a significant impact on indirect labour costs. For example, in the case of sickness decrease, there was a difference of +41 points and on reduced absenteeism of +28 points. Temporary groups, which cover a large range of issues, seem a good mechanism to reduce indirect labour costs. The reduction in indirect labour costs occurred particularly in those temporary groups dealing with the improvement of working conditions. Temporary groups which do not discuss working conditions were reckoned to achieve only a 20 per cent reduction in sickness rates; if this item was a strong issue for the group, the value increased to 49 per cent (+29). A similar effect can be observed on absenteeism (+29).

In comparison with the more developed forms of temporary consultative groups, the stronger forms of permanent consultation groups (e.g. quality circles) did not have a significantly higher effect on economic performance, indirect labour costs and employment, as Figure 7.5 shows. Neither the number of issues nor individual clusters of issues on customer relations, strategic developments or working conditions, had any performance impact. Performance was not influenced, either,

Figure 7.6: The effects of the scope of individual delegation - % of those responding 'yes'

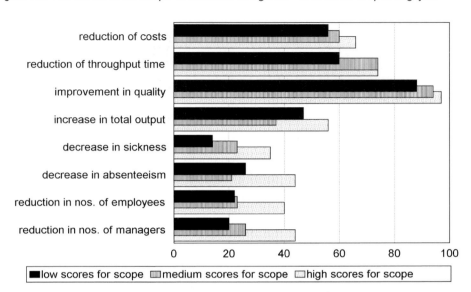

by the extent of autonomy given to the group, e.g. to decide on the group's composition and the issues to be discussed in the group.

*Individual delegation*

The practice of job design and job enrichment have been an important part of the debate on organisational development for more than 40 years. Table 7.1 has already shown that delegation to the individual had a significant impact on the economic performance of workplaces. More than 90 per cent of workplaces with job enrichment improved their quality, nearly 70 per cent reduced throughput time, 60 per cent reduced costs and more than 40 per cent increased output. The impact on indirect labour costs was lower but significant in a quarter of workplaces.

The overall scope of individual rights was covered in the questionnaire through three key dimensions:

- time (time keeping, absence control);

- co-ordination (dealing with customers and internal groups)

- process (scheduling of work, improving process)

The results are summarised in Figure 7.6 in an index of the overall scope of individual delegation in relation to key issues. The results show an interrelation between all indicators of economic performance and greater individual autonomy on the job. Workplaces with high scores for individual delegation achieved 97 per cent quality improvement – that is 10 percentage points higher than workplaces with low scores. Using the same comparisons, success in cost reduction increased by +10; throughput time by +14; and output increased by +9. The effects on indirect labour costs were even higher. Sickness decreases by +21 and absenteeism reduces by +18.

A more in-depth analysis, using the three different indicators shows that the positive effect on individual labour costs was, on one hand, related to a stronger control of the individual employee over his/her time keeping and attendance and, on the other, to more process control, for example, through more freedom in the scheduling of work. The stronger economic effects, however, were mainly related to the greater freedom of individuals to manage external customer relations and internal relations with other departments or groups.

*Group delegation*

Managers were asked whether group delegation was effective in reaching eight goals. The results in Table 7.1 show that the overall impact of group-delegation on the economic performance from the point of view of management was impressive. More than 90 per cent of managers saw improved product and service quality as a result of all forms of group delegation, 60 per cent saw cost reduction and improved throughput time and 58 per cent increased their output due to group delegation, which was also reckoned to reduce indirect costs. Absenteeism decreased in nearly 40 per cent of all workplaces, while sickness rates were lower in one third.

Chapter 4 introduced two models used to characterise group delegation: the 'Scandinavian' with high autonomy and a wide range of rights allotted to group members and, on the other hand, the 'Toyota' or 'lean production' with low group autonomy and few decision rights. Do workplaces with group delegation conforming to these types have different economic and employment effects? We have altogether three measures to characterise this form: *scope*, which indicates the range of group rights; *autonomy*, which covers the group's discretion to chose their members and decide their own discussion topics; and *intensity*, which combines both scope and autonomy to a measure that somewhat denotes the 'quality' of group delegation.

Figure 7.7 reports the results on the scope of rights in group delegation. The economic effect of groups with high scores would appear to be convincing as cost reduction increased from 44 per cent (low) to 62 per cent (high). This is a difference of +18 percentage points. Throughput time (+15); quality (+6); and increase in

Figure 7.7: The effects of the scope of group delegation - % of those responding 'yes'

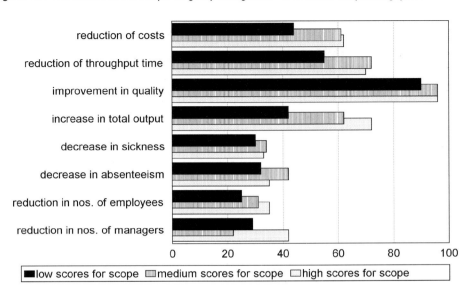

output (+20) also showed a strong relationship with the scope of issues the group could consider.

The employment situation is also affected, however. Stronger forms of group delegation had stronger negative employment impacts. Group delegation achieving high scores was accompanied, in one third of all workplaces, by general lay-offs and in over 40 per cent of workplaces with a delayering of management. Indirect labour costs, however, did not show any great variation with the scope of group work.

The autonomy of the group is a second key dimension defining group delegation. Figure 7.8 demonstrates that there was a strong impact of 'high autonomy' on high economic performance according to our respondents. More than 50 per cent of managers reported a cost reduction; 83 per cent reduced throughput time; 83 per cent increased output and 94 per cent increased quality. So 'high autonomy' groups were regarded very positively by management.

The greater the autonomy of the group, the greater the effects on employment, however. More than half of the workplaces with 'high autonomy' groups reduced their workforce (56 per cent) and half their middle managers. The percentage point difference to workplaces with low autonomy is +40 and +31.

Figure 7.8: The effects of the autonomy of group delegation - % of those responding 'yes'

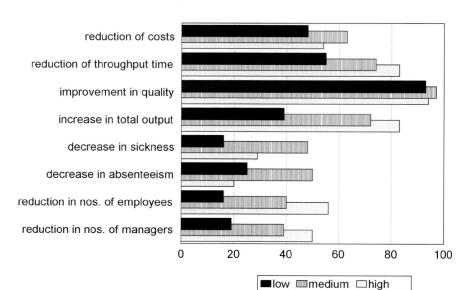

Figure 7.9: The effects of the intensity of group delegation - % of those responding 'yes'

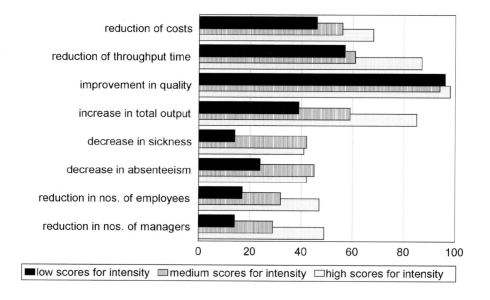

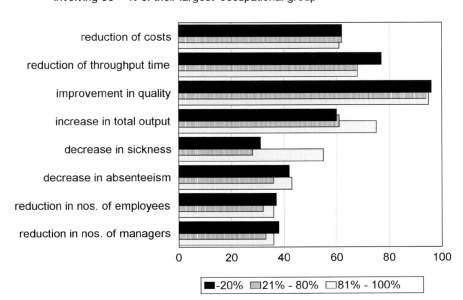

Figure 7.10: The effects of the coverage of group delegation - % of those responding 'yes' involving 50+ % of their largest occupational group

The reported significance of the overall measure of the intensity of group delegation is shown in Figure 7.9. Not surprisingly, in the light of the analysis of the two underlying effects in Figures 7.7 and 7.8, group delegation achieving high scores on this overall measure had a very strong economic and labour market effect. The theory, and often reported practice, of organisations which have delegated significant responsibilities to employees being more effective and productive receives additional support from the results of the EPOC survey.

Are these results due to the intensity of group delegation or to the level of workforce coverage within workplaces, i.e. the share of employees which work in groups? Compared to the intensity of group delegation, the influence of workforce coverage was much less clear (see Figure 7.10). The coverage dimension had hardly any systematic influence on direct economic effects or on the reduction in the number of employees and managers.

It was, however, very significant for the rates of sickness and absence decrease – workplaces with only small sections of the workforce involved in group delegation reported about a 30 per cent reduction of sickness and absenteeism, but this figure was more than 50 per cent where practically the whole workforce is engaged in group delegation.

There are two competing explanations for this result: (1) the decrease of sickness and absenteeism was the result of improved work circumstances and employee motivation through group delegation; (2) reduced sickness and absenteeism was the result of increased informal peer pressure from within the group and mutual control to conform to work rules. According to the data, the second explanation is more likely: the different intensity of group delegation (Figure 7.9) did not influence sickness rates, and only moderately influenced the absenteeism rate. The coverage of group delegation exerted a much higher influence on both sickness and absence rates. Under conditions of widespread group delegation, pervasive peer group control is a likely explanation.

Overall, comparing the effects of three dimensions of group delegation, it can be said that the scope is of particular importance for direct economic effects, whereas the coverage of has more social repercussions which, in turn, affect the economic outcomes indirectly.

## 7.4   Bench marking the scope and intensity of different forms of direct participation

*Economic effects*

The analysis of the economic effects of direct participation has so far been presented in three steps:

- effects of single forms of direct participation without any differentiation;

- effects of multiple forms of direct participation;

- effects of single forms of direct participation taking into account their scope

### Key findings:

- group delegation with high scores for scope was best on three dimensions: quality; throughput time; and increase in output

- 'arm's length' consultation, using suggestion schemes, attitude surveys and 'speak-up' schemes, was strongest on cost reduction and improved quality

- group delegation and 'arm's length' consultation with high scores for scope individually applied achieved superior results regardless of the scope of each single measure within a multiple form approach

To complete the analysis, we want to pull together these three levels by bench marking the effect of a multiple-form approach with high scores for scope against the best performing individual form for all four economic performance indicators. Table 7.2 looks at the impact of multiple forms. Column 1 includes the "best" individual form from Table 7.1; Column 2 presents the results from Figure 7.1 on workplaces applying 5 or 6 measures simultaneously and Column 3 the results from the workplaces using all six measures in parallel.

Where were the strongest economic effects? Table 7.2 suggests that the superiority of the multiple form approach was limited, – 76 per cent of workplaces reduced their costs and 78 per cent increased their output. This was 10 percentage points higher than the score for the "best" individual form on cost reduction and 20 percentage points on increased output. There was no variation as a result of a multiple form approach for quality and throughput time.

A similar bench marking exercise was applied in Table 7.3 comparing the "best" individual form from Table 7.1 and the application with high scores for the scope of. The last column includes the high scores for the intensity of group delegation. There is a clear message from Table 7.3: the strongest economic performance came from the two individual forms with the highest scores for scope, i.e.:

- group delegation with high scores for scope was best on three dimensions: quality – 98 per cent (+3); throughput time – 87 per cent (+18); and increase in output – 85 per cent (+27).

- 'arm's length' consultation, using suggestion schemes, attitude surveys and 'speak-up' schemes, was strongest on cost reduction (+15) and improved quality (+3).

If one now compares the effects of multiple forms of direct participation with group delegation and 'arm's length' consultation achieving high scores, it would seem that the latter achieved superior results regardless of the scope of each single measure within a multiple form approach.

*Indirect labour costs*

In this section we apply the same bench marking exercise to indirect labour costs. The effects of the "best" individual form on the reduction of sickness and absenteeism are compared with those of a multiple form approach in Table 7.2. It will be seen that there were **no** significant effects on these indicators and only a marginal effect on employment and delayering of management.

**Table 7.2 Bench marking the effects of the different forms of direct participation: "best" performing individual form versus multiple forms – % of those responding 'Yes'**

|  | "best" performing individual form | combination of 5-6 forms | combination of 6 forms |
|---|---|---|---|
| reduction of costs | 66 | 67 | 76 |
| reduction of throughput time | 69 | 70 | 68 |
| improvement in quality | 95 | 97 | 96 |
| increase in total output | 58 | 71 | 78 |
| decrease in sickness | 40 | 45 | 44 |
| decrease in absenteeism | 42 | 49 | 45 |
| reduction in no. of employees | 37 | 37 | 41 |
| reduction in no. of managers | 31 | 34 | 44 |

Table 7. 3 bench marks individual forms with high scores for scope against the "best" individual form from Table 7.1. The results are straight forward: 'arm's length' and temporary consultation groups with high scores outperformed all other direct participation forms. Temporary consultation groups achieved high scores for reduced absenteeism and the sickness rate in 60 per cent and 57 per cent of workplaces respectively. This is 17/18 percentage points above the bench mark. Such groups did not have a particular strong effect on reductions in sickness and absenteeism, however. The pattern of relation between multiple forms and single forms with high scores for scope were the same as for economic performance. The latter appear to have outperformed the former.

*Employment effects*

One key finding of the analysis is that strong economic effects were combined with strong negative employment effects. Therefore, it is not surprising that strong negative employment effect occurred in workplaces where there was 'arm's length' consultation with high scores, while the strongest effect on reducing managers was to be found in workplaces with group delegation with the greatest scope for employee initiative(see Table 7.3). Half of those workplaces also reduced the number of middle managers due to the introduction of group delegation. The bench mark was 18 percentage points lower.

## 7.5 The employment effects of direct participation in perspective

Previous sections have contained a first analysis of the possible employment impact of the introduction of different forms of direct participation. Table 7.1 showed a range of between 20 and 40 per cent of workplaces, which reported lay offs due to the introduction of different forms of direct participation. The effects increased with the scope of certain forms of direct participation, as has been demonstrated in Table 7.3. For example, two thirds of workplaces with wide scope for 'arms-length' individual consultation reduced the number of employees in the short term. Based on this result, a preliminary conclusion is that direct participation would not only be accompanied by generally positive economic performance effects, but also by negative employment effects in a significant number of workplaces.

## Key findings:

- there were more likely to be reductions in employment in workplaces *without* direct participation than those with

- although the introduction of direct participation was associated with reductions in employment in a third of workplaces, in half these cases the short term effect was compensated or over compensated in the medium term

This not the complete story, however; the analysis up to now has some serious limitations. The indicator used in Tables 7.1 and 7.3 measures only negative effects and gives no indication on a possible increase of employment or stable employment. It measures only a short term immediate effect of direct participation and gives no indication for the medium term. Many commentators argue that any short term rationalisation effect of direct participation would be made up in the medium term and lead to increased employment via increased competitiveness. The indicator provides also no information on the number of employees, which would be affected either way, and the response rate for this important indicator was just under 40 per cent.

In a more sophisticated analysis, we want to use the results of a second indicator on medium term employment trends in the workplace for the largest occupational group in the last three years. The response rate for this indicator is 96 per cent. The limitations of this indicator are that it does not measure an immediate and direct impact of direct participation. Medium term changes in the employment performance of organisations can be influenced by many factors inside and outside. It may be difficult to determine exactly the direct effect of the introduction of direct participation. Table 7.4 gives, first of all, an overall picture on the medium term employment trends in our workplaces. A quarter had reduced employment; more than a third increased employment and around 40 per cent had stable employment.

Table 7.4 confirms the initial findings of Chapter 3 in indicating a positive medium term employment impact of direct participation. The number of direct participation workplaces with a positive employment balance over three years is 35 per cent, 11 percentage points higher than in non-direct participation workplaces. Even though

**Table 7.3 Bench marking the effects of the different forms of direct participation: "best" performing individual form versus other individual forms – % of those responding 'Yes'**

| | "best" performing individual form | individual consultation: individual 'face-to-face' form | individual consultation: 'arms-length' | group consultation: temporary groups | group consultation: permanent groups | individual delegation | group delegation | |
|---|---|---|---|---|---|---|---|---|
| | | high scope | high scope | high scope | high scope | high scope | high scope | high intensity |
| reduction of costs | 66 | 56 | 81 | 62 | 59 | 66 | 62 | 68 |
| reductions of throughput time | 69 | 56 | 61 | 66 | 57 | 74 | 70 | 87 |
| improvement in quality | 95 | 96 | 98 | 95 | 96 | 97 | 96 | 98 |
| increase in total output | 58 | 44 | 50 | 70 | 56 | 56 | 72 | 85 |
| decrease in sickness | 40 | 38 | 49 | 57 | 47 | 35 | 33 | 41 |
| decrease in absenteeism | 42 | 35 | 49 | 60 | 43 | 44 | 35 | 42 |
| reduction in nos. of employees | 37 | 20 | 47 | 41 | 22 | 40 | 35 | 47 |
| reduction in nos. of managers | 31 | 21 | 33 | 26 | 26 | 44 | 42 | 49 |

a quarter (26 per cent) of all direct participation workplaces reduced their employment in the last 3 years, the number of non-direct participation workplaces with negative employment is 34 per cent, 8 percentage points higher. In general, direct participation workplaces in the 10 countries have come through the economic crisis of the mid-1990s much better than those workplaces which did not change their work organisation. In other words whilst, a significant minority of direct participation workplaces were involved in lay offs, there would, however, have been a high probability of higher rates of lay offs without any introduction of direct participation.

**Table 7.4 Medium term employment trends in workplaces *with* and *without* direct participation**

| *trends in number of* *employees in the last 3 years* | workplaces *without* direct participation | workplaces *with* direct participation |
|---|---|---|
| | % | % |
| increase | 24 | 35 |
| same | 41 | 39 |
| reduced | 34 | 26 |

In the next step, we want to combine the two indicators in order to optimise the information. Table 7.5 gives, first of all, a breakdown of the possible combinations of all direct participation workplaces with a negative short term employment impact: 53 per cent of these workplaces report, at the same time, a medium term reduction of employment; 30 per cent stable employment and 17 per cent increased employment.

**Table 7.5 Short term effects of direct participation and medium term employment trend in workplaces *with* and *without* direct participation**

| | short term negative employment impact of direct participation | |
|---|---|---|
| *trends in number of employees* *in the last 3 years* | yes % | no % |
| increase | 17 | 39 |
| same | 30 | 43 |
| reduced | 53 | 18 |

Table 7.6 identifies 6 types of workplaces by systematically combining the two indicators and giving a breakdown of the share of each type in the overall number of direct participation workplaces. Before, we had a share of 31 per cent of all direct participation workplaces with negative short term employment effects. The more sophisticated analysis shows that this figure can be broken down: 16 per cent of all

direct participation workplaces had a short term negative effect of direct participation *and* employee lay offs in the medium term (type 3). This is the real critical case, where the short term rationalisation effect of direct participation measures cannot be made up. In 9 per cent (type 2) or respectively 5 per cent (type 1) of all workplaces with a negative short term effect, the medium term employment trend in the direct participation workplaces is stable or improves. Considering all direct participation workplaces, positive or stable employment effects are more dominant (see e.g. types 4 and 5). Overall, nearly 60 per cent of all direct participation workplaces have no negative short term effect of direct participation and have increased or stabilised their employment in the last 3 years.

**Table 7.6 Categories of workplace with short term negative employment effects and medium term employment trends**

| | | |
|---|---|---|
| type 1 | *negative* short term effects of direct participation/ *positive* medium term employment trends | 5% |
| type 2 | *negative* short term effects of direct participation/ stable medium term employment trends | 9% |
| type 3 | *negative* short term effects of direct participation/ negative medium term employment trends | 16% |
| type 4 | *no negative* short term effects of direct participation/ *positive* medium term employment trends | 27% |
| type 5 | *no negative* short term effects of direct participation/ *stable* medium term employment trends | 30% |
| type 6 | *no negative* short term effects of direct participation/ *negative* medium term employment trends | 13% |

To summarise, the more sophisticated analysis revises the focus. The introduction of direct participation takes place in a majority of workplaces with a stable or positive medium term employment situation and with no short term negative employment effects. In a third of all direct participation workplaces short term lay offs occur. In half of those cases. however, there is compensation for this short term effect in the form of increased employment. Finally, it should be stressed again that due to the complexity of the subject and due to the previously mentioned methodological limitations, the results should be interpreted carefully.

In a last step of the analysis, we want to control the combination of short and medium term negative employment impacts for sector and workplace size. Table 7.7 concentrates particularly on types 1, 2 and 3 discussed above. It reveals first of all a weak sectoral variation. Industry and construction are the two sectors, where we find an above average number of workplaces, which combine a negative short term rationalisation effect of direct participation with increased lay offs in the medium term. Every fifth workplace in construction shows such a pattern and 18 per cent in industry. The other sectors are close to the average.

**Table 7.7  Categories of workplace with short term negative employment effects and medium term employment trends by sector**

|  | type 1 and type 2: *negative* short term effects of direct participation and *positive* or *stable* medium term employment trends | type 3: *negative* short term effects of direct participation and *negative* medium term employment trends |
|---|---|---|
|  | % of workplaces | % of workplaces |
| average all sectors | 14 | 16 |
| industry | 11 | 18 |
| construction | 9 | 20 |
| trade | 24 | 15 |
| services | 14 | 16 |
| non profit | 14 | 14 |

**Table 7.8  Categories of workplace with short term negative employment effect and medium term employment trends by size**

|  | type 1 and type 2: *negative* short term effect of direct participation and *positive* or *stable* medium term employment trend | type 3: *negative* short term effect of direct participation and *negative* medium term employment trend |
|---|---|---|
|  | % of workplaces | % of workplaces |
| average all sizes | 14 | 16 |
| under 50 | 11 | 18 |
| 50 - 99 | 9 | 20 |
| 100 - 199 | 24 | 15 |
| 200 - 499 | 14 | 16 |
| 500 plus | 14 | 14 |

We also controlled the employment effect for workplace size (see Table 7.8). Again we find a weak relationship. Only the larger workplaces, with more than 500 employees, show a stronger short term and medium term negative employment impact due to the introduction of direct participation. The lowest impact was in medium sized workplaces. To conclude, sector and workplace size have no strong impact on the overall result with regard to the combination of the short and medium term employment impact of direct participation.

## 7.6 A cross-national comparison of the effects of direct participation

So far, the analysis has focused on the ten-country trends. Experience shows that the country factor is, in an European comparative analysis, usually the single most important variable. However, this assumption is challenged by another hypothesis, which assumes that the introduction of new forms of work organisation combined with different forms, and penetration of direct participation which started in the mid 1980s has been steadily diffused throughout Europe. According to this hypothesis the conformity in the development of direct participation would be accompanied by a relative homogenous pattern of effects on the economic performance, indirect labour costs and on employment. Consequently only small country differences would occur.

### Key findings:

- the reported improvement in quality was universal and shows hardly any variation by country

- the strongest expansion effect was in three smaller countries on the Northern, Western and Southern periphery of Europe, the lowest in two large central EU countries (France and Germany).

- Swedish and Dutch workplaces were especially successful in reducing sickness, whereas particularly low effects were reported by French and Italian managers

- in Germany and Sweden almost half, and in Portugal and the UK 40 per cent, of the workplaces reported a reduction in employment due to the introduction of direct participation, whereas only one in twenty in France did

- the Netherlands and Denmark lead the way in absorbing the reductions in employment due to direct participation; Germany and Spain were the least successful

Table 7.9 gives an overview on the economic effects of direct participation in the ten countries. Improvement of quality is a widespread trend and shows hardly any variation by country. The other three factors, however, show strong variations. Germany, Portugal and the UK show the strongest impact on cost reduction (79 per cent – 71 per cent); whereas Denmark and France reported only a moderate impact (between 31 and 43 per cent). A reduction in throughput time was highest in Italy, Germany and Spain (between 88 and 70 per cent), lowest in France, the Netherlands and Denmark (between 22 and 47 per cent). The third indicator measures the perceived increase in output by management due to the introduction of direct participation. France and Germany are at the bottom with 21 and 34 per cent respectively. The highest positive impact, however, is perceived in Portugal, Sweden and Ireland (between 79 and 85 per cent). From a policy perspective, it is interesting to observe the strongest output change and expansion effect in three smaller countries on the Northern, Western and Southern periphery of Europe. The lowest expansion, however, was in two large central EU countries (France and Germany).

In order to structure and summarise the results, a typology based on rationalisation effects of direct participation (reduction of costs and reduction of throughput time) is used and an expansion effect, where direct participation combined with new forms of work organisation resulted in increased output. Table 7.10 classifies all ten countries according to these dimensions.

Six different types emerge. In Germany, direct participation leads to very strong rationalisation combined with a weak expansion in output. In France, it triggers off weak rationalisation accompanied by weak expansion. The positive combination of very strong expansion of output and strong rationalisation occurs in Portugal, Sweden, the UK and Ireland. These four countries have improved their competitiveness and have transformed this advantage into expansion. Italy shows a similar pattern with a stronger rationalisation effect, but a slightly lower output increase; in this case, the negative impacts on employment due to rationalisation are matched by a strong expansion of output. In the Netherlands and Denmark the relatively weak rationalisation impacts of direct participation are combined with a strong output increase.

**Table 7.9  The effects of direct participation by country – % of those responding 'Yes'**

|  | ten country average | DK | FR | GER | IR | IT | NL | POR | SP | SW | UK |
|---|---|---|---|---|---|---|---|---|---|---|---|
| reduction of costs | 60 | 43 | 31 | 79 | 57 | 61 | 59 | 71 | 65 | 62 | 71 |
| reduction of throughput time | 60 | 47 | 22 | 81 | 64 | 88 | 44 | 69 | 70 | 62 | 65 |
| improvement in quality | 92 | 88 | 85 | 94 | 95 | 98 | 94 | 96 | 96 | 95 | 92 |
| increase in total output | 58 | 60 | 21 | 34 | 79 | 59 | 59 | 85 | 57 | 84 | 77 |

**Table 7.10  The effects of direct participation by country: rationalisation and expansion – % of those responding**

| *expansion* | very strong (160-151) | strong (140-121) | weak (103-53) |
|---|---|---|---|
| | *rationalisation* | | |
| very strong (85-77) | | Portugal Sweden UK Ireland | |
| strong (60-57) | Italy | Spain | Denmark the Netherlands |
| weak (34-21) | Germany | | France |

One may argue that the different pattern of combined effects of rationalisation and expansion in the ten countries is a spurious relationship. In reality, the country differences are based on different patterns of the distribution of direct participation in the relevant countries. As different types of direct participation have a stronger impact on the economic performance, the country differences would be explained by the stronger impact of certain forms of direct participation (e.g. group delegation). To check this argument, we controlled the different effects of direct participation for group delegation in the ten countries. The results are presented in Table 7.11. Surprisingly, the results are the same as on the overall direct participation level (see Table 7.9) i.e. there is a specific country effect.

As for indirect labour cost effects, the expectations are confirmed that Sweden is particularly successful in this respect. Table 7.11 shows that around 70 per cent of Swedish workplaces reduced sickness and absenteeism along with direct participation . Dutch workplaces were also successful in reducing sickness (63 per cent), whereas in Spain, direct participation was important for the decrease of absenteeism (50 per cent). Particularly low effects on indirect labour costs by direct participation were perceived by French and Italian managers.

Employment effects are measured first of all via the two indicators reduction in number of employees' and 'reduction in number of managers'. Table 7.11 shows a strong variation in the number of workplaces in the 10 countries with a short term reduction of employment, due to the introduction of direct participation. In Germany and Sweden almost half of the workplaces reported such a reduction – Portugal and the UK reach 40 per cent. A particularly low effect was reported from France. Only one in twenty workplaces showed a reduction in the workforce due to the introduction of direct participation.

**Table 7.11  The effects of group delegation by country – % of those responding 'Yes'**

|  | ten-country average | DK | FR | GER | IR | IT | NL | POR | SP | SW | UK |
|---|---|---|---|---|---|---|---|---|---|---|---|
| reduction of costs | 57 | 54 | 28 | 77 | 60 | 64 | 59 | 59 | 47 | 61 | 75 |
| reduction of throughput time | 65 | 59 | 23 | 80 | 63 | 94 | 48 | 83 | 88 | 60 | 74 |
| improvement in quality | 94 | 91 | 94 | 94 | 94 | 96 | 94 | 94 | 89 | 94 | 91 |
| increase in total output | 63 | 70 | 26 | 38 | 88 | 57 | 62 | 92 | 65 | 86 | 88 |
| decrease in sickness | 42 | 34 | 17 | 38 | 30 | 18 | 63 | 28 | 21 | 69 | 49 |
| decrease in absenteeism | 43 | 36 | 26 | 38 | 42 | 31 | 39 | 33 | 50 | 70 | 41 |
| reduction in nos. of employees | 28 | 14 | 5 | 47 | 25 | 22 | 22 | 40 | 32 | 45 | 40 |
| reduction in nos. of managers | 31 | 18 | 4 | 33 | 25 | 17 | 18 | 17 | 22 | 53 | 31 |

The figures confirm a similar variation with regard to the reduction of managers, particularly middle managers. In 53 per cent of all Swedish workplaces direct participation measures have been accompanied by a reduction of managers. This is by far the highest figure in any of the ten countries. In Germany and the UK about a third of workplaces report such a reduction. The smallest impact is reported from France, Denmark, Italy, the Netherlands and Portugal.

In a last step, we want to go back to the more sophisticated analysis used in section 7.6 by combining the indicator of short term lay offs due to the introduction of direct participation with the medium term employment trends in the workplace. Table 7.12 gives a country breakdown of those workplaces which have reduced their labour force after the introduction of direct participation and have, at the same time, reduced their workforce in the last three years. This is the critical case, where short term rationalisation due to direct participation could not be compensated for. Not surprisingly, Germany has, with 27 per cent of all direct participation workplaces, the highest number of critical cases. In Sweden, the UK, Spain and Portugal, one in five workplaces were also faced with a reduction of employment in shrinking internal labour markets due to direct participation. At the other end of the scale are Denmark, France and the Netherlands, where only 1 out of 20 workplaces had a particular employment problem related to direct participation.

**Table 7.12  Categories of workplaces with short term negative employment effects and medium term employment trends by country**

|  | ten-country average | DK | FR | GER | IR | IT | NL | POR | SP | SW | UK |
|---|---|---|---|---|---|---|---|---|---|---|---|
| type 1 and type 2 | 15 | 9 | 3 | 19 | 12 | 11 | 16 | 21 | 13 | 23 | 22 |
| type 3 | 14 | 4 | 4 | 27 | 10 | 10 | 6 | 18 | 20 | 22 | 20 |

Another question is the flexibility of internal labour markets and how they react to lay offs in the short term due to direct participation. Table 7.12 shows that in Sweden, the UK, Portugal and Germany, the highest percentage of workplaces with a high internal flexibility were able to compensate for short term lay offs. This measure, however, is biggest because all these countries had high percentages of workplaces which were negatively affected by direct participation in the short term. A more appropriate measure would be the percentage of direct participation workplaces with flexible markets in relation to all direct participation workplaces with short term lay offs. In this respect the Netherlands and Denmark out-performed all other countries: they were able to absorb, in the medium term, around 70 per cent of all short term lay offs due to direct participation whereas, for example, Germany and Spain absorbed only 41 and 39 per cent respectively.

## 7.7  Summary and conclusions

Even allowing for the methodological limitations referred to in the introduction to this chapter, one thing seems very clear. The managers responding to the EPOC survey believe that direct participation works. Most forms of direct participation were viewed as having positive effects on a range of key indicators of economic performance and indirect labour costs. Consistent with their views on the most important forms of direct participation discussed in Chapter 4, the consultative forms such as suggestion schemes, speak-up schemes and project groups were also regarded as making as much contribution to good economic performance and reductions in indirect labour costs as group delegation allowing employees considerable scope for initiative. The public debate which has focused, nearly exclusively, on the economic advantages of group work is one sided and neglects the importance of other forms of direct participation.

More particularly, it seems that the greater the scope of direct participation, measured in terms of a wider coverage of issues in which employees are involved, the stronger the positive impact on economic performance and sickness and absenteeism. Multiple forms of direct participation are especially effective if they are built on single forms with substantial scope. This makes it even more poignant that these most effective forms of direct participation are seriously under-represented in workplaces in the ten countries. There is a massive gap between management rhetoric and practice

Also clear, as Chapter 6 has already demonstrated, is that our managers do not appear to see any incompatibility in pursuing functional flexibility and numerical flexibility strategies. The more extensive the scope of direct participation, the more accompanied it was likely to be by reductions in the number of employees and of managers.

This finding needs to be put into context, however. The introduction of direct participation takes place in a majority of workplaces with a stable or positive medium term employment trend and no short term negative employment effects of direct participation. Indeed, as Chapter 3 pointed out, the likelihood of a reduction in employment in workplaces *with* direct participation was less than that in those *without*. Also, although short term negative employment effects occurred in one third of direct participation workplaces, these are made good in half of them in the medium term.

Of the ten countries, Germany is hardest hit by short term and medium term reductions in employment. Denmark and the Netherlands out-perform all other countries as they were able to absorb 70 per cent of all lay offs associated with the introduction of direct participation within a flexible and growing internal labour market. The "ideal" scenario of strong expansion based on strong cost and process rationalisation can be found in 4 countries (Portugal, Sweden, the UK and Ireland).

## References

European Commission. 1997. Green Paper, *Partnership for a new organisation of work.*

Fröhlich, D. and U. Pekruhl. 1996: *Direct Participation and Organisational Change – Fashionable but Misunderstood? An analysis of recent research in Europe, Japan and the USA.* EF/96/38/EN. Luxembourg: Office for the Official Publications of the European Communities.

Regalia, I. 1995. *Humanise Work and Increase Profitability? Direct participation in organisational change viewed by the social partners in Europe.* EF/95/21/EN. Luxembourg: Office for the Official Publications of the European Communities

Womack, J.P., D.T. Jones and D.Roos. 1990: *The machine that changed the world*, New York: Rawson Associates.

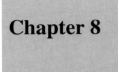

# Chapter 8

# The regulation of direct participation

The introduction of direct participation takes place in a regulatory framework, set not only by existing labour law, collective agreements and individual employment contracts, but also by informal rules and practices, which vary significantly between the 10 countries covered by the EPOC survey. A systematic overview of the patterns of regulation of workplace participation in Europe is given in EPOC's social partner study (Regalia, 1995:46). It distinguishes four types of regulation:

- mixed regulation of centralised agreements and legislation;

- statutory regulation;

- joint central regulation negotiated between the social partners;

- voluntarism.

The debate at the EU level has been stimulated by the European Commission's recently published Green Paper, *Partnership for a new organisation of work* (1997). In regard to regulation it makes four main points:

- The renewal of the organisation of work can only be achieved by the firms themselves, involving management and workers and their representatives'.

- It should be based on 'a partnership for the development of a new framework for the modernisation of the organisation of work taking account of the interests of both business and workers' with the objective to 'strike a balance between flexibility and security'.

- The word "framework" should be given a broad interpretation. It could include everything from the creation of a common understanding of the importance of new forms of work organisation, through joint declarations, to binding contractual or legal initiatives. The level and content of such a framework has to be clarified through discussions, in particular in the Social Dialogue.

- Such a partnership could make a significant contribution to achieving the objective of a productive, learning and participative organisation of work. It would be based on European values, which combine competition between firms and solidarity between citizens.

The regulation of direct participation proved to be one of the most sensitive issues to emerge from EPOC's social partner (Regalia, 1995:46) and literature (Fröhlich and Pekruhl, 1996). The results of the EPOC survey shed further light on the issue and, in particular, on the role of the various actors in the introduction of direct participation and on the effects of this role and the various types of regulation. The term 'regulation' is used here in a broad (and not solely legal) sense to denote the processes by which formal and informal rules governing direct participation are formulated and implemented.

The analysis tries to answer four main questions:

1. What is the impact of the existing pattern of employee representation in the ten countries (works councils, union representatives, collective agreements) on the introduction of direct participation? Does the presence of employee representatives impede or facilitate the introduction of direct participation? Or, is there a neutral relation between the direct and indirect forms of participation?

2. How is direct participation regulated at the workplace level? To what extent are works councils and union representatives effectively involved in the introduction and implementation of direct participation? Do we observe an inclusive and partnership approach as recommended by the Green Paper or do we find an exclusive approach, in which the introduction of direct participation is being controlled more or less unilaterally by management?

3. How are employees themselves informed and consulted *before* the introduction of direct participation? Are the interests of employees taken seriously by management and representative bodies? What is the relation between patterns of representative involvement and employee involvement *before* the introduction of direct participation? Does strong representative involvement go hand-in-hand with strong employee involvement or do we find a significant number of workplaces, where management tries to substitute extensive information and consultation of employees for representative involvement?

4. What are the economic and labour market effects of the regulation of direct participation? Does joint regulation in particular diminish the economic effects of direct participation, especially the negative employment effects, as unions and works councils seek to protect their members' interests? Or does regulation enhance economic performance and accelerate internal labour market adjustment?

## 8.1 Workplace regulation in context

It will be helpful to begin by reporting the key results on the patterns of employee representation in the 10 countries covered by the survey. Some of these results are not only important in defining the regulatory framework of direct participation, but also in informing the debate over the proposals for information and consultation within the national framework recently put forward by the European Commission (European Commission, 1997).

Figure 8.1 shows a significant difference in the extent of coverage of employee representatives in the ten countries. The two main institutions are works councils or joint consultation committees, on one side, and different forms of trade union representatives, on the other. In Sweden, nearly all workplaces (92 per cent) had representative bodies and most involved trade union representatives (85 per cent). Coverage was extensive in Italy, Spain and France as well. By far the lowest level of coverage of employee representatives was reported in Portugal. Only one third of Portuguese workplaces had representatives.

Overall, trade union organisations were more prevalent than works councils. Only in Germany, Italy, The Netherlands and Spain did works councils have a higher diffusion than trade union representatives. Contrary to conventional wisdom, however, Germany and The Netherlands showed a relatively low coverage of workplaces with works councils. There are different reasons for this. In Germany, the introduction of works councils is not mandatory above a certain size, but is triggered by the demand of employees; experience shows that, particularly in small and medium sized workplaces, employees are slow to use this right. In The Netherlands, the low coverage can be explained by the high percentage of small workplaces which responded to our survey; here too there is no mandatory obligation to establish works councils in these workplaces. If one compares workplaces of similar size throughout the 10 countries, The Netherlands had a coverage significantly above average for SMEs (see Huijgen, Benders and Nieuwkamp, 1997).

## Key findings:

- there were significant differences between the 10 countries in the presence of employee representatives and the coverage of collective agreements

- with the exception of three countries, however, (France and Portugal, where direct participation was more likely with a representative system, and Spain, where the opposite was the case), the incidence of direct participation appeared to be independent of the workplace regulation arrangements

A second important institutional feature is related to collective bargaining provisions. To what extent were the workplaces bound by a collective agreement covering all employees or a significant proportion? Not surprisingly, Table 8.1 shows large differences between the 10 countries. The highest rates of collective bargaining coverage were in Italy, Sweden and Spain where nearly every workplace was covered. By contrast, nearly two thirds of UK workplaces (64 per cent) and more than a half of Irish workplaces (56 per cent) in the survey were not covered. If one compares these results with the OECD study by Traxler (1994) our results deviate to a certain extent. In comparison, the EPOC figures for the UK were 36 per cent; whereas Traxler's were 47 per cent. There were also differences for Germany (EPOC, 81 per cent; Traxler, 90 per cent). These are most probably explained by the different dates of the figures. Traxler's figures are for 1990, whereas EPOC's are for 1996.

Figure 8.1: % of workplaces with employee representation - all respondents

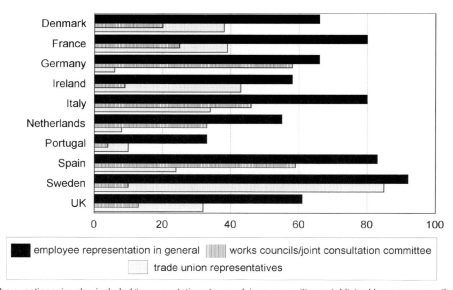

The questionnaire also included "representatives to an advisory committee established by management".

The degree of unionisation among the largest occupational group followed the expected pattern (see Table 8.1). The two Scandinavian countries topped the league. By far the lowest degree of union membership was to be found in France.

**Table 8.1 Unionisation and coverage by collective agreement – % of all respondents**

| | unionisation | | | | collective agreement | | |
|---|---|---|---|---|---|---|---|
| | no member | 1-29% | 30-69% | 70-100% | all employees | some employees | no coverage |
| ten-country average | 24 | 25 | 15 | 36 | 63 | 82 | 8- |
| Denmark | 1 | 6 | 9 | 85 | 41 | 35 | 24 |
| France | 47 | 40 | 10 | 3 | 87 | 5 | 8 |
| Germany | 25 | 41 | 23 | 11 | 66 | 15 | 19 |
| Ireland | 32 | 10 | 8 | 49 | 25 | 31 | 44 |
| Italy | 12 | 24 | 29 | 35 | 99 | 1 | 0 |
| Netherlands | 35 | 37 | 20 | 9 | 61 | 9 | 30 |
| Portugal | 34 | 32 | 20 | 14 | 67 | 6 | 27 |
| Spain | 15 | 54 | 19 | 11 | 75 | 22 | 3 |
| Sweden | 3 | 1 | 8 | 88 | 91 | 7 | 2 |
| UK | 47 | 18 | 13 | 23 | 18 | 8 | 64 |

Especially relevant to the policy debate is the percentage of workplaces in the 10 countries which had neither a representative body nor collective agreement coverage. Overall, 13 per cent of workplaces in the 10 countries had no collective representation of any kind. In Ireland and the UK, one third of workplaces were in this position. Very few workplaces were without representation in France (4 per cent), Sweden (Sweden 1 per cent) and Spain (1 per cent); and in Italy no respondents said they were without. As well as highlighting the limitations of voluntarism in providing collective representation, these results also question the perception of the superiority of the German and Dutch systems in comparison to other countries. Whereas in France, Italy and Spain nearly all workplaces were covered, in Germany and The Netherlands one in seven were not.

Moving on to the impact of these patterns on the introduction of direct participation, Table 8.2 presents the data on the relationship between collective bargaining and direct participation in the 10 countries. It suggests that the coverage and extent of coverage had little or no impact on the introduction of direct participation. Also, the presence of employee representatives (works councils, union representatives) did not appear to have any bearing on the diffusion of direct participation (see Table 8.3). The results of the effects of the degree of unionisation (see Table 8.4) complete the picture: they suggest a neutral relationship between direct participation and collective representation. To summarise, works councils, union representatives, degree of unionisation and collective bargaining neither hindered nor promoted the diffusion of direct participation in Europe.

**Table 8.2  Coverage by collective agreement in workplaces *with* and *without* direct participation- % of all respondents**

|  | all employees covered by collective agreements | some employees covered by collective agreements | no collective agreements |
|---|---|---|---|
| workplaces *with* direct participation | 81 | 78 | 82 |
| workplaces *without* direct participation | 19 | 22 | 18 |

**Table 8.3  Employee representatives in workplaces *with* and *without* direct participation- % of all respondents**

|  | workplaces *with* representatives | workplaces *without* representatives |
|---|---|---|
| workplaces *with* direct participation | 82 | 78 |
| workplaces *without* direct participation | 18 | 22 |

As for collective bargaining, the ten-country results are confirmed for most of the individual countries (see Table 8.5). Only Italy and Spain had a significantly higher number of workplaces without collective bargaining practising direct participation. The reverse was the case in the UK: the coverage by collective bargaining apparently had a positive effect on the introduction of direct participation.

**Table 8.4  Unionisation in workplaces *with* and *without* direct participation – % of all respondents**

|  | no members | 1% – 29% | 30% – 69% | 70% – 100% |
|---|---|---|---|---|
| workplaces *with* direct participation | 81 | 82 | 82 | 79 |
| workplaces *without* direct participation | 19 | 18 | 18 | 21 |

**Table 8.5  % of workplaces *with* direct participation and collective agreement coverage**

|  | all employees | no coverage |
|---|---|---|
| ten-country average | 80 | 86 |
| Denmark | 83 | 92 |
| France | 86 | 83 |
| Germany | 80 | 83 |
| Ireland | 84 | 89 |
| Italy | 82 | 100 |
| Netherlands | 89 | 91 |
| Portugal | 57 | 63 |
| Spain | 65 | 83 |
| Sweden | 89 | 100 |
| UK | 88 | 80 |

**Table 8.6  % of workplaces *with* direct participation and employee representation**

|  | workplaces *with* employee representatives | workplaces *without* employee representatives |
|---|---|---|
| ten-country average | 82 | 80 |
| Denmark | 82 | 77 |
| France | 90 | 73 |
| Germany | 82 | 79 |
| Ireland | 85 | 85 |
| Italy | 81 | 83 |
| Netherlands | 92 | 88 |
| Portugal | 74 | 55 |
| Spain | 60 | 84 |
| Sweden | 89 | 92 |
| UK | 83 | 81 |

The presence of employee representatives only had a significant influence on the introduction of direct participation in three countries. In France and in Portugal, workplaces *with* such representatives had more direct participation than those *without*. As shown in Table 8.6 the difference was nearly 20 percentage points. In France, one may interpret this result as an effect of the Auroux-laws. The opposite effect is shown in Spain, where not only collective bargaining coverage but also the presence of works councils or union representatives might be said to be an obstacle to the diffusion of direct participation. Generally speaking, however, with few exceptions in the ten countries, the diffusion of direct participation is neither significantly impeded nor promoted by existing collective regulation. The diffusion of direct participation, as Chapter 5 suggested, is a widespread trend based on economic motives relatively independent of the existing industrial relations system.

## 8.2. The involvement of employee representatives in the introduction of direct participation

The introduction of direct participation takes place in all 10 countries in the context of existing systems of representative participation. These systems are diverse in their structure, their practice and type and level of regulation. The key question is: how is direct participation regulated at the workplace level? To what extent are works councils and union representatives effectively involved in the introduction and implementation of direct participation? Do we observe an exclusive approach, in which the introduction of direct participation is being controlled more or less unilaterally by management, or an inclusive one, in which employee representatives are involved?

### Key findings:

- there was high level of employee representative involvement in the introduction of direct participation: 30 per cent of the workplaces reported extensive negotiations/ joint decision making; only 13 per cent did not involve their representatives

- the Scandinavian countries, followed by Germany, had the most extensive representative involvement; Portugal had the lowest level

In order to measure the precise extent of the involvement of employee representatives we used four indicators derived from previous European Foundation-sponsored research on representative participation in technological change (Fröhlich, Gill and Krieger, 1993). In.particular, we distinguished between:

- information

- consultation

- negotiations

- joint decision-making

Each indicator was measured on three dimensions:

- extensively

- limited

- not at all

In order to reduce the variety and complexity of the information, we combined all four indicators with each other and constructed a five dimensional scale representing the extent of involvement. The five dimensions were:

- no involvement

- limited information

- extensive information and limited consultation

- extensive consultation and limited negotiations

- extensive joint decision making/negotiations

This approach leaves some methodological questions open. What did management understand by 'limited information' or 'limited consultation'? Did 'extensive information' include timely and comprehensive information? Did 'extensive joint decision making' imply veto power on the part of employee representatives? Even so, as the previous research confirmed, it does enable a fairly systematic breakdown of process to be made.

The analysis starts with the workplaces with an employee representative system in place. Table 8.7 indicates a relative high level of involvement: 30 per cent of the workplaces reported extensive negotiations and high developed joint decision making, and a quarter of workplaces each had extensive information/limited consultation and extensive consultation. Only 13 per cent of workplaces with a representative system did not involve employee representatives in the introduction of direct participation. Based on these results, one can conclude that the introduction of direct participation is an inclusive process in a large majority of workplaces.

As expected from the previous research, the Scandinavian countries, followed by Germany, had the most extensive representative involvement. In Denmark 60 per cent and in Sweden 50 per cent of workplaces reported that employee representatives were involved as equal partners in the introduction of direct participation. In Germany, the works councils followed closely with 47 per cent.

By far the lowest level of involvement was in Portugal. Employee representatives were not involved in one third of workplaces where they were present. Surprisingly low also was the figure for The Netherlands, where a quarter of employee representatives were not involved and less than a fifth entered into negotiations. Ireland and the UK, the two voluntarist systems, showed a different pattern. In the light of the activities of the Irish government and the Irish Congress of Trade Unions in the promotion of direct participation and involvement of union representatives in this process since the beginning of 1990s, it is surprising that Ireland lagged behind the UK. In Ireland, employee representatives were not involved or received only limited information in a third of workplaces. In the UK, only 14 per cent of managers reported such low levels of participation, but the strength was extensive consultation with 44 per cent, which was the highest of all countries. The Italian results are also unexpected – nearly 40 per cent of Italian managers reported no or marginal involvement.

Table 8.7 deals with workplaces with systems of employee representation. In order to get an impression of the overall level of employee representative involvement, the results of Table 8.7 are combined with those of Table 8.1. The results are shown in Table 8.8 and the message is quite different.

**Table 8.7  The extent of employee representative involvement in the introduction of direct participation – % of workplaces with employee representation**

|  | no participation | limited information | extensive information/ limited consultation | extensive consultation | extensive joint decision making/ negotiations |
|---|---|---|---|---|---|
| ten-country average | 13 | 9 | 24 | 25 | 30 |
| Denmark | 5 | 1 | 9 | 25 | 60 |
| France | 16 | 8 | 38 | 18 | 20 |
| Germany | 8 | 7 | 17 | 21 | 47 |
| Ireland | 23 | 11 | 17 | 28 | 21 |
| Italy | 20 | 18 | 27 | 19 | 17 |
| Netherlands | 24 | 5 | 20 | 32 | 19 |
| Portugal | 32 | 18 | 5 | 36 | 9 |
| Spain | 13 | 16 | 20 | 25 | 27 |
| Sweden | 1 | 7 | 14 | 27 | 50 |
| UK | 7 | 7 | 24 | 44 | 18 |

A quarter of workplaces in the 10 countries did not involvement employee representatives in the introduction of direct participation . Half of these reflect the lack of employee representatives and half the lack of their involvement where they were present.

**Table 8.8  The extent of employee representative involvement in the introduction of direct participation – % of *all* workplaces with direct participation**

|  | no participation | limited information | extensive information/ limited consultation | extensive consultation | extensive joint decision making/ negotiations |
|---|---|---|---|---|---|
| ten-country average | 25 | 9 | 22 | 20 | 24 |
| Denmark | 22 | 3 | 10 | 21 | 44 |
| France | 22 | 8 | 37 | 16 | 17 |
| Germany | 29 | 5 | 15 | 18 | 34 |
| Ireland | 40 | 8 | 16 | 22 | 14 |
| Italy | 25 | 18 | 22 | 17 | 17 |
| Netherlands | 39 | 8 | 18 | 19 | 16 |
| Portugal | 44 | 8 | 15 | 19 | 14 |
| Spain | 19 | 13 | 23 | 24 | 22 |
| Sweden | 3 | 7 | 17 | 29 | 45 |
| UK | 19 | 12 | 24 | 27 | 19 |

**Table 8.9  Employee representatives involved in consultation, negotiation or joint decision-making in the introduction of direct participation – % of workplaces *with* employee representatives**

|  | works councils/ joint consultation committee | trade union | both |
|---|---|---|---|
| ten-country average | 68 | 17 | 13 |
| Denmark | 45 | 48 | 7 |
| France | 62 | 13 | 24 |
| Germany | 95 | - | 5 |
| Ireland | 37 | 58 | 5 |
| Italy | 52 | 19 | 30 |
| Netherlands | 76 | - | 24 |
| Portugal | - | 100 | - |
| Spain | 93 | 3 | 3 |
| Sweden | 4 | 77 | 19 |
| UK | 27 | 60 | 13 |

Table 8.8 also shows that Sweden was by far the most participative country: only 3 per cent of workplaces with direct participation did not involve employee representatives in its introduction. The other extreme is represented by Ireland and Portugal; over 40 per cent of workplaces with direct participation did not involve unions or works councils in its introduction. Again, The Netherlands and Germany show high levels of non-involvement in comparison to France, Spain and the UK.

Another important question concerns the channel of negotiation and joint decision-making. To what extent were works councils and joint consultation committees involved as opposed to trade union representatives? Table 8.9 gives the answers. Spain, Germany, The Netherlands and France showed the predominance of works councils, whereas in Portugal, Sweden and the UK trade union representatives were most important. In Italy, France and The Netherlands both channels were used.

## 8.3 The involvement of employees in the introduction of direct participation

The successful introduction of direct participation does not only depend on the involvement of employee representatives, but also on the extent to which employees are informed and consulted. How does this take place? Are the interests of employees taken seriously by management and representative bodies?

What is the relation between patterns of representative involvement and employee involvement in the introduction of direct participation? Does strong representative involvement go hand-in-hand with strong employee involvement or do we find a significant number of workplaces where management tries to substitute extensive information and consultation for employees representative involvement? What channels of communication are used by management? Does management inform employees via its own channels, or does it rely on representative bodies, such as works councils?

### Key findings:

- there was a relatively high level of employee consultation before the introduction of direct participation; employees were extensively consulted in more than one quarter of workplaces and to a limited extent in more than 50 per cent

- Sweden and Denmark had the highest levels of employee involvement and Portugal the lowest

- the most preferred channel of communications was the management chain

In order to measure the involvement of employees in the introduction of different forms of direct participation, we used a five dimensional scale with an ascending order:

- no involvement
- limited information
- extensive information
- limited consultation
- extensive consultation

The survey results, which are presented in Table 8.10, indicate a relatively high level of employee consultation before the introduction of direct participation. In more than one quarter of the workplaces, all employees were 'extensively' consulted and in more than 50 per cent to a 'limited extent' consulted. In one out of 10 workplaces, however, even our managers admitted that employees were neither informed nor consulted before the introduction of direct participation.

Some important differences emerge by country which might have been expected. Sweden and Denmark had a high level of employee involvement. The lowest was in Portugal where nearly one in five workplaces said employees were neither informed nor consulted. Denmark had the highest level of extensive consultation (50 per cent) followed by France (nearly 40 per cent. The two countries characterised by voluntarism had the stronger levels of employee involvement. Both the UK and Ireland were above the 10 country average with a third of workplaces practising extensive consultation.

**Table 8.10 The extent of employee involvement in the introduction of direct participation – % of workplaces *with* direct participation**

|  | no involvement | limited information | extensive information | limited consultation | extensive consultation |
|---|---|---|---|---|---|
| ten-country average | 10 | 8 |  | 51 | 28 |
| Denmark | 5 | 6 | 5 | 38 | 50 |
| France | 8 | 5 | 2 | 40 | 39 |
| Germany | 10 | 8 | 9 | 51 | 24 |
| Ireland | 12 | 9 | 4 | 45 | 33 |
| Italy | 15 | 10 | 1 | 54 | 17 |
| Netherlands | 13 | 8 | 4 | 54 | 22 |
| Portugal | 18 | 8 | 3 | 54 | 13 |
| Spain | 4 | 10 | 8 | 61 | 21 |
| Sweden | 3 | 5 | 4 | 58 | 31 |
| UK | 10 | 8 | 3 | 48 | 33 |

**Table 8.11  Channels of communication with employees in the introduction of direct participation – % of respondents with employee representatives**

|  | employee representatives only | management channels only | both |
|---|---|---|---|
| ten-country average | 10 | 56 | 34 |
| Denmark | 3 | 68 | 29 |
| France | 10 | 48 | 43 |
| Germany | 9 | 55 | 37 |
| Ireland | 7 | 65 | 27 |
| Italy | 15 | 63 | 23 |
| Netherlands | 2 | 64 | 34 |
| Portugal | - | 83 | 17 |
| Spain | 15 | 52 | 33 |
| Sweden | 16 | 43 | 41 |
| UK | 7 | 63 | 30 |

As for the channels of communications, Table 8.11 shows our managers preferred to use their own. 56 per cent of workplaces organised meetings with senior management and supervisors and only 1 in 10 workplace relied solely on employee representatives. A significant proportion (34 per cent) used both channels.

Of the 10 countries, Portuguese managers relied almost exclusively on their own channels (83 per cent) and employee representatives were not used at all. The greatest exclusive use of employee representatives was in Italy, Spain and Sweden (15-16 per cent). The most reliant on the range of channels were France (43 per cent) and Sweden (41 per cent).

**Table 8.12  Means of communication with employees in the introduction of direct participation – % of workplaces *with* direct participation**

|  | company newspaper | leaflet/ brochures | videos |
|---|---|---|---|
| ten-country average | 17 | 30 | 8 |
| Denmark | 17 | 12 | 1 |
| France | 21 | 20 | 10 |
| Germany | 14 | 42 | 2 |
| Ireland | 14 | 23 | 5 |
| Italy | 9 | 8 | 2 |
| Netherlands | 27 | 41 | 7 |
| Portugal | 13 | 21 | 4 |
| Spain | 7 | 28 | 3 |
| Sweden | 29 | 41 | 4 |
| UK | 20 | 32 | 22 |

Table 8.12 shows that, overall, less than 10 per cent of workplaces used videos to inform their employees. This form of communication was particularly popular in the UK, however, where nearly one in four workplaces used it. The most common means of information were leaflets and brochures (30 per cent overall). The greatest use of this approach was in Germany, Sweden and The Netherlands (more than 40 per cent). A very low application, however, was observed in Italy and Denmark. Regular workplace newspapers were considered less important than leaflets (17 per cent overall). The greatest use of newspapers was, again, in The Netherlands and in Sweden and lowest in Spain and Italy.

Taking the three means of communications together, one can conclude that extensive use was made of written or visual communication in the UK, Sweden, The Netherlands and Germany especially. Overall, traditional written forms of communication remained more important than more recent visual ones.

## 8.4   The extent of the involvement of employee representatives *and* employees

Another important aspect is the combined extent of representative and employee involvement in the introduction of direct participation. Does extensive consultation of employees go hand-in-hand with extensive consultation of employee representatives and/or extensive negotiations and effective joint decision-making? Or is there a tendency for workplaces to substitute extensive employee information and consultation for employee representative involvement?

### Key findings:

- extensive involvement of employee representatives went together with the consultation of employees

- the two Scandinavian countries had the highest levels of joint involvement; Portugal, France and Italy had the lowest

The construction of the indicator for the extent of combined representative and individual employee involvement in the introduction of direct participation is fairly complex, but measurement was basically on five dimensions:

- no involvement

- limited involvement

- extensive involvement

- limited consultation

- extensive consultation

Employee representative involvement also had five dimensions:

- no involvement

- limited information

- extensive information/limited involvement

- extensive consultation/limited negotiations or joint decision-making

- extensive joint decision-making or negotiations

Based on this '5 by 5' grid, four types were derived:

- *non-participative*, which includes all 4 combinations with 'no involvement' and 'limited information';

- *substitutive*, which comprises 'no information' and 'limited information' in the case of employee representative involvement and 'extensive information' and all forms of employee information and consultation;

- *middle of the road*, which represents all combinations of 'employee information' and consultation with 'extensive information' of employee representatives;

- *highly participative* which includes all extensive forms of consultation and joint decision making of employee representatives and the different forms of employee consultation before the introduction of direct participation.

**Table 8.13  The extent of combined involvement of employee representatives *and* employees in the introduction of direct participation – % of workplaces with employee representatives**

|  | "non-participative" | "substitutive" | "middle of the road" | "highly participative" |
|---|---|---|---|---|
| ten-country average | 8 | 12 | 22 | 59 |
| Denmark | 1 | 6 | 9 | 84 |
| France | 13 | 11 | 38 | 38 |
| Germany | 8 | 8 | 18 | 66 |
| Ireland | 11 | 24 | 18 | 47 |
| Italy | 15 | 18 | 29 | 38 |
| Netherlands | 5 | 20 | 21 | 54 |
| Portugal | 33 | 33 | 8 | 25 |
| Spain | 8 | 18 | 25 | 49 |
| Sweden | 4 | 6 | 15 | 75 |
| UK | 7 | 8 | 30 | 55 |

The results of the analysis, which are presented in Table 8.13, show that nearly 3 out of 5 workplaces in the ten countries were in the *highly participative* group and less than 10 per cent in the *non-participative*. The *substitutive* group, in which the emphasis was on employee information and consultation, comprised only 12 per cent of the workplaces with direct participation *and* employee representatives

Of course, because these results only include workplaces with direct participation *and* employee representatives, they give an overly-positive impression of the state of the extent of combined employee representative and employee involvement. Table 8.8 shows that a quarter of workplaces with direct participation had no involvement of employee representatives and 9 per cent gave limited information to them. The overall figure for the *non-participative* group was, therefore, close to 20 per cent and the extent of *highly participative* workplaces under 50 per cent. Even so, the overall figures bode reasonably well for a renewal of the organisation of work based on the involvement of management, employees and employee representatives across the EU.

As for the individual countries, the two Scandinavian countries again stand out. Hardly any workplaces were *non-participative*, while between 84 and 75 per cent of workplace were *highly participative*. Germany followed in third place with two-thirds of workplaces being *highly participative*. Surprisingly, perhaps, the UK and The Netherlands had a similar level of combined involvement in workplaces with employee representation. The second country with a voluntarist tradition, Ireland, had a significantly lower level of combined involvement than the UK, but one of the largest *substitutive* groups. The lowest extent of participatory practice was found in Portugal, which is not surprising given previous results. Interestingly, one-third of Portuguese workplaces were in the *substitutive* group. Considering that this group was particularly prominent in Ireland, it suggests the strong influence of overseas-owned multinational companies in both countries. France and Italy were also below the ten-country average for the *highly participative* group by 20 percentage points.

To conclude, despite the overall positive results on the degree of involvement and its importance for a partnership approach, three important qualifications have to be made:

- Portugal, France and Italy had a much lower level of combined involvement.

- The *substitutive* approach appears to be a feature of countries with a strong multinational company presence.

- Regulation does not necessarily mean high levels of combined involvement; where there were employee representatives, the 'lowly-regulated' UK had a higher level of combined involvement than the 'highly-regulated' France.

## 8.5 The effects of employee representative involvement

The previous sections have given an overview of the extent of the involvement of employee representatives and employees in the introduction of direct participation. This section builds on sections 7.8 and 7.9 in the previous chapter, to provide an analysis of the impact of different forms of involvement on direct participation itself, its economic performance and its employment effects. Does involvement diminish the economic effects of direct participation and, in particular, moderate any negative employment effects? Or does it enhance economic performance and accelerate internal labour market adjustment?

### Key findings:

- strong forms of representative participation were associated with direct participation with wide scope; and vice versa

- one fifth of managers regarded the involvement of representatives as 'very useful' and more than two thirds found it 'useful'

- the involvement of employee representatives in the introduction of direct participation was also associated with reductions in the number of employees in general and managers in particular

As a first step the relationship between the extent of employee representative involvement and the overall scope of direct participation was analysed. Do the strong forms of involvement of employee representatives go hand-in-hand with the more intensive practice of direct participation, giving employees greater opportunity to influence their own immediate work situation, or do employee representatives pose barriers to the practice of these forms? The results from previous EPOC research suggested that employee representatives were neutral in regard of the decision to practice direct participation or not. Once the decision had been taken by management to go ahead, however, they usually pushed for what many trade union officials interviewed in the EPOC social partner study regarded as 'real' direct participation, which enabled employees to make a significant contribution to their work.

Table 8.14 confirms that this was the case. Strong forms of employer representative involvement were to be found in workplaces with high scores for the scope of direct participation; whereas low scores were most frequent in workplaces without such involvement. Works councils and union representatives were in most cases 'agents of change' rather than barriers to the development of the more intensive practice of direct participation.

**Table 8.14  The extent of employee representative involvement and overall scope of direct participation – % of workplaces with employee representatives**

| | scores for *scope of direct participation* | | |
| --- | --- | --- | --- |
| | low | medium | high |
| no involvement | 63 | 18 | 19 |
| limited information | 66 | 23 | 11 |
| extensive information/ limited consultation | 58 | 29 | 14 |
| extensive consultation | 51 | 25 | 24 |
| extensive negotiation/ joint decision | 44 | 25 | 31 |

How useful is the involvement of employee representatives in the introduction of direct participation in the view of our managers? The results in Table 8.15 suggest their evaluation in workplaces with employee representation and the practice of joint regulation was very positive. Overall, one fifth of managers regarded the involvement of representatives as 'very useful' and more than two thirds found it 'useful'. Eleven per cent said there was 'no effect'. Of the 10 countries, management was most positive in Denmark and the least positive in France. In the latter, a quarter saw no positive effect and no usefulness in the involvement of employee representatives, and two per cent even regarded them as a hindrance. Given the other findings for this country, the Portuguese result was especially surprising: Thirty eight per cent of managers regarded the involvement of works councils as 'very useful'. A possible explanation is the existence of a 'dual' system in this country. Managers in many workplaces may be critical and suspicious of employee representative involvement and may seek to avoid it. In others, however, where employee representation was accepted, their usefulness in the introduction of direct participation was likely to be recognised.

An important question concerns the relationship between the extent of involvement of employee representatives and its perceived usefulness by management. Table 8.16 confirms a clear trend: workplaces with extensive consultation or extensive negotiations/joint decision-making, registered the highest appreciation by management. The opposite is also true: if employee representatives received only 'limited information', their involvement was seen by more than 40 per cent of managers as being without any effect or even being a hindrance (6 per cent). The message is clear: extensive forms of employee representative involvement was most useful in the introduction of direct participation.

**Table 8.15 Usefulness of employee representative involvement in the introduction of direct participation – % of workplaces with employee representatives**

|  | "very useful" | "useful" | "no effect" | "hindrance" |
|---|---|---|---|---|
| ten-country average | 21 | 67 | 11 | 1 |
| Denmark | 41 | 54 | 6 | - |
| France | 18 | 54 | 26 | 2 |
| Germany | 21 | 67 | 9 | 3 |
| Ireland | 24 | 70 | 6 | - |
| Italy | 7 | 81 | 9 | 3 |
| Netherlands | 20 | 70 | 9 | 1 |
| Portugal | 38 | 62 | - | - |
| Spain | 16 | 70 | 13 | 1 |
| Sweden | 17 | 75 | 9 | - |
| UK | 26 | 61 | 11 | 2 |

**Table 8.16 The extent and usefulness of employee representative involvement in the introduction of direct participation – % of workplaces with employee representatives**

|  | limited information | extensive information/ limited consultation | extensive consultation | extensive joint decision/ negotiation |
|---|---|---|---|---|
| "very useful" | 1 | 8 | 24 | 25 |
| "useful" | 52 | 58 | 69 | 67 |
| "no effect" | 41 | 34 | 5 | 7 |
| "hindrance" | 6 | 1 | 3 | 3 |

In order to measure the relationship between the extent of employee representative involvement and the effects of direct participation, we used the same three sets of indicators already presented in Chapter 7:

The first covers indicators of economic performance:

*   cost reduction;
*   reduction of throughput time;
*   improvement of quality of product or service;
*   increase in output.

The second includes two indicators of indirect labour cost variables which featured strongly in the debate on direct participation in the 1960s and 1970s:

- decrease in sickness;

- decrease in absenteeism.

The third embraces two possible 'negative' labour market indicators resulting from the introduction of direct participation:

- reduction in number of employees;

- reduction in number of managers.

Table 8.17 presents the data on the relationship between employee representative involvement and impact of direct participation on economic performance Three out of the four indicators showed no systematic variation with the extent of the involvement: reduction in throughput times, quality improvement and output increase seemed to be independent of the extent of this involvement. However, improvement in cost reduction went hand-in-hand with more extensive employee representative involvement. Workplaces with no involvement reduced their costs, due to the introduction, of direct participation by 46 per cent. If workplaces negotiated or management and unions were involved in taking joint decisions on direct participation, the percentage moved up to 67 per cent. In other words, it seems that an indicator equating with rationalisation was significantly influenced by an inclusive approach to the introduction of direct participation.

Table 8.17 also suggests no systematic variation between the extent of employee representative involvement and the effects on indirect labour costs. Only the two extremes varied. Workplaces with no such involvement reported a significantly lower effect of direct participation on decrease in sickness and absenteeism than workplaces with high levels of involvement.

A particularly sensitive question for management, trade unions and policy makers is the effect of regulation on changes in employment at the workplace level due to the introduction of direct participation. Does the extent of involvement of works councils and unions lead to protection of their constituents against negative employment effects or are unions 'forced' to take an active role in the restructuring of the workplace, co-managing organisational change with management and getting involved in possible lay offs and delayering, due to the introduction of direct participation?

Table 8.17 suggests that employee representatives were involved in the restructuring of workplaces. Workplaces with no employee representative involvement laid off employees due to the introduction of direct participation to a much lesser extent (19 per cent) than those with extensive consultation (37 per cent) or negotiations/joint-decision making (36 per cent). As for the reduction of managers, there appears to be an even stronger relationship: the proportion of workplaces increases from 5 per cent (no participation) to 32 per cent (negotiations).

**Table 8.17  The extent of employee representative involvement in the introduction of direct participation and the effects of direct participation – % of workplaces with employee representatives**

|  | no involvement | limited information | extensive information/ limited consultation | extensive consultation | extensive negotiation/ joint decision |
|---|---|---|---|---|---|
| reduction of costs | 46 | 43 | 57 | 65 | 67 |
| reduction of throughput time | 73 | 62 | 68 | 67 | 66 |
| improvement in quality | 96 | 89 | 92 | 92 | 97 |
| increase in total output | 54 | 40 | 47 | 57 | 53 |
| decrease in sickness | 33 | 9 | 25 | 26 | 45 |
| decrease in absenteeism | 30 | 38 | 37 | 24 | 43 |
| reduction in nos. of employees | 19 | 25 | 19 | 37 | 36 |
| reduction in nos. of managers | 5 | 15 | 18 | 24 | 32 |

To summarise, the involvement and particularly the extensive involvement of employee representatives in the introduction of direct participation in the 10 countries accelerated the tendency to reduce the number of employees and managers. Indeed, Table 8.18 suggests a strong relationship between successful cost reduction and the extent of employee representative involvement.

Clearly, these are very controversial conclusions and so it is important to note that there are three significant qualifications:

- The indicators used on economic and labour market performance have some methodological limitations (see section 7.1 in the previous chapter).

- The analysis is bi-variant and the results have to be checked by a multi-variant approach.

- Employment effects have been measured so far only in terms of short run reductions in the number of employees and managers; a further analysis in terms of the medium term employment situation will be given in section 8.10.

## 8.6 The effects of employee involvement

Not surprisingly, the EPOC literature review found that many commentators emphasised the importance of the involvement of employees themselves, and not just their representatives, in the *successful* introduction of direct participation. How does employee involvement in the introduction of direct participation influence direct participation and its economic and labour market effects? Table 8.18 indicates a clear relationship between good practice, in terms of informing and consulting with employees, and the scope of direct participation.

Extensive consultation of employees went together with the introduction of forms of direct participation, such as semi-autonomous working groups, with a wide scope for decision making. The opposite was the case in workplaces with no employee involvement. More than three quarters of these had low scores for the scope of direct participation. Extensive employee consultation appears to have had the same effect on direct participation, therefore, as the extensive involvement of employee representatives .

## Key findings:

- extensive consultation of employees went together with the introduction of the more intense forms of direct participation with a wide scope of decision-making

- the more employees were informed and consulted, the greater managers thought the economic effects

**Table 8.18  The extent of employee involvement in the introduction of direct participation and the scope of direct participation – % of workplaces**

| scores for scope | no involvement | limited information | extensive information | limited consultation | extensive consultation |
|---|---|---|---|---|---|
| low | 78 | 65 | 68 | 62 | 35 |
| medium | 11 | 22 | 26 | 18 | 25 |
| high | 11 | 13 | 6 | 20 | 40 |

Table 8.19 suggests that workplace performance was not influenced by employee involvement in respect of improved throughput time and quality. The biggest differences occurred between workplaces *with* and *without* employee involvement in respect of cost reduction and output increase. Direct participation was accompanied by increased output in 13 per cent of workplaces without consultation. However, if workplaces consulted their employees before the introduction, the output increased in 63 per cent of workplaces (+50 percentage points). A smaller increase occurred in cost reduction (+13). In the view of our managers, good information and consultation practice with employees before the introduction of direct participation seems to pay an economic dividend .

**Table 8.19  The extent of employee involvement in the introduction of direct participation and the effects of direct participation – % of workplaces**

| | no involvement | limited information | extensive information | limited consultation | extensive consultation |
|---|---|---|---|---|---|
| reduction of costs | 47 | 54 | 69 | 65 | 60 |
| reduction of throughput time | 61 | 69 | 42 | 66 | 64 |
| improvement in quality | 90 | 87 | 98 | 91 | 96 |
| increase in total output | 13 | 58 | 15 | 47 | 63 |
| decrease in sickness | 15 | 13 | 14 | 33 | 44 |
| decrease in absenteeism | 16 | 17 | 11 | 37 | 48 |
| reduction in nos. of employees | 28 | 24 | 16 | 31 | 34 |
| reduction in nos. of managers | 23 | 14 | 14 | 21 | 35 |

Indirect labour costs might also be expected to be reduced by involving employees in the introduction of direct participation. Table 8.19 suggests that sickness decrease showed a 29 percentage point difference between *non-participative* workplaces and those with extensive consultation. The decrease in absenteeism followed the same trend (+32). Indirect labour cost were reduced, if employees were involved in the introduction of direct participation. The observed positive effects on economic performance and indirect labour costs would appear to confirm, therefore, the basic assumptions of good human resource management.

Looking at the employment indicators, the results are at first glance surprising. Employee representative involvement had a significant impact on the reduction of employees on the introduction of direct participation. The difference was 17 percentage points between workplaces with and without full union or works council involvement. For employee involvement, this difference was reduced to +6 points (see Table 8.19). The same trend can be observed in regard of delayering. The difference between the two extremes of employee representative involvement was (+27), whereas in the case of employee involvement this difference is reduced to +12 points. How do we interpret these results? Information for employees is seen by management as good practice independent of the need for adaptation and rationalisation. It seems that, if a workplace has to reduce the workforce, many managers fall back on a significant involvement of employee representatives in order to achieve greater legitimacy for the outcome.

## 8.7   The effects of employee *and* employee representative involvement

To complete the analysis of the relationship between the extent of involvement in the introduction and the effects of direct participation, we focus in this section on a combined index of employee representative and employee involvement.

The effect on direct participation is clear (see Table 8.20) and in line with the results in sections 7.7 and 7.8 in Chapter 7.

In regard of economic performance and the effect on indirect labour costs (see Table 8.21) two results are significant:

- workplaces which were *non-participative* were significantly out performed by workplaces which had involvement;

- workplaces with a combination of strong employee representative and strong employee involvement did not systematically out perform workplaces with other combinations – there is no one way, it seems, of achieving high performance.

One result from Table 8.20 is clear, however: workplaces which were *highly participative* experienced by far the strongest negative employment effects.

**Key findings:**

- workplaces, which had no participative culture were significantly out performed by workplaces which had participation

- there does not appear to be one "best" way to achieve high performance; workplaces with strong representative *and* employee involvement did not systematically out perform those with other combinations of employee and representative participation

**Table 8.20  Combined employee representative and employee involvement in the introduction of direct participation and effects of direct participation – % of workplaces with employee representatives**

|  | "non-participative" | "substitutive" | "middle of the road" | "highly participative" |
|---|---|---|---|---|
| reduction of costs | 37 | 51 | 57 | 62 |
| reduction of throughput time | 59 | 69 | 68 | 65 |
| improvement in quality | 76 | 99 | 90 | 95 |
| increase in total output | 28 | 57 | 50 | 52 |
| decrease in sickness | 3 | 27 | 24 | 38 |
| decrease in absenteeism | 8 | 40 | 34 | 37 |
| reduction in nos. of employees | 7 | 17 | 18 | 34 |
| reduction in nos. of managers | 5 | 11 | 18 | 31 |

## 8.8 The employment effects of the joint regulation of direct participation

The analysis in sections 8.4 to 8.6 focused on the relationship between the regulation of direct participation and the short term labour market effects of the introduction of direct participation. The result was a clear and unambiguous relation between strong employee representative involvement and a reduction in the number of employees in general and managers in particular. It remains an open question whether these lay offs would have occurred, in any event, in these workplaces without significant involvement of employee representatives.

To what extent were these reductions compensated for or even over-compensated in the medium term? A description of the methodology used and its limitations can be found in Chapter 7. Table 8.21 gives an overview of the typology constructed on the basis of the systematic combination of short and medium term employment effects. Where there were negotiations and joint decision-making between management, unions or works councils, the number of workplaces with negative short and medium term employment effects increased from 16 per cent to 20 per cent (type 3). However, in 45 per cent of the workplaces experiencing lay offs in the short term, the overall employment situation stabilised in the medium term (type 1 and type 2 in relation to the total of type 1 to type 3).

A similar pattern occurs in workplaces with extensive employee representative and employee involvement. Twenty one per cent of these workplaces had a negative employment record in both the short and medium terms. However, 38 per cent of workplaces with a short term negative effect reported increases in employment in the medium term.

Comparing the effects of the different levels of involvement in the introduction of direct participation on employment is even more revealing. The data, which are presented in Table 8.22, show that between 7 and 10 per cent of workplaces with low or high scores for the levels of information of employee representatives experienced a negative employment impact in the short **and** medium term. Workplaces with extensive involvement, by contrast, reduced their employees in one out of five cases. A similar difference emerges in Table 8.22 in the case of combined employee representative and employee involvement. High levels of employee representative and combined employee representative-employee involvement, it seems, went hand-in-hand with above average negative short and medium term employment effects.

There are two possible explanations for these findings. One is that managers in workplaces with strong negative employment effects tended to involve employee representatives and employees in the decision-making on direct participation to a higher degree probably out of a need for legitimacy. The other is that employee representatives themselves sought an active role in the adjustment process. By becoming involved in the introduction of direct participation and any consequent lay offs, downsizing and delayering, they were trying to minimise the impact on their members and/or the constituency of the works council. These explanations, of course, are not mutually exclusive; there may well have been a mix of both.

**Table 8.21** Categories of workplaces with short term negative employment effects and medium term employment trends - % of workplaces with negotiation/joint-decision-making and "high participative" involvement of employee representatives *and* employees

| | all workplaces *with* direct participation | negotiations/ joint decision | "high participative" |
|---|---|---|---|
| type 1 *negative* short term effect of direct participation/ *positive* medium term employment trends | 5 | 6 | 5 |
| type 2 *negative* short term effect of direct participation/ *stable* medium term employment trends | 9 | 10 | 8 |
| type 3 *negative* short term effect of direct participation/ *negative* medium term employment trends | 16 | 20 | 21 |
| type 4 *no negative* short term effect of direct participation/ *positive* medium term employment trends | 27 | 25 | 25 |
| type 5 *no negative* short term effect of direct participation/ *stable* medium term employment trends | 30 | 28 | 29 |
| type 6 *no negative* short term effect of direct participation/ *negative* medium term employment trends | 13 | 11 | 12 |

**Table 8.22** Employee representative/employee involvement in the introduction of direct participation in workplaces with negative short term effects of direct participation *and* negative medium term employment trends – % of workplaces with employee representatives[1]

negative short term effect of direct participation and negative medium term employment trends

| employee representative involvement | | combined employee representative *and* employee involvement | |
|---|---|---|---|
| no involvement | 0 | "non-participative" | 3 |
| limited information | 10 | "substitutive" | 3 |
| extensive information/consultation | 7 | "middle of the road" | 8 |
| extensive consultation | 20 | "highly participative" | 21 |
| extensive negotiation/ joint-decision-making | 20 | | |

[1] Some cells of the table include a small number of respondents.

## 8.9  Summary and conclusions

The EPOC survey results suggest that the diffusion of direct participation in Europe is based on economic motives relatively independent of the existing systems of collective regulation of industrial relations. There seems to be a neutral relationship between direct participation and collective representation. Inasmuch as works councils, union representatives, degree of unionisation and collective bargaining neither hinder nor promote the diffusion of direct participation in Europe, the results confirm one key message of the EPOC social partners study: organised labour in Europe is not a barrier to organisational change. More positively, the results indicate a relatively high level of employee representative involvement in the introduction of direct participation: 30 per cent of the workplaces reported extensive negotiations and highly developed joint decision-making; a quarter of workplaces provided extensive information; only 13 per cent of the workplaces with an established employee representative system did not involve these representatives in the process of introduction of direct participation. Organisational change, it seems, is an inclusive process in the large majority of workplaces.

The extent of employee information and consultation about the introduction of direct participation is high. Considering the combined practice of employee representative-employee involvement one can conclude that the pre-conditions exist for a partnership approach to the development of a new framework for the modernisation of the organisation of work. Strong forms of employee representative involvement go together with a wide scope of direct participation; whereas a narrow scope was most frequent in workplaces without such involvement. Employee representatives were, in most cases, regarded as 'agents of change' rather than 'barriers to progress'.

The extent of employee representative involvement has, in the opinion of managers, no negative effect on the positive economic performance effects of the introduction of direct participation. The effect on reducing direct costs and indirect labour costs is beneficial. Good information and consultation practice seems to pay an economic dividend. Extensive employee representative and combined employee representative-employee involvement also go hand-in-hand with any negative short and medium term employment effects of direct participation, however.

There are two possible interpretations of the last finding, which are not mutually exclusive. Managers in workplaces with strong negative employment effects tend to involve employee representatives and employees to a greater degree than those in workplaces with fewer problems of internal labour market adjustment. A second interpretation is that employee representatives seek an active role in the adjustment process in order to minimise the impact on their members and/or the constituency of the works council.

## References

European Commission. 1997. Green Paper, *Partnership for a new organisation of work.*

European Commission. 1997. Consultation document for the Community social partners concerning *Information and Consultation of Workers within the National Framework.*

Fröhlich, D., C. Gill and H. Krieger 1993: *Workplace Involvement in Technological Innovation in the European Community*, volume I: *Roads to Participation*, Luxembourg: Office for the Official Publications of the European Communities.

Fröhlich, D. and U. Pekruhl. 1996: *Direct Participation and Organisational Change – Fashionable but Misunderstood? An analysis of recent research in Europe, Japan and the USA.* EF/96/38/EN. Luxembourg: Office for the Official Publications of the European Communities.

Huijgen, F., J. Benders and B. Nieuwkamp. 1997. 'Direct Participation in the Netherlands. An outline of the interim results of the EPOC survey questionnaire'. Paper presented to Conference on Direct Employee Participation organised by the Netherlands Ministry of Social Affairs and Employment in cooperation with the European Foundation for the Improvement of Living and Working Conditions, Amsterdam, 10-11 April 1997.

Regalia, I. 1995. *Humanise Work and Increase Profitability? Direct participation in organisational change viewed by the social partners in Europe.* EF/95/21/EN. Luxembourg: Office for the Official Publications of the European Communities.

Traxler, F. 1994. 'Collective Bargaining: levels and coverage', *OECD Employment Outlook.* Paris: Organisation for Economic Co-operation and Development.

# Chapter 9

# The significance of qualification and training

The fundamental assumption underlying the practice of direct participation is that more use is going to be made of employees' skills and knowledge in order to achieve higher productivity, greater flexibility and better product quality. As the European Commission states in its Green Paper on new forms of work organisation: 'In traditional economic thinking, labour is a factor of production similar to land and capital – a cost to be reduced. In a knowledge based economy, however, people represent a key resource. Organisations are valued not only on the basis of their products or machines but primarily on the knowledge-creating capacity of the workforce, the people who work for them, how they work, what work means to them'. (p.3). Skills and knowledge of the workforce are used in particular to:

- overcome problems in highly automated production processes, where the limits, shortcomings and inflexibility of new technologies become more and more evident (Brödner 1997)

- exploit tacit knowledge and every-day experience to practice continuous improvement in work processes and product quality (Womack/Jones/Roos 1990)

- plan tasks and allocate work with a view to increasing flexibility in new business processes (Brödner/Pekruhl 1991)

- cope successfully with the problems of technical and organisational change by involving employees actively in the change process (Cummings/Markus 1979)

Other things being equal, some of these goals could be reached by tapping the employee's every-day knowledge and some basic skills. It is not unfair to assume, however, that the results can be improved if those employees were also qualified. Workers' self-management in flexible business units means that those managing their own work not only need information about the operations process as a whole but also to be qualified in specific process and planning methods. Coping with the problems of new technology requires a broad basic technical education as well as specialised knowledge.

Moreover, such qualification is held not only to improve the use of human capabilities but also to be an important factor in job satisfaction. Employees with a wide scope of action (and with the qualification to use this scope) are more likely to be content with their work than unskilled workers (Ulich 1994). Thus, qualification has been considered to be a basic condition of both humanised work and work motivation and employee commitment.

As EPOC's literature survey revealed (Fröhlich and Pekruhl 1996), however, there is an ongoing debate about the nature and the extent of the qualification and training required for the economic success of direct participation. The practice of direct participation can go together with rudimentary employee qualification. For example, members of work groups in the Japanese Toyota plants (and in their twin factories in some American and European transplants) only receive three days on-the-job-training until they can carry out all tasks in one particular group and participate in quality circles improving work processes (Berrgren 1992). The question is whether this limited direct-participation-low-qualification approach is more efficient than work systems with comprehensive forms of direct participation based on a broad qualification of the workforce.

Also at issue is the training required for group consultation and group delegation. Many commentators, the EPOC literature review revealed, emphasised the 'social dimension' of group activities and the need they imposed for 'social skills'. Here the questions that need to be addressed are whether the training for direct participation of (1) employees and (2) management influences the economic effects of group delegation and group consultation.

These themes provide the subject of the first three sections of this chapter. The fourth briefly describes some conditions affecting skill requirements and the application of training: sector, size, industrial relations considerations and gender.

## 9.1 Qualification requirements

Our respondents were asked to rate the level of qualification required of their largest occupational group on a scale running from 1 to 5, where '1' meant a high level of qualification and '5' little or no qualification. Of course, this cannot provide an exact measurement of qualification demands, since all answers necessarily are related to the particular situation in a certain business sector. Thus we do not know what 'high qualification' or 'low qualification' mean in absolute terms (e.g.

duration and level of education), but we are able to compare the relative level of qualification requirements.

## Key findings:

- the proportion of workplaces with direct participation requiring high qualification was double that in those without and the greater the scope of direct participation, the stronger was the demand for high qualification

- high qualification enhanced the economic benefits of direct participation – especially the ability to achieve cost reductions

- the number of high-qualification workplaces reporting direct participation was completely successful was more than double that of those employing an unqualified workforce

Table 9.1 shows the overall distribution of answers to this question for workplaces that apply at least one direct participation measure (direct participation-workplaces) and for those workplaces that do not apply any direct participation measure (non-direct participation-workplaces). Maybe it is most informative to have a closer look at the two extremes, i.e. 'very low' and 'very high' qualification. One quarter of all workplaces practising direct participation reported they needed a very highly qualified workforce, whereas only about 5 per cent say that they could manage their business with unqualified employees. Evidently, qualification is a very important factor for direct participation: in 80 per cent of workplaces practising direct participation the level of required qualification is medium or higher. The proportion *with* direct participation requiring high qualification is double that in workplaces *without*.

As Figure 9.1 confirms, country differences are most apparent for Denmark, at one extreme, and for Spain and the UK, at the other. While in Denmark the demand for very high qualification is almost twice as high (46 per cent) as the ten-country average, it is the opposite for the other two countries. High qualification is used only to a very limited extent in Spain (13 per cent) and the UK (13 per cent). Moreover, a comparatively large number of managers (16 per cent) in the UK declared they could run their business with an unqualified workforce. The case of Portugal and Spain is also interesting. While Spanish managers seemed to be pursuing a low-qualification strategy, in Portugal the number of workplaces with very high qualification requirements is well above the average (39 per cent). Taking in account case study reports, together with the findings in Chapter 4, it seems fair to assume that a major consideration is the presence of multinational companies bringing with them operating concepts demanding high qualification.

**Table 9.1 Qualification requirements – all respondents**

|  | very high (1) % | 2 % | 3 % | 4 % | very low (5) % |
|---|---|---|---|---|---|
| workplaces *with* direct participation | 23 | 30 | 27 | 14 | 5 |
| workplaces *without* direct participation | 11 | 29 | 29 | 20 | 12 |

Significantly, the results suggest, there might be a competitive disadvantage for workplaces following a low qualification strategy in their approach to direct participation. As Figure 9.2 reveals, cost reduction was achieved in almost two thirds of those workplaces requiring a highly qualified workforce but only in about one third of those that do not. If we assume that the costs of qualified employees are considerably higher than for an unskilled staff, one message becomes evident. Qualification pays; in spite of higher wages, cost reduction is more likely to be achieved by direct participation if the workforce is qualified.

The proportion of workplaces reporting the reduction of throughput times is also much higher in the high-qualification workplaces, whereas quality improvements and an increase in total output only were only slightly affected. Another important message of Figure 9.2 is that direct participation-workplaces whose largest occupational group is highly qualified tend to reduce the number of employees (26 per cent) less often than other workplaces (39 per cent). There are two possible explanations for this phenomenon: one is that high-qualification workplaces are more successful on the market so they can compensate higher productivity with an increased production of goods or services; the other is that the increase of productivity on its own is less important in these workplaces than other cost reduction factors or other considerations such as flexibility and quality.

A decrease in sickness and absenteeism is more likely to be achieved in workplaces with very low qualification requirements. A possible explanation is that direct participation has a stronger impact on changes in working conditions in low-qualification workplaces than higher ones, and that these changes of working conditions positively influence sickness and absenteeism. In the absence of detailed information about the workplaces, a definitive answer is not possible.

Figure 9.1: Qualification requirements - % of respondents with
direct participation by country

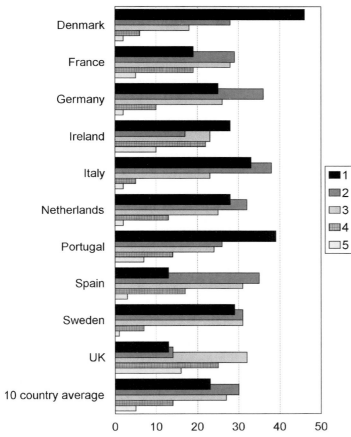

Note: 1 = very high: 5 = very low

Table 9.2 confirms what has already been indicated by looking at the single economic effects of direct participation: the overall success of direct participation is estimated much more positively – twice as high for 'completely successful' – by managers who employ a qualified.

The level of qualification required does not relate to the basic form of direct participation. Regardless which of these six forms is applied, the qualification needed on average remains the same. This suggests the demand for qualification is a result of direct participation itself without taking in account the various

Figure 9.2: Qualification requirements and the effects of direct participation - % of respondents with direct participation

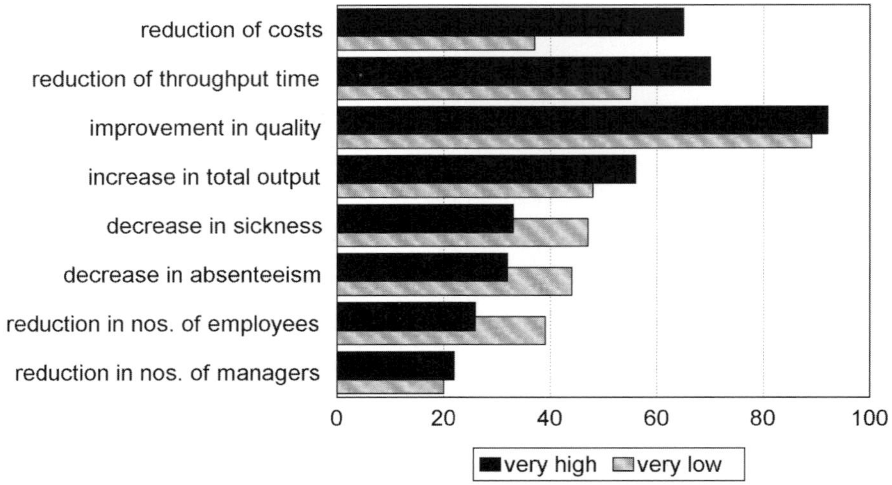

circumstances and particular conditions direct participation is embedded in. However, there is a correlation between the measures of the overall scope of direct participation and qualification requirements: The workplaces scoring highly (34 per cent) for the scope of direct participation more often needed a highly skilled workforce than those with low scores (20 per cent) (Table 9.3).

**Table 9.2 Qualification requirements and the success of direct participation**

|  |  | level of qualification required | |
|---|---|---|---|
|  |  | very high (1) | very low (5) |
|  |  | % | % |
|  | completely successful | 46 | 22 |
| was direct participation | very successful | 45 | 54 |
| a success? | moderately successful | 8 | 21 |
|  | not very successful | 1 | 4 |

**Table 9.3  Qualification requirements and overall scope of direct participation**

|  |  | very high | very low |
|---|---|---|---|
|  |  | % | % |
| overall scope of | low | 20 | 5 |
| direct participation | high | 34 | 4 |

## 9.2   Training as a basis for direct participation

Since employee qualification plays a crucial role in the implementation and success of direct participation, it might be expected that training for direct participation would be no less important. Even if the organisation's staff has been well qualified before the introduction of direct participation, there are most likely additional skills that have to be achieved by those employees whose capabilities and competencies now shall be used to largely extended degree in direct participation work systems. These new skills are in particular:

- professional skills, since direct participation in most cases means taking over new tasks on the same level (job enlargement) or on a higher level (job enrichment). Moreover, because employees gain new responsibilities for the entire work process they have to learn about the interrelations between single departments and the production process

- methodological competencies, i.e. management-know-how for planning of work and processes; capabilities and techniques to develop ones own creativity; self-learning-techniques; the ability to participate in discussions

- social skills, because direct participation in many cases implies co-operation in groups.

### Key findings:

- two-thirds of respondents agreed that direct participation requires considerable investment in vocational training; even more (82 per cent) agreed that training in the social skills for direct participation is a high priority

- the wider the scope of direct participation, the more likely managers agree that investments in vocational and social skills training are significant

To make the best use out of this co-operation and to be able to cope with the problems that usually arise in every group, employees have to be able to communicate, i.e. to exchange knowledge, information, ambitions and emotions, and to solve problems like group pressure, informal leadership.

In the words of the Green Paper: 'The new forms of work organisation require a much better educated and trained workforce, including in particular management. The flexibility and adaptability of skills are key ... It is hardly possible to over-estimate the importance of action in this area' ( p.7-8). This importance of workforce training is acknowledged by most managers in direct participation-workplaces, as Table 9.4 indicates. Sixty seven per cent of all those managers marked the following statement to be significant or very significant: 'direct participation requires considerable investment in vocational training'. Even more workplaces (82 per cent) agreed with the assertion that 'training in the social skills necessary for direct participation has to be a high priority'.

**Table 9.4 Statements about training in direct participation workplaces**

|  | very significant | significant | not significant |
|---|---|---|---|
|  | % | % | % |
| vocational training | 18 | 50 | 33 |
| social skills training | 29 | 53 | 18 |

Quite interestingly, in most of those countries in which the qualification requirements, i.e. the recent average level of workforce qualification, are already comparably high, the vocational training is not estimated as *very* significant (Table 9A.23 in Appendix 3): Only 9 per cent of Dutch and Danish managers and 12 per cent of Swedish respondents think that vocational training is very important against the ten-country average of 18 per cent. On the other hand, Spanish managers seem to be quite aware that at their workplaces there is a considerable lack of qualification which has to be overcome: 24% of those managers say that vocational training is very important. Much less awareness can be found amongst managers in the UK. While the actual workforce qualification at UK workplaces is the lowest of the 10 countries in the survey, vocational training is not assessed as very significant either: only 15 per cent of all managers agree with this statement; 43 per cent of British mangers even say that vocational training is not important (average 33 per cent).

As Table 9A.24 in Appendix 3 shows, there are also substantial country differences with respect to the estimated need for social skills training. Since there are no obvious explanations for these variances, we will point only at those countries which deviate from the average: The high significance of social skill training is acknowledged by a high proportion of managers in France (37 per cent), Germany (35 per cent), Portugal (36 per cent) and Spain (37 per cent) but only by 16 per cent of Dutch managers and 19 per cent of managers in the UK. Overall, 29 per cent of all respondents say that social skills training is very significant.

Tables 9.5 and 9.6 below show that there is a clear relationship between the scope of direct participation at the workplace and the acknowledgement of both vocational and social skills training, i.e. the higher the scope of direct participation in an organisation, the more likely managers agree with the statement that investment in vocational and social skills training are very significant or at least significant. This again supports the message: successful direct participation has to be based on sufficient employee qualification.

**Table 9.5  The scope of direct participation and statements about vocational training**

| scope of direct participation | statements about vocational training | | |
|---|---|---|---|
| | very significant | significant | not significant |
| | % | % | % |
| low | 16 | 49 | 35 |
| medium | 17 | 47 | 36 |
| high | 24 | 56 | 21 |

**Table 9.6  The scope of direct participation and statements about social skills training**

| scope of direct participation | statements about social skills training | | |
|---|---|---|---|
| | very significant | significant | not significant |
| | % | % | % |
| low | 27 | 55 | 18 |
| medium | 30 | 47 | 23 |
| high | 35 | 51 | 13 |

## 9.3  Social skills training – group consultation

The emphasis on training holds true in particular for those forms of direct participation involving groups of employees. Especially important here are methodological and social skills. These kind of skills are rarely topics in 'normal' training courses. To find out more about training for these special qualifications we concentrated our questions about training on these aspects rather than vocational training . We asked those workplaces with either group consultation measures (in temporary or permanent groups) or group delegation about the intensity of and the issues covered by this training.

Only about 50 per cent of workplaces who apply group consultation in temporary or permanent groups provide special training courses for their employees (Table 9.7). Most of these courses only included one particular topic and only a minority covers the whole field. There is a substantial gap between saying and doing according to Table 9.6 above, more than 80 per cent of managers in direct participation workplaces said that training in social skills should have a high priority, but only a few actually carried out such courses. On the other side, there also is a more optimistic interpretation of the results: all the same 50 per cent of workplaces who consulted employees on a group basis provided training for special skills that rarely had been a part of traditional curricula.

## Key findings:

- Only a half of workplaces with the group forms of consultation provide social skills training for their employees

- respondents giving employees social skills training were more likely to estimate direct participation 'completely successful' than those that did not

**Table 9.7  Training for temporary and permanent group consultation: number of topics covered**

|                   | training for temporary group consultation % | training for permanent group consultation % |
|-------------------|:---:|:---:|
| no training       | 48  | 51  |
| 1 topic           | 22  | 27  |
| 2 topics          | 20  | 14  |
| 3 topics or more  | 10  | 8   |

There are very few country differences to be found. Worth a mention is that Irish workplaces seem to be very active in the field of workforce training for temporary groups (73 per cent of all Irish workplaces who have this kind of group consultation) and that Portugal is lacking behind a little bit (38 per cent) when it comes to training activities for permanent groups.

As Table 9.8 reveals, the duration of this training – we asked for the time spent for training in the last year – in most cases was 1 to 5 days (35 per cent with permanent groups and 45 per cent with temporary groups). About one fifth of the workplaces in each category run courses which were either longer or shorter. The relatively high number of no answers might indicate that workplaces had carried out training courses at the time of the introduction of direct participation, but had no training going on within the last year.

**Table 9.8  Training for temporary and permanent group consultation: duration in days**

|  | training for temporary group consultation % | training for permanent group consultation % |
|---|---|---|
| 1 day or less | 19 | 21 |
| between 1 and 5 days | 45 | 35 |
| more than 5 days | 15 | 17 |
| no answer | 21 | 27 |

All of the training areas we asked about have been part of training activities (see Table 9.9). It is not possible to identify one area which is of particular importance. Obviously all topics are relevant in a considerable number of workplaces:

**Table 9.9  Training for temporary and permanent group consultation: topics covered**

|  | training for temporary group consultation % | training for permanent group consultation % |
|---|---|---|
| data collection | 27 | 23 |
| presentation skills | 19 | 17 |
| inter-personal skills | 26 | 22 |
| group dynamics | 22 | 18 |

Does training of the workforce have a positive effect on the economic results of group consultation? In order to find out more about this relationship we combined the variables 'training duration' and 'number of topics' in a new variable called 'training intensity'. A high training intensity means that the duration of the courses is comparably high *and* the number of topics tackled above the average; low training intensity means short duration training with very limited content.

Tables 9.10 and 9.11 suggest that social skills training has clear positive effects on the economic results of group consultation. Workplaces giving special courses to their employees are more likely to estimate direct participation as 'completely successful' than workplaces without any training. This correlation is stronger for temporary groups than for permanent groups. While for permanent groups the intensity of training does not play a crucial role – it seems to be important that *any* training is provided – high training intensity makes a difference for direct participation in temporary groups: 56 per cent of workplaces with such a high training intensity say direct participation is completely successful while there is almost no difference between 'low training intensity' and 'no training'.

**Table 9.10**     **Intensity of training for temporary group consultation**

|  |  | training intensity | | |
|---|---|---|---|---|
|  |  | low % | high % | no training % |
|  | completely successful | 27 | 56 | 32 |
| was direct participation a success? | very successful | 61 | 37 | 56 |
|  | moderately successful | 11 | 7 | 11 |
|  | not very successful | 0 | 0 | 1 |

**Table 9.11**     **Intensity of training for permanent group consultation**

|  |  | training intensity | | |
|---|---|---|---|---|
|  |  | low % | high % | no training % |
|  | completely successful | 50 | 49 | 39 |
| was direct participation a success? | very successful | 39 | 46 | 42 |
|  | moderately successful | 10 | 3 | 14 |
|  | not very successful | 0 | 2 | 5 |

## 9.4   Social skills training – group delegation

Looking at the topics, the duration and the effects of training provided for group delegation, the findings are very similar to those described above for groups that are only consulted by management. Therefore we will not repeat all the arguments but only present the particular data (Tables 9.12 to 9.15).

In summary, 46 per cent of all workplaces that introduced group delegation for their largest occupational group provide particular training courses, most of these courses last 1 to 5 days, and all the topics we asked about are covered to about the same extent. A high intensity of training makes it much more likely that direct participation is assessed as 'completely successful'.

As previous chapters have pointed out, group delegation looms especially large in the debate on direct participation: it is supposed to be the most advanced form of direct participation and, moreover, the core of those new forms of integrated approaches such as 'lean organisation and TQM. However, as Chapter 4 reminded us, there are considerable differences between the intensity of various forms of group delegation. As well as the scope of rights and the degree of autonomy, qualification and training are important as well. Taking these additional factors into account, we can distinguish two opposite types of group delegation: on the one hand, we find groups whose rights and scope for decision making are quite limited, the qualification of the staff is comparably low and there is little or no particular investment in workforce training. On the other, we have semi-autonomous groups who are managing themselves to a large extent. These groups might also be expected to be a highly qualified in order to be able to cope with new tasks. Appropriate labels for these two models, as Chapter 4 has already suggested, might be 'Scandinavian' and 'Toyota'.

## Key findings:

- less than half of workplaces with group delegation provided social skills training for their employees

- respondents giving employees social skills training were more likely to estimate group delegation "completely successful" than those that did not

- the 'Scandinavian' model of group delegation (high-intensity delegation+ qualified workforce +high training intensity) was judged to be more successful than the 'Toyota' (low-intensity delegation +medium or low employee skills+ low training intensity)

- less than two per cent of workplaces matched the 'Scandinavian' model

**Table 9.12 Training for group delegation: number of topics covered**

|  |  | training for group delegation |
|---|---|---|
|  |  | % |
|  | no training | 54 |
| no of topics covered by training | 1 topic | 20 |
|  | 2 topics | 16 |
|  | 3 topics or more | 10 |

**Table 9.13 Training for group delegation: duration of training**

|  | training for group delegation |
|---|---|
|  | % |
| 1 day or less | 27 |
| between 1 and 5 days | 50 |
| more than 5 days | 16 |
| no answer | 7 |

**Table 9.14  Training for group delegation: topics covered**

|  | training for group delegation |
|---|---|
|  | % |
| data collection | 20 |
| presentation skills | 23 |
| inter-personal skills | 16 |
| group dynamics | 19 |

**Table 9.15  Intensity of training for group delegation**

|  |  | training intensity | | |
|---|---|---|---|---|
|  |  | low % | high % | no training % |
|  | completely successful | 34 | 58 | 38 |
| was direct participation a success? | very successful | 49 | 33 | 48 |
|  | moderately successful | 11 | 7 | 13 |
|  | not very successful | 7 | 2 | 1 |

Significant questions are whether the 'Scandinavian' model is more successful than its 'Toyota' counterpart, and whether there are significant differences by country.

In our context the two types are defined as follows:

- *Toyota*: the intensity of group delegation is low, the qualification requirements are medium or lower, and the training intensity is low or zero;

- *Scandinavian* model: the intensity of group delegation is high, the qualification requirements are high or very high, and the training intensity is high.

Of course, this definition of fundamentally different types of group delegation refers to "ideal" models, as they can be derived from case description found in literature. These ideal models have been chosen to demonstrate the basic differences between types of group delegation. There are many workplaces practising group work to be found in between these two extremes. However, this does not mean that the 'Toyota' and the 'Scandinavian' models do not exist in reality. Most of the widely-publicised cases (e.g. Volvo Udevalla, ABB, EKATO, Johnson Control) discussed at conferences and in management journals meet the above definition of the 'Scandinavian' model, while some mass-production enterprises with assembly-line group work would fit the 'Toyota'.

The conclusion to be drawn from Table 9.16 and Figure 9.3 is clear: in the opinion of the two sets of sponsors, the 'Scandinavian' model seems to much more successful than the 'Toyota' equivalent. Almost half of all managers who applied the former said direct participation was a complete success, whereas only one fifth of the workplaces with the other model made this statement. Fifteen per cent of the 'Toyota-type' workplaces are very pessimistic (direct participation has been not very successful), whereas none of the workplaces with the 'Scandinavian' model were. Even so, there is a relative success for the 'Toyota' model as well.

**Table 9.16  Types of group delegation and economic success**

|  |  | type of group work | |
|---|---|---|---|
|  |  | *Toyota* | *Scandinavian* |
|  |  | % |  |
|  | completely successful | 20 | 48 |
| was direct participation | very successful | 56 | 44 |
| a success? | moderately successful | 9 | 8 |
|  | not very successful | 15 | 0 |

Figure 9.3: The effects of different types of group delegation - % of respondents with other forms

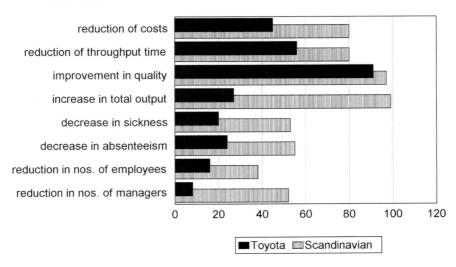

Also, if we look at the single effects of direct participation, the 'Scandinavian' model appears to be the indisputable winner. In all categories of economic effects the figures are much higher for the 'Scandinavian' than for the 'Toyota' model. For example, while a total output increase is achieved by almost all workplaces (99 per cent) applying the former, less than one third (27 per cent) with the latter did so. In many categories the results for the 'Scandinavian' model are more than twice as high as for the 'Toyota'.

However, as Table 9.17 reveals, cases of the 'Scandinavian' model are very much the exception. The proportion of workplaces matching the conditions outlined above is less than 2 per cent. Even in Sweden only 5 per cent of workplaces appear to apply it. This finding is a further confirmation for one of the most important conclusions from our survey: there is a broad gap between the obvious success of advanced forms of direct participation, on the one hand, and the adoption of them, on the other.

**Table 9.17  Diffusion of the *Scandinavian* model of group work**

| ten-country average | DK | FR | GER | IR | IT | NL | POR | SP | SW | UK |
|---|---|---|---|---|---|---|---|---|---|---|
| % | % | % | % | % | % | % | % | % | % | % |
| 1.4 | 1.6 | 0.2 | 0.6 | 0.3 | 1.6 | 1.6 | 1.0 | 0.2 | 4.6 | 1.0 |

## 9.5   Management training for direct participation

Most commentators agree that the work roles of managers, particularly of middle management, will change in the process of organisational restructuring through direct participation. The extent of this change and the management functions affected vary with the type of direct participation implemented. Most obviously, the forms of group consultation and, perhaps even more so, group delegation are having the strongest impacts on the work of managers. As already mentioned at the beginning of this chapter, the management role – at least for first-line supervisors – tends to shift from a directive towards a coaching and facilitating role. Managers become team organisers and communicators between teams and between teams and other units in the organisation. There obviously is a need for (middle) managers to be prepared for these conditions and learn to cope with the new situation: middle management need to learn and assume new roles in the organisation. Also, as 'team managers', their social skills tend to become more important than their technical skills.

## Key findings:

* workplaces providing employees with training for direct participation typically do the same for managers

* the impact of the training of managers for direct participation is regarded as positive as that of the training of employees

In order to find out whether these new management skills had been subject of management training activities, we used the same questions for managers as we did for workforce training. Since the forms and extent of management training is almost the same with all three forms of group participation, we aggregated the answers and only give a general overview about all three forms.

As a rule, it can be said that those workplaces that apply workforce training for direct participation also provide similar training for managers. Moreover, high training intensity for the workforce most often correlated with high training intensity for management. Looking at Tables 9.18 to 9.20 the results are quite familiar because they are rather similar to the findings on workforce training. The only difference is that the number of topics which is covered by management training and the duration of this training is very slightly higher than it is for employee training.

**Table 9.18  Management training: number of topics covered**

|  |  | % |
|---|---|---|
|  | no training | 43 |
| no of topics covered by training | 1 topic | 19 |
|  | 2 topics | 18 |
|  | 3 topics or more | 20 |

**Table 9.19  Management training: duration in days**

|  | % |
|---|---|
| 1 day or less | 16 |
| between 1 and 5 days | 37 |
| more than 5 days | 18 |
| no answer | 29 |

**Table 9.20  Management training: topics covered**

|                     | %  |
|---------------------|----|
| data collection     | 34 |
| presentation skills | 33 |
| inter-personal skills | 34 |
| group dynamics      | 28 |

Thus, it is no surprise that the impact of management training on the economic effects of direct participation (Table 9.21) is about the same as for employees. This means the positive effects of training cannot clearly be connected to one group *or* the other, but it must be said that the combination of both is a factor which influences the economic effects of direct participation.

**Table 9.21  Intensity of management training**

|                              |                        | training intensity | | |
|------------------------------|------------------------|--------|----------|--------|
|                              |                        | low %  | medium % | high % |
|                              | completely successful  | 38     | 48       | 34     |
| was direct participation a success? | very successful | 46     | 41       | 54     |
|                              | moderately successful  | 11     | 10       | 11     |
|                              | not very successful    | 5      | 1        | 1      |

## 9.6   The skill-oriented workplace

As already mentioned when discussing the 'Toyota' and 'Scandinavian' models of group delegation, there are a number of workplaces employing a well qualified workforce *and* investing both in workforce and management training. In a more general view (i.e. not focusing on particular forms of group delegation) these workplaces could be called 'skill-oriented':

### Key findings:

- only about 9 per cent of workplaces in the survey might be said to be 'skill-oriented'

- direct participation in 'skill-oriented' workplaces was more likely to be judged 'completely successful' than in other workplaces

- the level of qualification at these workplaces is high or very high

- the training intensity, i.e. the duration and scope of training courses, is high both for management and employees

About 9 per cent of all workplaces in the survey comply with these criteria. Differences by country were hardly significant.

After what has been said about the impacts of either qualification or training it is no surprise that 'skill-oriented' workplaces perform much better than the rest. 55 per cent of managers from these workplaces assess direct participation as very successful, but only 37 per cent of all the other managers agree with this statement (Table 9.22). Looking at the single economic effects of direct participation the 'skill-oriented' workplaces perform better in all categories (Figure 9.4).

**Table 9. 22  The skill-oriented workplace and economic success**

|  |  | skill-oriented workplaces % | other workplaces % |
|---|---|---|---|
|  | completely successful | 55 | 37 |
| was direct participation | very successful | 38 | 50 |
| a success? | moderately successful | 7 | 11 |
|  | not very successful | 0 | 2 |

Figure 9.4: The effects of the skill-oriented workplace

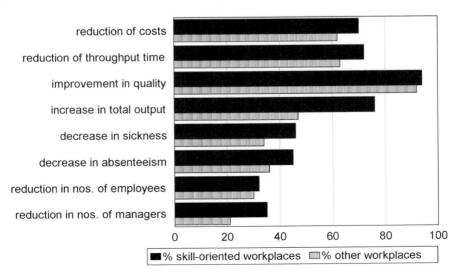

The most striking differences appear when managers are asked whether there was an ´increase in total output´ as an effect of direct participation. The answer to this question is 'yes' at 76 per cent of all 'skill-oriented' workplaces but only at 47 per cent of the other workplaces. A very tentative and quite speculative interpretation of this difference would be that 'skill-oriented' workplaces are better prepared to create new products and develop new markets, thus being able to increase their total output. This would be quite a strong indicator for positive labour market effects of qualification and training.

## 9.7    The significance of key structural variables

In this first overview of the results of the EPOC survey we are concentrating on the immediate connections between qualification, training, direct participation and the economic effects of direct participation. However, in this section we will give a very brief review of other factors affecting qualification requirements and training efforts in direct participation-workplaces.

All of the following statements about qualification requirements are valid for those workplaces that apply at least one direct participation measure (direct participation-workplaces); all statements about the 'skill-oriented' workplace regard workplaces with either consultation or group delegation.

### Key findings:

- services stand out – the demand for high qualification and the incidence of training for direct participation was greater in some sectors (professional services) than others (retail and catering/hotels)

- there was *no* significant relationship between the size of workplace and qualification requirements but training for group delegation was much more likely in large workplaces

- the number of workplaces not bound by a collective agreement requiring little or no workforce qualification was twice as high (11 per cent) as the average (5 per cent), but the intensity of training was only slightly affected by industrial relations considerations

- allowing for sector, the higher the share of women at the workplace, the lower are the qualification requirements and the skill orientation

*Sector*

While workplaces in the industrial sector all in all are close to the average level of qualification requirements, the service sector is split in two parts (see Table 9A.25

in Appendix 3). On the one hand, we find a high demand for very high qualification in the professional services (39 per cent, average for all direct participation-workplaces 23 per cent), in health and welfare (32 per cent) and, of course, in education (62 per cent). On the other hand, the need for high skills is very low in catering/hotels (8 per cent) and retail trade (15 per cent). Corresponding to this last figure the amount of workplaces that can work with an unqualified workforce is highest in the retail sector (12 per cent, average 6 per cent).

Also if we look at the dissemination of 'skill-oriented' workplaces (see Table 9A.26 in Appendix 3), the service sector shows the extremes: 20 per cent of all workplaces (with any form of group direct participation) in education and 21 per cent in the banking and insurance sector, but almost no workplace in recreation/leisure or catering/hotels can be labelled as skill-oriented.

*Size*

As Table 9A.27 in Appendix 3 shows, there is no obvious relationship between the size of the workplace (i.e. the size of the largest occupational group) and qualification requirements, if we look at workplaces with more than 50 employees in the largest occupational group. However, at smaller workplaces the qualification requirements are considerably above the average.

Skill-orientation, i.e. high qualification requirements plus a high training intensity, is much more likely to be found (19 per cent) in workplaces with more than 1000 employees (Table 9A.28 in Appendix 3).

*Industrial relations*

Among those workplaces not bound by a collective labour agreement the number of workplaces that required little or no workforce qualification is twice as high (11 per cent) as the average (5 per cent). Similar results are found in workplaces with no union members (10 per cent).

Training intensity is only slightly affected by industrial relations considerations. There is a smaller proportion of workplaces without any training with union representatives (47 per cent, average 56 per cent) and high training intensities are more likely in workplaces with a works council (29 per cent, average 24 per cent). The training intensity is also greater in highly unionised workplaces.

*Gender*

At first glance the figures in Tables 9A.29 and 9A.30 in Appendix 3 are quite surprising. Neither qualification requirements nor skill-orientation, it seems, are related to the percentage of women in the largest occupational group. But, of course, there are sector effects producing these results: in general, more women are working in sectors with a high average of qualification requirements and skill-orientation (like banking/insurance or education), while in large sectors with lower skill requirements (e.g. industry or construction) men are dominant. Looking at single sectors shows the result that might have been expected: The higher the share of women at the workplace, the lower are the qualification requirements and the skill orientation.

This can be exemplified by looking at two typical sectors with low and high women employment. As Table 9A.31 in Appendix 3 reveals, in manufacturing the amount of workplaces requiring very high qualification is more than four times higher in male-dominated workplaces (i.e. where the percentage of women was less than 10 per cent) than in women-dominated workplaces (where the percentage of women was above 75%). Just the opposite holds true for workplaces with very low qualification requirements. The number of 'skill-oriented' workplaces (see Table 9A.32 in Appendix 3) is almost twice as high in male-dominated workplaces than in organisations with a large female workforce. This impact of gender on qualification requirements and skill orientation is even more drastic in banking/insurance (see Tables 9A.33 and 9A.34 in Appendix 3): more than 40 per cent of male-dominated workplaces in this sector are high-qualification-workplaces, whereas this is the case in only 8 per cent of those female-dominated; the proportion of 'skill-oriented' workplaces was also almost five times higher in the male-dominated part of the sector.

## 9.8   Summary and conclusion

The findings of the EPOC survey presented in this chapter confirm general expectations. Direct participation requires qualification and training. The demand for qualification and training was positively associated with the scope of direct participation – one third of respondents with high scores for the overall scope of direct participation required a very highly qualified workforce, whereas only one in five with limited scope and one in ten of those not practising direct participation did so. Also qualification and training were reckoned to be significant influences on the economic effects of direct participation. High employee qualification and high training intensity made it much more likely that direct participation was completely successful and that various economic benefits of direct participation were attained.

More particularly, the chapter illuminates the debate about the different forms of group work. The 'Scandinavian' model (high-intensity group delegation+ qualified workforce + high training intensity) was judged to be more successful than the 'Toyota' equivalent (low-intensity group delegation+ medium or low employee skills + low training intensity) in the eyes of their respective sponsors. This puts into even sharper relief the finding that the 'Scandinavian' model is to be found in only a very small minority of workplaces (less than 2 per cent) across the 10 countries.

Finally, the chapter confirms that there are apparently very unequal opportunities between men and women. Allowing for sector, the higher the share of women at the workplace, the lower are the qualification requirements and the 'skill orientation'.

## References

Berrgren, C. 1992: *Alternatives to lean production. work organisation in the Swedish auto industry*, Ithaca, New York: Cornell University, ILR Press.

Brödner, P. (1997): *Der überlistete Odysseus. Über das zerrüttete Verhältnis von Menschen und Maschinen*. Berlin: edition sigma.

Brödner, P. and U. Pekruhl (1991): *Rückkehr der Arbeit in die Fabrik. Wettbewerbsfähigkeit durch menschenzentrierte Erneuerung der Produktion*. Gelsenkirchen: IAT

Cummings, Th.G. and M.L. Markus (1979): A socio-technical systems review of organizations. In: C.L. Cooper (ed.): *Behavioral problems in organizations*. Englewood Cliffs: Prentice Hall.

European Commission. 1997. Green Paper, *Partnership for a new organisation of work*.

Fröhlich, D. and U. Pekruhl. 1996: *Direct Participation and Organisational Change – Fashionable but Misunderstood? An analysis of recent research in Europe, Japan and the USA*. EF/96/38/EN. Luxembourg: Office for the Official Publications of the European Communities.

Ulich, E. (1994): *Arbeitspsychologie*. Stuttgart: Poeschl.

Womack, J.P., D.T. Jones and D.Roos. 1990. *The machine that changed the world*. New York: Rawson Associates.

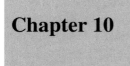

# Chapter 10  Remuneration systems

The term "remuneration system" refers here to the methods used to pay employees. There are two basic approaches:

- wages can be fixed, i.e. employees are paid on an hourly or monthly basis, without reference to how they perform, as long as they conform to their contracts with the organisation.

- wages can vary according to the performance and behaviour of employees.

The most prominent example of a performance-related pay system is payment by results: individual employees achieve wage bonuses according to the amount of output or the time they take to produce it. Although output might continue to play a role in work organisation involving direct participation, it might be expected that there would be other considerations, which are equally or even more important and which can be influenced by more complex remuneration systems:

- team work – the performance of the group as a whole may be much more significant for the organisation's success than individual employee's performance, which means that some form of collective bonus may be appropriate.

- organisational performance – the performance of the organisation may be a critical consideration leading to the application of some form of financial participation such as profit sharing or share ownership.

- quality – the quality of goods and services is likely to be increasingly significant even where output is important; it is rarely promoted by payment by results systems.

- flexibility – in many cases it is a willingness of employees to be flexible, to change jobs, for example, that the organisation wishes to encourage.

- qualification and skills – the organisation may wish to attract a highly qualified workforce or to motivate existing employees to take part in training courses in order to improve their skills.

- commitment – underpinning most of the other considerations is the need not for the compliance of employees but their commitment; how to promote commitment through the remuneration system is a major issue.

Throughout Europe, EPOC's literature review (Fröhlich and Pekruhl, 1996) reported, a number of cases can be cited where new forms of pay system are implemented and organisations report very positive effects. Some managers even argue that newly adopted pay systems are a necessary precondition for direct participation. It is a message, too, which the European Commission's Green Paper, *Partnership for a new organisation of work*, seems to have taken to heart: 'how to adapt wage systems along with organisational structures on which they are based', is deemed to be one of the critical issues public authorities and the social partners have to face up to (Executive Summary).

A key first task in this chapter, since there is so little systematic data about the subject, is to give an overview of the types of remuneration-systems applied in the workplaces in the 10 countries covered by the EPOC survey. The second is to establish what changes, if any, were made to the remuneration system to support the practice of direct participation.

The treatment is necessarily brief. The EPOC survey was not designed to get detailed information on pay systems. The same goes for the implications of national systems of regulation, which must be largely ignored.

## 10.1 Patterns of remuneration systems

Figure 10.1 suggests that most of the special components of remuneration systems are more frequent in workplaces *with* rather than *without* some form of direct participation. This is particularly true for components reflecting skills and qualification, which are applied in almost 50 per cent of direct participation-workplaces but in only one third of their non-direct participation counterparts. This would appear to support the conclusions of Chapter 9 that employee skills are a crucial factor in the functioning of direct participation. Bonuses for individual attitudes, team volume of output and profit sharing schemes are slightly more prominent in workplaces *with* direct participation , while bonuses for individual performance and share ownership are equally applied.

## Key findings:

- remuneration systems in workplaces *with* direct participation tended to be more complex than those *without*

- pay for skills and qualification was particularly prevalent in workplaces with direct participation

Table 10.1 suggests that, as well as differences due to particular national systems of regulation, which are not our concern here, there are some very particular results worthy of report:

- pay for qualification was by far most prominent in Germany (75 per cent of direct participation-workplaces). Germany also had the highest proportions with individual bonuses for output – Germany, it seems, is the country of payment by results systems.

- profit sharing schemes were very popular in France (43 per cent) and in the UK (38 per cent).

- the UK, as well as being prominent for profit sharing, was the only country with a considerable number of workplaces with share ownership schemes (22 per cent). It can be said, in other words, that direct participation is most likely to go together with financial participation the UK than the other countries.

Figure 10.1: Types of remuneration systems - % of all respondents

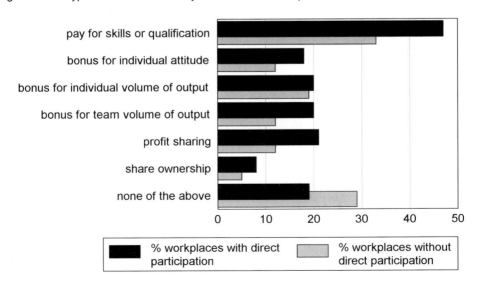

- bonuses for group volume of output were much more frequent in Italy (39 per cent) than other countries.

- Sweden was prominent on account of having the highest proportion of workplaces *not* paying any special bonuses (49 per cent).

**Table 10.1  Types of remuneration systems by country – respondents practising direct participation**

|                              | DK | FR | GER | IR | IT | NL | POR | SP | SW | UK |
|------------------------------|----|----|-----|----|----|----|-----|----|----|----|
|                              | %  | %  | %   | %  | %  | %  | %   | %  | %  | %  |
| pay for skills or qualification | 29 | 50 | 75 | 23 | 29 | 50 | 33 | 25 | 19 | 37 |
| bonus for individual attitude | 9 | 16 | 25 | 16 | 19 | 13 | 14 | 13 | 8 | 14 |
| bonus for individual volume of output | 12 | 14 | 27 | 14 | 22 | 11 | 14 | 22 | 7 | 18 |
| bonus for team volume of output | 18 | 12 | 14 | 22 | 38 | 9 | 5 | 21 | 22 | 25 |
| profit sharing | 9 | 43 | 11 | 7 | 5 | 13 | 5 | 11 | 15 | 38 |
| share ownership | 6 | 6 | 3 | 3 | 2 | 4 | 5 | 12 | 1 | 22 |
| no special pay system | 41 | 16 | 13 | 38 | 14 | 34 | 38 | 29 | 49 | 17 |

Key questions about the origins of these country differences cannot be explored here, but one thing seems clear from the data and the more detailed analysis undertaken. There is no obvious connection between the different forms of direct participation and the remuneration system. For example, it might have been expected that individual bonuses would more often be found in the case of individual delegation and consultation, whereas group bonuses and profit sharing schemes would go along with group consultation and group delegation. There is no such relationship, however .

## 10.2  Direct participation and remuneration systems

The implementation of the group forms of direct participation usually involves the most fundamental change in work organisations. Our respondents were therefore asked the introduction of any of these forms was accompanied by a change of the organisation's remuneration system.

## Key findings:

- a quarter of workplaces introducing direct participation on a group basis changed their remuneration system

- the most frequently cited and effective changes involved bonuses for team volume of output

- pay for flexibility was also frequently cited and deemed very effective

It emerges that almost one quarter of workplaces introducing direct participation in the ten countries changed their pay system. Figures are highest for those workplaces which introduced permanent group consultation (25 per cent) and somewhat lower for temporary group consultation (22 per cent) and group delegation (17 per cent).

Figure 10.2 suggests that changes in pay systems were not equally spread across the 10 countries. There were three countries to the fore: Italy, Sweden and the UK. From Italy, almost one third of all respondents with one or more of the three forms of group forms of direct participation report that they changed their remuneration system – which might help to explain why team based bonuses were especially prominent in Italy, given many of the changes in remuneration systems (more than 40 per cent) were aimed at the introduction of this very feature (see below). Another very active country is Sweden. Looking at the change activities here it might be expected that the relatively high number of Swedish workplaces not applying any special remuneration system will decrease over time. Finally, it is worth mentioning that in the UK almost 50 per cent of all workplaces who had introduced consultation with permanent groups changed their pay system.

Even if the figures are somewhat lower in the other countries, a change of remuneration systems was reported by many of our respondents. This is of particular interest. Evidently, there is a growing recognition of the need for change, notwithstanding that pay systems in many countries are subject to tight legal regulations and wage agreements between the social partners.

What is the nature of the changes in remuneration systems? Table 10.2 provides us with an overview for all three forms of group participation. Most remarkable seems to be the fact that almost 50 per cent of workplaces changing their remuneration systems because of the introduction of direct participation are now paying bonuses for team volume of output. Around 50 per cent are running profit sharing schemes as well. Collective bonuses are quite frequent, too, with both forms of group consultation. Overall, then, and perhaps not surprisingly, collective bonuses appear

Figure 10.2: % of workplaces changing their remuneration systems on the introduction of direct participation

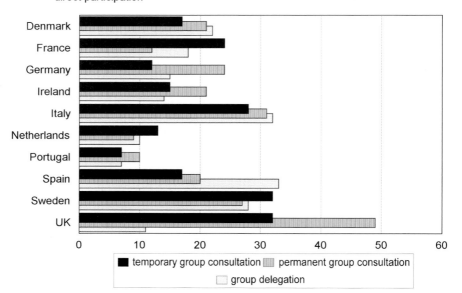

to be the most frequent changes in remuneration systems accompanying the introduction of the group forms of direct participation.

Adjustments in the payment for skills and qualification are made in about one third of workplaces changing their remuneration systems. As already mentioned in Chapter 9, this development is due to the rising importance of employee qualification in direct participation work-systems. Pay for uncertified skills is slightly more frequent than pay for qualifications formally certified. It might be asked whether this is a trend that is to the detriment of the workforce: uncertified skills are subject to management discretion and can hardly be fixed in a formal wage agreement.

All the other aspects of remuneration systems (with the exception of share ownership, which does not seem to be very widespread) are the subject of change in a substantial number of cases too. Particularly noteworthy is that pay for quality and pay for flexibility are introduced in a considerable number of workplaces. Very little information about payment for these two variables emerged in the EPOC literature review – there would appear to be a gap here that needs to be filled in order to support organisations thinking of going down this route.

In the light of the detailed discussion in the previous three chapters, our final comments are reserved for any links between changes in remuneration system and the effects of group delegation. Table 10.3 shows the differences in the reported effects on the by-now familiar indicators depending on whether the relevant change in pay systems had (+) or had not (-) taken place. Especially significant are the consequences of pay for flexibility. This kind of payment had the most significant impact on 'cost reduction': 89 per cent of workplaces introducing pay for flexibility reported that they reduced their costs. Also very high is the effect on the decrease of absenteeism (87 per cent). It seems fair to assume that employees' responsibility for flexibility, coupled with the reward for achieving it, is a strong motivation. Most remarkably, pay for flexibility is reckoned to be even more successful, as an indirect measure to lower the rate of absenteeism, than the attempt to influence employees' attitudes directly by individual bonuses.

**Table 10.2  Changes in remuneration systems involved in the introduction of direct participation**

|  | temporary group consultation | permanent group consultation | group delegation |
|---|---|---|---|
|  | % | % | % |
| changes involving personal skills – not certified | 39 | 31 | 37 |
| changes involving skills – formally certified | 18 | 35 | 26 |
| bonuses relating to individual attitude | 26 | 18 | 30 |
| bonuses relating to individual volume of output | 20 | 26 | 34 |
| bonuses relating to flexibility | 18 | 22 | 18 |
| bonuses relating to team volume of output | 41 | 36 | 46 |
| bonuses relating to quality | 31 | 27 | 34 |
| profit sharing | 18 | 24 | 46 |
| share ownership | 5 | 11 | 3 |

Bonuses for team volume of output appeared to be another very effective way of promoting employee performance. Team bonuses scored highly particularly in three categories (cost reduction, reduction of throughput times, and increase of total output).

**Table 10.3 % of workplaces by changes in remuneration system and the effects of group delegation**

| | | reduction of costs % | reduction of through put time % | improvement in quality % | increase in total output % | decrease in sickness % | decrease in absenteeism % | reduction in nos. of employees % | reduction in nos. of managers % |
|---|---|---|---|---|---|---|---|---|---|
| changes involving personal skills - not certified | - | 59 | 64 | 98 | 57 | 44 | 46 | 24 | 26 |
| | + | 79 | 65 | 97 | 76 | 47 | 73 | 39 | 46 |
| changes involving skills -formally certified | - | 65 | 64 | 98 | 60 | 36 | 51 | 26 | 26 |
| | + | 70 | 67 | 97 | 72 | 68 | 65 | 36 | 47 |
| bonuses relating to individual attitude | - | 60 | 67 | 97 | 59 | 37 | 49 | 28 | 31 |
| | + | 80 | 58 | 99 | 76 | 66 | 72 | 34 | 39 |
| bonuses for individual volume of output | - | 62 | 62 | 97 | 60 | 42 | 54 | 23 | 29 |
| | + | 78 | 74 | 99 | 75 | 56 | 58 | 43 | 45 |
| bonuses for team | - | 50 | 38 | 98 | 55 | 45 | 49 | 27 | 29 |
| | + | 83 | 89 | 98 | 79 | 45 | 64 | 33 | 38 |
| bonuses for flexibility | - | 59 | 65 | 98 | 62 | 39 | 46 | 23 | 27 |
| | + | 89 | 54 | 97 | 73 | 60 | 87 | 48 | 56 |
| bonuses for quality | - | 59 | 62 | 97 | 55 | 38 | 39 | 18 | 25 |
| | + | 78 | 69 | 98 | 79 | 57 | 82 | 46 | 45 |
| profit sharing | - | 50 | 38 | 97 | 55 | 45 | 49 | 27 | 29 |
| | + | 83 | 89 | 98 | 79 | 45 | 64 | 33 | 38 |
| share ownership | - | 66 | 64 | 98 | 63 | 45 | 56 | 28 | 33 |
| | + | 82 | 76 | 90 | 88 | 50 | 50 | 48 | 43 |

## 10.3 Summary and conclusion

Remuneration systems in workplaces *with* direct participation tended to be more complex than in those *without*. Pay for skills and qualification was particularly prevalent in workplaces with direct participation. Changes to remuneration systems as a result of the introduction of one or other of the group forms of direct participation were reported in about one quarter of workplaces. The most significant changes were bonuses for the team volume of output; these were the most frequently cited change and the one associated with those forms of direct participation having the greatest economic effects. Pay for flexibility, a relatively new concept, was also a frequently mentioned change and also seemed to be very effective.

### References

European Commission. 1997. Green Paper, *Partnership for a new organisation of work.*

Fröhlich, D. and U. Pekruhl. 1996: *Direct Participation and Organisational Change – Fashionable but Misunderstood? An analysis of recent research in Europe, Japan and the USA.* EF/96/38/EN. Luxembourg: Office for the Official Publications of the European Communities.

# Chapter 11    Conclusions and implications

The results of the EPOC survey have significant implications for both theory and practice. The implications for the many scientific debates will be discussed in other, more appropriate places, such as academic journals. The focus here is on their relevance for policy makers and practitioners. Reference is made to EPOC's social partner (Regalia, 1995) and literature (Fröhlich and Pekruhl, 1996) studies as well as the survey results.

## 11.1  Grounds for optimism ... and concern?

For those who wish to promote direct participation either because they believe it is an important ingredient in enhancing the quality of working life or because they think it will help to improve business performance, the EPOC survey results must be a cause of both optimism and concern. Optimism is justified because it would appear that around four out of five workplaces in the 10 countries – many more than it was thought – have some form of direct participation. The managers in large numbers of organisations appear to be aware of the concept of direct participation and, more importantly, practise one or other or a number of its forms. They do so primarily for economic considerations, but are also aware of the importance of improving the quality of working life as well. The widespread practice also suggests that direct participation is not wholly dependent on sector or task complexity or particular institutional arrangements – potentially, in other words, its application would appear to be universal.

Most importantly, the managers responding to the EPOC survey also believe that direct participation works. Each of the forms of direct participation was viewed as having positive effects on a range of key indicators of economic performance, such as quality, output, costs and through-put times, on absenteeism and sickness, and on reductions in the number of employees and managers. Overall, the verdict of respondents on direct participation was that it had been very successful.

For practitioners, in particular, the EPOC survey results have some extremely significant implications. It is not just that direct participation works or that it does not seem to be dependent on specific circumstances. Practising one form intensively also seems to be better than several forms to a limited extent. Measures of direct participation such as suggestion schemes, speak-up schemes and project groups are also as important for good economic performance and for reductions in labour costs as the group work which has dominated the policy as well as the scientific debate. The key message is that the greater the responsibility given to employees, the better the results.

Some of the ingredients of success are also clear. One is qualification and training. High employee qualification and vocational training intensity make it much more likely that direct participation will be successful in achieving the various benefits of direct participation. Similarly, direct participation is more likely to be successful if there is training of employees and managers for direct participation. Here the evidence from the EPOC survey is at one with that from EPOC's literature study – training in social skills, and not just vocational training, is very important and needs to embrace managers as well as employees.

A second ingredient is employee involvement in the introduction of direct participation. The EPOC survey results confirm the importance of employee and employee representative involvement in the regulation of direct participation in order to improve both the quality of the participation itself and its economic and social effects. Far from being a barrier to progress, it seems, employee representatives are agents of change. The greater their involvement, in terms both of form and extent (and this applies particularly to negotiation and joint decision-making), the more the indicators of effects were positive.

There is also an indication that some forms of remuneration help to make the practice of the various forms of direct participation more effective. Pay for flexibility and bonuses for team volume of output were two forms, in particular, appearing to have a positive impact on the indicators of economic performance.

As well as giving grounds for optimism, however, the results of the EPOC survey also raise several causes of concern. A significant minority of workplaces in the EPOC survey, one in five, do not practise any form of direct participation. More importantly, many of those that do might be said to be pursuing a partial approach. Relatively few – around one in seven – report having the five or six forms which might have been expected from organisations with an integrated approach. The coverage of group consultation and group delegation is also less than 50 per cent of the workplace's largest occupational group in most cases. The scope of much of the direct participation which is practised is rather limited as well. Indeed, when the total population of the workplaces in the survey is taken into account, the proportion with high scores for scope reaches double figures in the case of one form of direct participation only, that of individual delegation.

Although it is difficult to make comparisons with other surveys because of their different nature and extent, it seems that there has been an increase in the incidence of direct participation in Europe in recent years. Yet it is a moot point whether Europe has closed the gap with Japan and the USA identified in EPOC's literature study. This is especially so in the case of Japan, where group work, for example, was found to be practised by more than 90 per cent of large companies in industry and more than 80 per cent in services.

This brings us to a finding of the EPOC survey which is especially deserving of comment. It is that only a very small number (around two per cent) of organisations in the 10 EU member countries were pursuing what, for many commentators, has come to be regarded as the near-ultimate form of work organisation: the 'Scandinavian' model simply defined for present purposes as high-intensity group work + qualified workforce + high training intensity. This is particularly surprising given that their respective sponsors judged the 'Scandinavian' model to be more successful than the 'Toyota' equivalent of low-intensity group work + medium or low employee skills + low training intensity. The finding is at one, however, with the results of asking managers which, in their opinion, was the most important form of direct participation. In most countries, the consultative forms were regarded as more important than the delegative. Even many managers who practised group work did not necessarily regard it as the most important form.

Other areas of concern involve the ingredients which managers themselves identified as important in the success of direct participation. One is training. Around half the workplaces in the EPOC survey with one or other of the group forms offered no training in the social skills for direct participation. Another is regulation. There was no employee representative involvement of any kind in the introduction of direct participation in around a quarter of the workplaces. Employee representatives were not even present in many workplaces. Most surprisingly, employees themselves were not involved in the introduction of direct participation in one in 10 workplaces and received only limited information in a similar proportion.

These concerns relate to the average for the 10 countries. Many have to be magnified considerably for a number of the individual countries. There is great unevenness in the diffusion of the incidence and scope of direct participation, along with training and regulation, across the 10 countries. Most obviously, while there may not be a clearly identifiable 'Northern' European pattern, there does appear to be a 'Southern' European one embracing Italy, Portugal and Spain: the incidence and scope of direct participation in these countries were noticeably lower in many workplaces.

The weight to be put these findings depends on their interpretation. An optimistic, interpretation would emphasis process. Direct participation is difficult. It may be that in many organisations the practice of direct participation is relatively new and in the experimental stage. There is some evidence for this in the findings: just over 60 per cent or workplaces reported that the relevant form had been introduced within the last five years. Also consistent with this interpretation is the finding that group delegation is regarded as the most important form of direct participation in Sweden, where it has a long history, and in Portugal and Spain, where it can be associated with a proportionately larger number of green field sites introducing this form at the very beginning of their operations.

An equally plausible, and perhaps more realistic, interpretation is that differences in the incidence and scope of direct participation are to be expected. In particular, the 'Scandinavian' model which informs the political and scientific debate may not have universal application and is therefore unlikely to be adopted by a majority of managers. Much thinking in the area, after all, makes some heroic assumptions about changes in markets, for example, the end of mass production and the extent of flexible specialisation required, which are simply not supported by the evidence. The same is true of the relative insignificance of costs. There is also a tendency to be sector blind, with a focus on industry rather than services, where the bulk of the work force is employed.

The question of 'choice' also has to be brought into the equation. In some cases, choice may be a matter of principle – managers may be reluctant to give up control and, in particular, rely too much on the delegative forms of direct participation which do not leave the initiative with them. In other cases, it may be a matter of contingency – direct participation takes time and effort and managers may think that the costs are likely to outweigh the benefits given the specific technology of operations or the demands on them in terms of short-term profitability.

The more detailed analysis of the EPOC survey results which is planned will help to illuminate some of these issues. The attempt to identify, with the help of statistical techniques, whether there are particular sets of conditions associated with workplaces with different scopes and intensities of direct participation is likely to be especially helpful. It should enable the development of a more informed view of what can realistically be expected so far as the diffusion of these forms and intensities is concerned.

## 11.2  The policy challenges

Our comments in this final section are directed at the challenges confronting policy makers in the area and take as their starting point the European Commission's Green Paper, *Partnership for a new organisation of work*, adopted in April 1997. The Green Paper emphasises that the modernisation of the organisation of work can only be achieved by the firms themselves, involving management and workers and their representatives. Policy makers nonetheless have an important role to play in developing policies which 'support rather than hinder organisational renewal' and which 'strike a productive balance between the interests of business and the interests of workers' (p. 2). The Green Paper suggests that these policy challenges can be summarised in one question: 'how to reconcile security for workers with the flexibility which firms need'? (Executive Summary). It goes on to suggest that this raises a number of issues for the public authorities and social partners across the spectrum of employment, education and social policy areas:

- how to organise the necessary training and retraining, so that the workforce can meet the increasing needs for skills and competence

- how to adapt social legislation to take account of new employment trends

- how to adapt wage systems along with organisational structures on which they are based

- how to adapt working time arrangements in the light of the new situation

- how to take advantage of the new employment trends with regard to equal opportunities

- how to develop more flexible organisations in the public services

- how to provide adequate support to firms, in particular small firms, who wish to change, but lack the resources or expertise to do so.

The Green Paper also emphasises the role of partnership in bringing about change. In particular, it invites the social partners and public authorities to 'build a partnership for the development of a new framework for the modernisation of work'. The word framework, the Green Paper adds, should be given a broad interpretation:

It could include everything from the creation of a common understanding of the importance of the new forms of work organisation, through joint declarations, to binding contractual or legal initiatives. The level and content of such a framework has to be clarified through discussion in the social dialogue (Executive Summary).

The EPOC survey results confirm that the Green Paper's summary point – the need to reconcile security for workers with the flexibility of firms – is likely to be an especially sensitive issue. Not surprisingly in the light of the case study evidence in EPOC's literature review, many of the workplaces introducing direct participation in the EPOC survey (around a third) reported that one of the effects was a reduction in the number of employees in general and managers in particular – and the more extensive the practice, it seems, the more likely they were to report so. Furthermore, and less expected, employee representatives were more likely to be involved in the introduction of forms of direct participation involving reductions in employment.

These apparently bizarre findings bring us to one of the most critical set of results of the EPOC survey. Direct participation may have led to a reduction in employment in around a third of workplaces. In half of these cases, however, any short-term reduction seems to have been compensated or over compensated for by stable or increased employment in the medium term. Furthermore, and most fundamentally, the workplaces *without* direct participation were more likely to report a reduction in medium term employment than those *with*.

The implication is that the case for direct participation and other forms of modernisation will not be as easy to present as many commentators have implied. Most importantly, they cannot be honestly presented as something from which everyone gains – although on balance the employment prospects are likely to be *better* in those workplaces which make changes than those that do not, some employees will be losers in the short run. To pretend otherwise is likely to lead to cynicism and an undermining of the much-needed employee support.

The Green Paper's emphasis on qualification and training is important here: providing employees with opportunities to acquire knowledge and skills, so that they can find alternative employment, should the number of jobs be reduced in their present workplace, is one of the key ways of helping to reconcile security and flexibility. A major problem, however, as Chapter 9 has confirmed, is that there currently appear to be very unequal opportunities between men and women. Allowing for sector, the higher the share of women at the workplace, the lower are the qualification requirements and the 'skill orientation' of the workplaces in the EPOC survey.

It is also possible to say something about the means of bringing about change suggested by the Green Paper: the building of a partnership for a new organisation of work. The results of the EPOC survey confirm the findings of its literature and social partner reviews. At workplace level, direct participation has greater effects and is more successful where employee representatives are involved in its implementation. Moreover, the greater the involvement, in the form of extensive joint decision-making, the greater the effects and the success.

It is not difficult to understand why this should be so. The views of employees, most commentators agree, are vital to the success of changes in work organisation. In the absence of a representative 'voice', there is a danger that these views are not expressed for fear of antagonising managers or are ignored. Trust is also essential: trust depends on the legitimacy of decisions and joint regulation is one of the most tangible ways of expressing such legitimacy. Put negatively, managers who do not involve employee representatives run the risk of giving the impression they have something to hide.

One implication is that, if they want to maximise the effects of changes in work organisation, policy makers will have to address the representation 'gap' that exists in many workplaces in EU member countries. A significant minority of workplaces (around a third), the EPOC survey results suggest, do not have any employee representation at workplace level. It is in this connection that the European Commission's (1997) recent proposals for information and consultation within the national framework take on a particular significance. Some progress on these would seen to be a prerequisite for the successful promotion of new forms of work organisation.

The EPOC survey results, along with the findings of its literature and social partner reviews, suggest that it is not just the workplace which is important, however. The wider context is also significant. The Netherlands and Sweden stand out on a number of counts: the incidence, scope, intensity and effects of direct participation. It is difficult to escape the conclusion that this reflects the wider context of support. Replication of this context at the EU level is not going to be easy – the interest in new forms of work organisation in both countries is long-standing and is rooted in a wide variety of institutional arrangements. Even so, two features of their experience would appear to be especially relevant: an over-arching understanding or framework agreement between the social partners giving legitimacy to the project; and major public campaigns of practical support such as that run by the Swedish Work Life Fund in the first half of the 1990s. At the very least, careful study of the recent experience of these countries, taking account of the *failures* as well as the *successes*, could pay handsome dividends.

Our final comments take us back to the previous section and are concerned with the fundamental challenge which is implicit rather than explicit in the Green Paper: that of persuading European management to advance down the road of direct participation. Not necessarily, it must be emphasised, to adopt any particular form, but to introduce the forms that are appropriate and to maximise their scope and, in the case of group delegation, their intensity. It is management across the board, in industry as well as services, that apparently needs to be persuaded. It is not primarily, as the Green Paper seems to imply, a question of management in the public services and SMEs. Indeed, the EPOC survey results suggest management in the public services is often in the vanguard of the practice of direct participation. The gap between the rhetoric and reality of direct participation, as the managers have illustrated so clearly in their own responses, is substantial in every sector.

The challenge is fundamental because it cannot be assumed that, left to their own devices, this is a route that management will automatically take. Changing work organisation, the various strands of the EPOC project have clearly established, is difficult and time-consuming, especially in the case of 'brown-field' operations, and the pay back may not be so obvious or immediate as reducing costs. Such change is none the less essential, for the reasons the Green Paper spells out, if the organisation is to survive and prosper in the interests of society at large as well as its managers, employees and shareholders in an increasingly competitive world.

As well as demonstrating the magnitude of the challenge, the EPOC survey results also underline the complexities of meeting it. The promotion of "best practice" – bench-marking as it has become to be known – and legislation have traditionally been seen as the two major ways of raising awareness as well as, in the case of legislation, establishing rights and obligations. Both figure in the Green Paper. Yet examples of "best practice" and legislation, the EPOC survey results suggest, have been relatively insignificant in leading management to introduce direct participation. While it would be wrong to exaggerate the importance of these findings – the relative absence of legislation and collective agreements dealing with direct participation may be a consideration – it is a reminder that these two approaches, though necessary, are unlikely to be sufficient.

Received wisdom has it that, in management of change situations, one looks to a particular individual or group to exercise a leadership role. In the present circumstances, of a campaign to modernise work organisation across the EU, there is a strong case to be made for encouraging multinational companies to take on such a role in conjunction with networks of SMEs. Multinational companies, as EPOC's literature study established, have been in the forefront of developments in work organisation; they have the networks and resources to learn from and implement 'best practice' from around the world. Most importantly, as the EPOC survey has confirmed, they have a major presence in many EU member countries, including Italy, Portugal and Spain, where the incidence and scope of direct participation are noticeably lower in many workplaces. Above all, multinational companies have a very special relationship with SMEs. It is not just that many SMEs depend on supplying, subcontracting and outsourcing from large companies, but also that the latter depend on the quality of services and supplies from the former. Very often too the relationship is embedded in the local community, which reinforces the logic of mutual support.

The enormous potential of the leadership role of multinational companies is clearly demonstrated in the European Round Table of Industrialists' report on the ways in which practical partnerships between large and small companies can help to stimulate job creation (ERT, 1997). The 43 case studies illustrate the benefits of such partnerships in five areas: 'buying and selling', 'positive restructuring', 'SME support', 'training and education', and 'local focus'. In each case, as well as the specific details of the case studies, a number of general principles of "best practice" are drawn which are intended to have general application. A major EU-wide campaign involving multinational companies, in conjunction with SMEs, targeted on innovation in work organisation could considerably speed up the diffusion of new working practices as well as help to improve their suppliers', and therefore their own, performance in the process.

## References

European Commission. 1997. Green Paper, *Partnership for a new organisation of work*.

European Commission. 1997. Consultation document for the Community social partners concerning *Information and Consultation of Workers within the National Framework*.

European Round Table of Industrialists. 1997. *A Stimulus to Job Creation: Practical partnerships between large and small companies*. Brussels: ERT.

Fröhlich, D. and U. Pekruhl. 1996: *Direct Participation and Organisational Change – Fashionable but Misunderstood? An analysis of recent research in Europe, Japan and the USA*. EF/96/38/EN. Luxembourg: Office for the Official Publications of the European Communities.

Regalia, I. 1995. *Humanise Work and Increase Profitability? Direct participation in organisational change viewed by the social partners in Europe*. EF/95/21/EN. Luxembourg: Office for the Official Publications of the European Communities.

# Appendix 1    The EPOC Project

The Project's Research Group comprises the following:

Alain Chouraqui* (Coordinator, 1992-95)
LEST-CNRS, Aix-en-Provence

Dieter Fröhlich*
ISO-Institut, Cologne

Adelheid Hege*
IRES, Paris

Fred Huijgen*
Nijmegen Business School

John Geary
Graduate School of Business, University College, Dublin

Ulrich Pekruhl*
Institut Arbeit und Technik, Gelsenkirchen

Ida Regalia
IRES-Lombardia, Milan

Keith Sisson*
IRRU, Warwick Business School (Coordinator, 1995-)

Georges Spyropoulos*
formerly ILO

Hubert Krieger*
European Foundation for the Improvement of Living and Working Conditions

Kevin O'Kelly*
European Foundation for the Improvement of Living and Working Conditions

* involved in the writing of the interim report on the results of the EPOC
  questionnaire survey

The Group has also benefited from the contributions of Goran Brulin and Horst Hart of the Swedish Work Environment Fund as well from the advice of the members of the EPOC Advisory Committee including representatives of ETUC, UNICE, national governments, the European Commission and the International Labour Organisation.

## The EPOC objectives

The objectives of the investigation have been expressed in the form of a number of questions which any project on direct participation should ideally seek to answer:

1. The 'WHO' of direct participation: who is practising direct participation - how diffuse is it; which sectors; which industries; which firms; which countries; and which group of workers (gender, ethnicity and skill categories). How does Europe compare with the USA and Japan?

2. The 'WHEN' of direct participation: how recent is its introduction and what does this tell us about 'why' it was introduced. Here it will be interesting to examine if direct participation is adopted at points of transition (crisis or modernisation) in an organisation and/or during normal periods of operation.

3. The 'WHY' of direct participation: to 'test' the main motives for its introduction i.e. management's interest in competitivenss, flexibility and performance (TQM and lean production); union demands for an improvement in quality of working life; employees' 'post-materialistic' values; state initiation and/or sponsorship for direct participation.

4. The 'HOW' of direct participation: how did it come to assume the shape(s) it has - the processes involved in its development. How was it introduced and implemented - what participation is there in the introduction of direct participation? Are trade union representatives and/or employees permitted to participate?

5. The 'WHICH' of direct participation: what form does direct participation assume and what issues are significantly influenced by employee participation; how closely aligned are they with existing labels/concepts e.g. quality circles, autonomous work groups, etc.

6. The 'EFFECT' of direct participation: both objective (if possible) and perceived on organisational performance; how have people's working lives changed; how have hierarchical and authority relations changed; are employees working 'harder' and/or more 'effectively'? Have employees' attitudes changed? Another crucial issue is direct participation's relationship to forms of indirect (representative) participation: does direct participation erode or strengthen existing institutional forms of employee participation and representation? Of course as well as the intended effects, we will also have to consider direct participation's unintended consequences? There is no need to anticipate these at this stage.

7. The 'SUCCESS' or 'FAILURE' of direct participation: how is each defined by the actors concerned. Is success or failure associated with trade union involvement, or with a strategic approach to other HR/IR issues such as training and communications?

## EPOC Publications

*Main*

These reports can be purchased from the Office of Official Publications of the European Communities, Luxembourg:

Fröhlich, D. and U. Pekruhl. 1996: *Direct Participation and Organisational Change - Fashionable but Misunderstood? An analysis of recent research in Europe, Japan and the USA.* Number and price to be confirmed.

Geary, J. and K. Sisson. 1994: *Conceptualising Direct Participation in Organisational Change. The EPOC Project.* EF/94/23/EN. Price (excluding Vat) in Luxembourg ECU 8.50.

Regalia, I. 1995. *Humanise Work and Increase Profitability? Direct participation in organisational change viewed by the social partners in Europe.* EF/95/21/EN. Price (excluding Vat) in Luxembourg ECU 25.

Sisson, K. 1996. *Coming to terms with Direct Participation: A summary of the first phase results of the EPOC project.* Number and price to be confirmed.

*Working Papers*

These are available free of charge on request from the European Foundation:

Geary, J. and K. Sisson. 1995: *Direct Participation in Organiational Change - Introducing the EPOC project*. Dublin: European Foundation for the Improvement of Living and Working Conditions, Working Paper No. WP/94/18/EN.

Pekruhl, U., A. Schnabel and K. Weishaupt. 1995: *Direct Participation Bibliography. Results from a data base research. The EPOC Project*, Dublin: European Foundation for the Improvement of Living and Working Conditions, Working Paper No. WP/95/34/EN.

Regalia, I. and C. Gill. 1995. *Direct Participation: how the social partners view it - A comparative study of 15 countries*. Dublin: European Foundation for the Improvement of Living and Working Conditions, Working Paper No. WP/95/73/EN.

*Country Studies - Volume 1*. Dublin: European Foundation for the Improvement of Living and Working Conditions, Working Paper No. WP/95/35/EN.

*Country Studies - Volume 2*. Dublin: European Foundation for the Improvement of Living and Working Conditions, Working Paper No. WP/96/03/EN.

The following individual country studies are also available:

Albertijn, M. 1994: *The Development of Direct Participation. Belgium*, Dublin: European Foundation for the Improvement of Living and Working Conditions, Working Paper No. WP/94/49/EN.

Als, G. 1994: *Luxembourg: a model of consensus*, Dublin: European Foundation for the Improvement of Living and Working Conditions, Working Paper No. WP/95/06/EN.

Carrieri, M. 1994: *La partecipazione diretta in Italia. La posizione delle parti sociali*, Dublin: European Foundation for the Improvement of Living and Working Conditions, Working Paper No. WP/95/07/EN.

Cristóvam, M.L. 1994: *The positions of the social partners on direct participation. The case of Portugal*, Dublin: European Foundation for the Improvement of Living and Working Conditions, Working Paper No. WP/95/71/EN.

Flecker, J. 1994: *Participative work organisation in Austria. The position of the social partners*, Dublin: European Foundation for the Improvement of Living and Working Conditions, Working Paper No. WP/95/69/EN.

Geary, J., C. Rees and K. Sisson. 1995: *Management-Initiated Direct Participation. United Kingdom*, Dublin: European Foundation for the Improvement of Living and Working Conditions, Working Paper No. WP/95/03/EN.

Jacobi, O. and A. Hassel. 1993: *The Union and Management Positions on Direct Worker Participation in Europe. The German Report*, Dublin: European Foundation for the Improvement of Living and Working Conditions, Working Paper No. WP/95/67/EN.

Lund, R. 1994: *The primacy of collective agreements. Denmark*, Dublin: European Foundation for the Improvement of Living and Working Conditions, Working Paper No. WP/94/33/EN.

Miguélez Lobo, F. and C. Llorens Serrano. 1994: *La posiciòn de los actores sociales ante la participatiòn directa. Informe Español*, Dublin: European Foundation for the Improvement of Living and Working Conditions, Working Paper No. WP/95/72/EN.

Nikola-Lahnalammi, T. and T. Alasoini. 1994: *Direct participation in a centralised industrial relations system. Finland*, Dublin: European Foundation for the Improvement of Living and Working Conditions, Working Paper No. WP/94/34/EN.

O'Kelly, K. 1995: *A Joint Approach to direct Participation. Ireland*, Dublin: European Foundation for the Improvement of Living and Working Conditions, Working Paper No. WP/95/01/EN

Tchobanian, R. 1994: *Les positions des partenaires sociaux face à la participation directe en France*, Dublin: European Foundation for the Improvement of Living and Working Conditions, Working Paper No. WP/95/68/EN.

Tollhagen, R. 1995: *A History of Work Environment Innovation. Sweden*, Dublin: European Foundation for the Improvement of Living and Working Conditions, Working Paper No. WP/95/02/EN.

Van der Meché, P., B. van Beers, M. van der Veen and W. Buitelaar. 1994: *Direct Participation in Organizational Change. The Netherlands*, Dublin: European

Foundation for the Improvement of Living and Working Conditions, Working Paper No.: WP/94/48/EN.

Vervelacis, T. 1994: *The Positions of the Social Partners on Direct Participation. The case of Greece*, Dublin: European Foundation for the Improvement of Living and Working Conditions, Working Paper No. WP/95/70/EN.

For summaries of the roundtable discussions in Dublin in February 1995 and in Lisbon in June 1996, see *P+ (European Participation Monitor)*.

# Appendix 2

# The EPOC survey questionnaire

**THE ORGANISATION OF WORK:**

**Questionnaire: A survey into the role of direct participation in organisational change**

**Fall 1996**

Dear Sir, Madam,

Work and the organisation of work is undergoing constant change. Some organisations have introduced forms of indirect participation involving employee representatives, others have more direct practices such as quality circles or group or team work, again others prefer not to have such work practices in their workplaces.

The European Union wants to gain an insight into the degree in which organisations deal with forms of participation by employees. Therefore, a cross section of organisations in the EU member states is selected to participate in a survey on this subject.

This survey is commissioned by the European Foundation for the Improvement of Living and Working Conditions, which is an autonomous body of the European Union with representation on its Administrative Board of the national employer and trade union organisations and of the governments of the Member States. The Foundation was established by the Council of Ministers in 1975 with a mandate to initiate research into all aspects of living and working conditions within the European Union. The Foundation is based in Dublin, Ireland. The survey is a part of a wider Foundation study into direct participation practices and organisational change.

The questionnaire asks information on the organisation, business or institution itself and the degree of participation in the organisation of the work. All questions are to be answered for the workplaces to which the questionnaire has been sent. The questionnaire is addressed to the general manager, who either fills out the questionnaire himself/herself, or passes it on to the most appropriate person in the organisation.

Most questions can be answered by ticking a box for the chosen answer in this manner:

The names and addresses of the workplaces were selected at random. The data obtained will be analysed on an aggregate basis. Thus the anonymity of the responding organisations is guaranteed.

We would be grateful for your participation in this very important survey. Filling out the questionnaire will take less than 30 minutes. After completion of the questionnaire please send it in the freepost return envelope to our affiliated GfK office in the Netherlands: Intomart in Hilversum.

Thank you for your co-operation.

## A. The workplaces' activities and labour force

**1. In which of the following sectors is this workplace active?**
*Please, indicate the ONE sector accounting for the LARGEST part of your activities.*

- mining ☐
- transport, warehousing and communications ☐
- manufacturing industry (please specify ) ☐

| |
|---|
| |

- process industry (please specify ) ☐

| |
|---|
| |

- banking/insurances ❏
- professional services ❏
- public utilities ❏
- public administration ❏
- construction and installation ❏
- education ❏
- wholesale ❏
- (public) health and social welfare ❏
- retail trade ❏
- culture and recreation/leisure ❏
- catering, hotels ❏
- other (please specify) ❏

2.  **What is the status of this workplace?**
    - totally independent ❏
    - totally or partly owned by domestic company/ institution ❏
    - totally or partly owned by company/institution ❏
    - based in EU ❏
    - totally or partly owned by non-EU company / institution ❏

3.  **Is this workplace a:**
    - private company ❏
    - state or semi-state owned company/institution ❏

4.  **Is this workplace active in the:**
    - profit sector ❏
    - non-profit sector ❏

5.  **Is this workplace bound by a collective labour agreement?**
    - yes, for all employees ❏
    - yes, but not for all employees ❏
    - no ❏

6.  **Over the previous three years, has this workplace:**
    - opened as a new operation ❏
    - transferred ownership within the private sector ❏
    - transferred ownership from the public to the private sector ❏
    - none of the above ❏

7. **Which of the following BEST describes the competition for the products and/or services of this workplace?**
   - no competition ❏
   - only domestic competition ❏
   - domestic competition with little foreign competition ❏
   - both domestic and foreign competition ❏

8. **Over the past three years, has this competition:**
   - declined ❏
   - stayed the same ❏
   - increased slightly ❏
   - increased significantly ❏
   - none of the above ❏

9. **Which of the following initiatives have been taken by the management of this workplace in the last three years?**
   *Please tick **all** that apply from the following list.*
   - working time reduction ❏
   - working time flexibility ❏
   - down sizing ❏
   - flattening of management structures ❏
   - outsourcing ❏
   - back to core business ❏
   - greater involvement of lower level employees ❏
   - strategic alliances ❏
   - installing of team-based-work organisation ❏
   - product innovation ❏
   - new information technology ❏
   - automation ❏
   - job rotation ❏
   - other (please specify) ❏

10. **Thinking of competitive success, how important are the following features of the main products and/or services of this workplace?**

| | very important | somewhat important | not important |
|---|---|---|---|
| - price | ❏ | ❏ | ❏ |
| - quality | ❏ | ❏ | ❏ |

- variety ❑ ❑ ❑
  **(i.e. customising products or services)**
- service ❑ ❑ ❑
  **(i.e. availability, speed of delivery)**

11. **What proportion of the total costs of this workplace are labour costs?**
    - less than 25% ❑
    - 25% to 49% ❑
    - 50% to 74% ❑
    - 75% and more ❑

12. **What is the total number of employees, including full time and part-time, permanent and temporary, who presently work at or from this workplace?**

    total number of employees: [                    ]

## B. The largest occupational group

*ALL FOLLOWING QUESTIONS ASK ABOUT THE EMPLOYEES
IN THE LARGEST OCCUPATIONAL GROUP*

13. **Would you please indicate which one of the following occupational categories has the LARGEST number of non-managerial employees at this workplace?**
    - production; operational ❑
    - commercial; sales; marketing ❑
    - medical; social care ❑
    - transport; warehousing; distribution ❑
    - educational ❑
    - personal services; catering ❑
    - administrative; clerical ❑
    - repair and maintenance ❑
    - technical ❑
    - other (please specify) ❑

    [                                        ]

**14.** **How many employees are working in this largest occupational group?** *(as indicated in Q. 13)*

**15.** **What is the number of women in this largest occupational group?**

**16.** **How does the number of employees in the largest occupational group (Q. 14) compare to three years ago?**

- there has been an increase ❑
- about the same ❑
- there has been a reduction ❑

**17.** **Has the composition of the largest occupational group been affected in the last three years by one or more of the following?**

| | yes | no |
|---|---|---|
| - increase in proportion of people working part-time | ❑ | ❑ |
| - increase in proportion of people working on | ❑ | ❑ |
| - temporary contract | | |
| - increase in absolute number of woman | ❑ | ❑ |

**18.** **Over the past three years has the largest occupational group been directly affected by:**

- major changes in work organisation involving new plant/machinery/equipment/automation ❑
- major changes in work organisation NOT involving new plant/machinery/equipment/automation ❑
- increase in subcontracting of their activities ❑

**19.** **Please indicate if employees in the largest occupational group receive any of the following as part of their wages:**

- components reflecting skill/qualifications ❑
- bonuses related to individual attitude ❑
- bonuses for individual volume of output ❑
- bonuses for team volume of output ❑
- none of the above ❑

**20.** **Please indicate if employees in the largest occupational group are eligible for membership of the following:**

- profit sharing schemes ❑
- share ownership schemes ❑
- none of the above ❑

21. **Are there any of the following REPRESENTATIVES of the employees in the largest occupational group recognised for the purposes of consultation/ negotiation and or joint decision making at this workplace?**

- trade union representatives ❑

- representatives elected to a works council ❑

- representatives to an advisory committee established
  by management ❑

- none of the above ❑

22. **Roughly, what proportion of the employees in the largest occupational group do you think are trade union members?**

%

23. **Thinking of the WORK ORGANISATION of the employees in the largest occupational group, how would you rate the following dimensions on a scale running from 1 to 5:**
*whereby **1** means that you totally agree with the statement on the left hand side, and **5** means that you totally agree with the statement on the right hand side. Figures in between: 2, 3 and 4 can also be used. You tick one box per line.*

| work involves range of different tasks | | | work involves repetition of a single task | |
|:---:|:---:|:---:|:---:|:---:|
| ❑1 | ❑2 | ❑3 | ❑4 | ❑5 |

| pace of work is independent of technology | | | pace of work is dependent on technology | |
|:---:|:---:|:---:|:---:|:---:|
| ❑1 | ❑2 | ❑3 | ❑4 | ❑5 |

| work is essentially a team activity | | | work is essentially an individual activity | |
|:---:|:---:|:---:|:---:|:---:|
| ❑1 | ❑2 | ❑3 | ❑4 | ❑5 |

| a high level of qualification is required | | | little or no qualifications required | |
|:---:|:---:|:---:|:---:|:---:|
| ❑1 | ❑2 | ❑3 | ❑4 | ❑5 |

| recruits have to be trained to do the job | | | recruits are already trained to do the job | |
|:---:|:---:|:---:|:---:|:---:|
| ❑1 | ❑2 | ❑3 | ❑4 | ❑5 |

C. **The practice of direct participation:**

For purposes of this survey we distinguish two forms of direct participation in the largest occupational group:

- Consultative participation - management encourages non-managerial employees in the largest occupational group at work place level to make their views known on work-related matters, but retains the right to accept or reject them **(consultation).**

- Delegative participation - management gives non-managerial employees in the largest occupational group at work place level increased responsibility to organise and do their jobs without reference back **(decision making).**

Both forms of direct participation relate to non-managerial employees in the largest occupational group either as **individuals** or as **groups** and refers to the immediate work task, work organisation and working conditions.

Direct participation (DP) is to be distinguished from indirect or representative participation through trade unions and works councils. There is also a strong contrast with financial participation, i.e. profit-sharing and share ownership.

24a. **Does the management seek the views of or CONSULT with INDIVIDUAL non-managerial employees in the largest occupational group about work related matters in one or more of the following ways?**

|  | yes | no |
|---|:---:|:---:|
|  | ❏ | ❏ |
| - regular meetings with immediate manager | ❏ | |
| - regular training and development review meetings | ❏ | |
| - regular performance review meetings | ❏ | |
| - speak up scheme involving 'counsellor' or 'ombudsman' | ❏ | |
| - attitude surveys | ❏ | |
| - suggestion scheme | ❏ | |

**24b. Does the management seek the views of or CONSULT with non-managerial employees in the largest occupational group on a GROUP basis on work related matters in one or more of the following ways?**

|  | yes | no |
|---|---|---|
|  | ❏ | ❏ |

regular meetings with:
- groups with a specific task, on a ongoing basis
  (i.e. quality circles) ❏
- groups with a specific task, on a temporary basis
  (i.e. project groups) ❏

**24c. Has the management given INDIVIDUAL non-managerial employees in the largest occupational group the right to make DECISIONS on how their OWN work is performed without reference to immediate manager for one or more of the following?**

|  | yes | no |
|---|---|---|
|  | ❏ | ❏ |

- scheduling of work ❏
- quality of product or service ❏
- improving work processes ❏
- dealing with 'internal' customers ❏
- dealing with external clients ❏
- time keeping ❏
- attendance ❏
- working conditions ❏

**24d. Has the management given to formally introduced GROUPS the right to make DECISIONS on how their work is performed on a GROUP basis without reference to immediate manager for one or more of the following?**

|  | yes | no |
|---|---|---|
|  | ❏ | ❏ |

- allocation of work ❏
- scheduling of work ❏
- quality of work ❏
- time keeping ❏
- attendance and absence control ❏
- job rotation ❏
- co-ordination of work with other internal groups ❏
- improving work processes ❏

*IF YOU ONLY TICKED "NO" ON ALL QUESTIONS 24A, 24B, 24C
AND 24D: GO TO QUESTION 68; OTHERS GO TO QUESTION 25*

25. *IF ANY YES ON Q. 24A PLEASE ANSWER Q. 25A - Q. 27, OTHERS
GO TO Q. 28*

**25a. On what issues and how often are the views of INDIVIDUAL employees
in the largest occupational group sought?**

|  | regularly | sometimes | never |
|---|---|---|---|
| work organisation | ❏ | ❏ | ❏ |
| working time | ❏ | ❏ | ❏ |
| health & safety | ❏ | ❏ | ❏ |
| training & development | ❏ | ❏ | ❏ |
| quality of product or service | ❏ | ❏ | ❏ |
| customer relations | ❏ | ❏ | ❏ |
| changes in technology | ❏ | ❏ | ❏ |
| changes in investment | ❏ | ❏ | ❏ |
| other (please specify) | ❏ | ❏ | ❏ |

26. **How long ago was the practice of INDIVIDUAL CONSULTATION
introduced in this workplace?**
- 0 - 2 years ago ❏
- 2 - 5 years ago ❏
- 5 -10 years ago ❏
- more than 10 years ago ❏

27. **What were the main motives for introducing the practice of individual
consultation in this workplace?**
need to improve quality of product or service ❏
pressure to reduce costs ❏
pressure to reduce throughput times ❏
desire to encourage continuous improvement ❏
belief that employees have right to participate ❏
desire to improve quality of working life ❏
demands from employees ❏
demands from employee organisations ❏
examples elsewhere in the organisation ❏
examples in other companies ❏
requirements of legislation ❏

requirements of collective agreement ❑

other (please specify) ❑

> [blank box]

28. **IF ANY YES ON Q. 24B PLEASE ANSWER Q. 28a - 41, OTHERS GO TO Q. 42**

28a. **On what issues and how often are the views of employees in the largest occupational group sought on a GROUP basis?**

| | regularly | sometimes | never |
|---|---|---|---|
| work organisation | ❑ | ❑ | ❑ |
| working time | ❑ | ❑ | ❑ |
| health & safety | ❑ | ❑ | ❑ |
| training & development | ❑ | ❑ | ❑ |
| quality of product or service | ❑ | ❑ | ❑ |
| customer relations | ❑ | ❑ | ❑ |
| changes in technology | ❑ | ❑ | ❑ |
| changes in investment | ❑ | ❑ | ❑ |
| other (please specify) | ❑ | ❑ | ❑ |

> [blank box]

29. **Thinking of the practice of GROUP CONSULTATION, please indicate which of the following statements BEST describes current practice.**
   - **involvement of employees in groups is:**
     - voluntary ❑
     - compulsory ❑
     - both ❑
   - **composition of groups is decided by:**
     - management ❑
     - group ❑
     - both ❑
   - **issues to be discussed by groups are decided by:**
     - management ❑
     - group ❑
     - both ❑

30. **How many employees in the largest occupational group are involved in the practice of group consultation?**

number ☐

31. **What proportion of this number (Q. 30) is female?**

proportion (%) ☐

32. **How long ago was the practice of group consultation introduced in this workplace?**
    - 0 - 2 years ago ☐
    - 2 - 5 years ago ☐
    - 5 - 10 years ago ☐
    - more than 10 years ago ☐

33. **What where the main motives for introducing the practice of group consultation in this workplace?**
    - need to improve quality of product or service ☐
    - pressure to reduce costs ☐
    - pressure to reduce throughput times ☐
    - desire to encourage continuous improvement ☐
    - belief that employees have right to participate ☐
    - desire to improve quality of working life ☐
    - demands from employees ☐
    - demands from employee organisations ☐
    - examples elsewhere in the organisation ☐
    - examples in other companies ☐
    - requirements of legislation ☐
    - requirements of collective agreement ☐
    - other (please specify) ☐

34. **Does the group have a leader?**
    - yes, all groups ☐
    - yes, some groups ☐
    - no (GO TO Q. 36) ☐

35. **The leader of the group is chosen by:**
    - management ☐
    - group ☐
    - both ☐

36. **Does the group propose changes in the organisation and/or planning of work?**
    - yes, frequently ❑
    - yes, sometimes ❑
    - yes, rarely ❑
    - no, never (GO TO Q. 38) ❑

37. **Who decides whether or not to implement changes?**
    - management ❑
    - group ❑
    - both ❑

38. **Has the management organised any training of <u>employees</u> and/or <u>managers</u> in the following areas to support its consultation activities?**

    |  | employees | managers |
    |---|---|---|
    | - processes of data collection and analysis | ❑ | ❑ |
    | - presentation skills | ❑ | ❑ |
    | - interpersonal skills | ❑ | ❑ |
    | - groups dynamics | ❑ | ❑ |
    | - other (please specify) | ❑ | ❑ |

    |  |  |
    |---|---|
    |  |  |

    *IF YOU DID NOT TICK ANY BOX IN Q.38: GO TO Q.40*

39. **Approximately how much time was spent in the last year on the training per individual employee and manager?**

    |  | per employee | per manager |
    |---|---|---|
    | - less than one day | ❑ | ❑ |
    | - about a day | ❑ | ❑ |
    | - between 1 and 5 days | ❑ | ❑ |
    | - more than 5 days | ❑ | ❑ |

40. **Has the management made any changes to the remuneration system to support its consultation activities?**
    - yes ❑
    - no (GO TO Q. 42) ❑

41. **Do these changes in the renumeration system involve:**
    - changes in the renumeration structure involving:
      - personal skills (not certified) ❑
      - qualifications/task skills (formally certified) ❑

- bonus payments relating to:
  - individual attitude ❑
  - individual volume of output ❑
  - team/group volume of output ❑
  - flexibility ❑
  - quality ❑
- forms of financial participation:
  - profit sharing ❑
  - share ownership ❑
  - other (please specify) ❑

**42.** *IF ANY YES ON Q.24C PLEASE ANSWER Q. 42A - 43, OTHERS GO TO Q. 44*

**42a. How long ago was the practice OF INDIVIDUAL DECISION MAKING introduced in this workplace?**
- 0 - 2 years ago ❑
- 2 - 5 years ago ❑
- 5 -10 years ago ❑
- more than 10 years ago ❑

**43. What were the main motives for introducing the practice of <u>individual decision making</u> in this workplace?**
- need to improve quality of product or service ❑
- pressure to reduce costs ❑
- pressure to reduce throughput times ❑
- desire to encourage continuous improvement ❑
- belief that employees have right to participate ❑
- desire to improve quality of working life ❑
- demands from employees ❑
- demands from employee organisations ❑
- examples elsewhere in the organisation ❑
- examples in other companies ❑
- requirements of legislation ❑
- requirements of collective agreement ❑
- other (please specify) ❑

**44.** *IF ANY YES ON Q. 24D, PLEASE ANSWER Q. 44A-56, OTHERS GO TO Q.57*

**44a. Thinking of the practice of <u>GROUP DECISION</u> MAKING, please indicate which of the following statements BEST describes current practice.**

- involvement of employees in groups is:
  - voluntary ❑
  - compulsory ❑
  - both ❑
- composition of groups is decided by:
  - management ❑
  - group ❑
  - both ❑
- issues to be discussed by groups are decided by:
  - management ❑
  - group ❑
  - both ❑

**45. How many employees in the largest occupational group are involved in the practice of group decision making in this workplace?**

number [          ]

**46. What proportion of this number (Q. 45) is female?**

proportion (%) [          ]

**47. How long ago was the practice of group decision making introduced in this workplace?**

- O - 2 years ago ❑
- 2 - 5 years ago ❑
- 5 - 10 years ago ❑
- more than 10 years ago ❑

**48. What where the main motives for introducing the practice of group decision making in this workplace?**

- need to improve quality of product or service ❑
- pressure to reduce costs ❑
- pressure to reduce throughput times ❑
- desire to encourage continuous improvement ❑
- belief that employees have right to participate ❑
- desire to improve quality of working life ❑
- demands from employees ❑
- demands from employee organisations ❑
- examples elsewhere in the organisation ❑
- examples in other companies ❑

- requirements of legislation ❏
- requirements of collective agreement ❏
- other (please specify) ❏

<table>
<tr><td></td></tr>
</table>

**49. Does the group have a leader?**
- yes, all groups ❏
- yes, some groups ❏
- no (GO TO Q. 51) ❏

**50. The leader of the group is chosen by:**
- management ❏
- group ❏
- both ❏

**51. Does the group propose changes in the organisation and/or planning of work?**
- yes, frequently ❏
- yes, sometimes ❏
- yes, rarely ❏
- no, never (GO TO Q. 53) ❏

**52. Who decides whether or not to implement changes?**
- management ❏
- group ❏
- both

**53. Has the management organised any training of <u>employees</u> and/or <u>managers</u> in the following areas to support its decision-making activities?**

|  | employees | managers |
|---|---|---|
| - processes of data collection and analysis | ❏ | ❏ |
| - presentation skills | ❏ | ❏ |
| - interpersonal skills | ❏ | ❏ |
| - groups dynamics | ❏ | ❏ |
| - other (please specify) | ❏ | ❏ |

|  |  |
|---|---|
|  |  |

*IF YOU DID NOT TICK ANY OF THE ITEMS IN Q.53: GO TO Q.55*

**54.** **Approximately how much time was spent in the last year on the training per individual employee and manager?**

|  | employees | managers |
|---|---|---|
| - less than one day | ❏ | ❏ |
| - about a day | ❏ | ❏ |
| - between 1 and 5 days | ❏ | ❏ |
| - more than 5 days | ❏ | ❏ |

**55.** **Has the management made any changes to the renumeration system to support its decision-making activities?**

| | |
|---|---|
| - yes | ❏ |
| - no (GO TO Q. 57) | ❏ |

**56.** **Do these changes in the renumeration system involve:**

- changes in the renumeration structure involving:
  - personal skills (not certified)    ❏
  - qualifications/task skills (formally certified)    ❏

- bonus payments relating to:
  - individual attitude    ❏
  - individual volume of output    ❏
  - team/group volume of output    ❏
  - flexibility    ❏
  - quality    ❏

- forms of financial participation:
  - profit sharing    ❏
  - share ownership    ❏
  - other (please specify)    ❏

**57.** **`Which form of direct participation do YOU consider the most important form of DP at your workplace?**

| | |
|---|---|
| - consultation with individual employees(Q. 24a) | ❏ |
| - consultation with employees in groups (Q.24b) | ❏ |
| - decision making by individual employees (Q. 24c) | ❏ |
| - decision making by groups (Q. 24d) | ❏ |

*Of the four forms of dp listed in Q.57, please answer the following questions (58-67) in respect of the form which you indicated was the MOST IMPORTANT in encouraging participation at this workplace.*

58. **Which managerial function (a) and level (b) was primarily responsible for initiating the introduction of the most important direct participation practice.**

   a) **function:**
   - production and operations ❑
   - personnel and human resources ❑

   b) **level:**
   - senior management at higher level ❑
   - senior management at this workplace ❑
   - middle management at this workplace ❑
   - first-line management at this workplace ❑

59. **To what extent were the following involved in the introduction of the most important practice of dp?**

|  | extensively | limited | not at all |
|---|---|---|---|
| - employers' organisations | ❑ | ❑ | ❑ |
| - external consultants | ❑ | ❑ | ❑ |
| - state agencies | ❑ | ❑ | ❑ |
| - other (please specify) | ❑ | ❑ | ❑ |

60. **To what extent were employees informed and/or consulted about the initiative to introduce this most important practice of direct participation?**

|  | extensively | limited | not at all |
|---|---|---|---|
| - informed | ❑ | ❑ | ❑ |
| - consulted | ❑ | ❑ | ❑ |

61. **By which of the following means were employees informed or consulted?**
   - regular company newspaper ❑
   - leaflets / brochures / memos ❑
   - videos ❑
   - trade union representatives ❑
   - meetings of groups of employees led by senior managers ❑
   - meetings of groups of employees with own supervisors ❑
   - work council representatives ❑
   - other (please specify) ❑

**62. To what extent were employee REPRESENTATIVES informed, consulted, involved in negotiations, or joint decision making about the introduction of the most important practice of participation?**

| | extensively | limited | not at all |
|---|---|---|---|
| - informed | ❑ | ❑ | ❑ |
| - consulted | ❑ | ❑ | ❑ |
| - involved in negotiations | ❑ | ❑ | ❑ |
| - involved in joint decision making | ❑ | ❑ | ❑ |

*IF ANY NEGOTIATION OR JOINT DECISION MAKING IN Q. 62:*

**63. With whom did this negotiation/joint decision making take place?**

| | |
|---|---|
| - a works council | ❑ |
| - trade union representatives | ❑ |
| - other (please specify): | ❑ |

```



```

*IF ANY INFORMATION, CONSULTATION NEGOTIATION OR JOINT DECISION MAKING IN Q. 62:*

**64. To what extent did this involvement influence the design and implementation of the most important DP practice?**

| | |
|---|---|
| - a great deal | ❑ |
| - somewhat | ❑ |
| - very little | ❑ |
| - not at all | ❑ |

**65. To what extent was this involvement:**

| | |
|---|---|
| very useful | ❑ |
| useful | ❑ |
| no effect | ❑ |
| a hindrance | ❑ |
| a significant hindrance | ❑ |

**66. On which of the following did the introduction of DP activities at this workplace have an effect?**

| | yes | no |
|---|---|---|
| - general reduction of costs | ❑ | ❑ |
| - reduction of throughput times | ❑ | ❑ |
| - improvement of quality of product or service | ❑ | ❑ |
| - increase in total output | ❑ | ❑ |

- decrease in sickness    ❑    ❑
- decrease in absenteeism    ❑    ❑
- reduction in numbers of employees    ❑    ❑
- reduction in numbers of managers    ❑    ❑
- other (please specify)    ❑    ❑

**67. Overall, how successful would you say DP has been in meeting its objectives?**

- completely successful    ❑
- moderately successful    ❑
- not very successful    ❑
- not at all successful    ❑

## D. General opinion on direct participation (DP)

**68. Finally, thinking of the practice of DP, do YOU agree or disagree with the following statements?**

|  | agree | disagree |
|---|---|---|
| - 'DP plays a major role in competitiveness' | ❑ | ❑ |
| - 'DP does not change the fundamental need for managers to use established means of reward and discipline' | ❑ | ❑ |
| - 'DP enhances the role and influence of middle managers'. | ❑ | ❑ |
| - 'DP helps employees to feel involved in the firm' | ❑ | ❑ |
| - 'DP reduces the need for trade unions and other systems of employee representation' | ❑ | ❑ |

**69. Here are some statements about the conditions necessary for DP to work. Thinking of the practice of DP, please indicate how significant IN YOUR VIEW each of the following factors is.**

|  | very significant | significant | not significant |
|---|---|---|---|
| - 'DP requires a long time period for planning and implementation' | ❑ | ❑ | ❑ |
| - 'Active promotion by senior managers is a pre-condition of successful 'DP' | ❑ | ❑ | ❑ |

- 'DP involves radical changes in the
  role of middle managers' ❑ ❑ ❑
- 'DP requires considerable investment
  in vocational training' ❑ ❑ ❑
- 'Training in the social skills necessary
  for DP has to
  be a high priority' ❑ ❑ ❑

70. **Do you expect to introduce within the next two years in your organisation any of the following (other) forms of non-managerial DP as defined in Q. 24a-24d?**

|                                                          | yes | no |
|----------------------------------------------------------|-----|----|
| - consultation with individual employees (Q.24a)         | ❑   | ❑  |
| - consultation with employees on a group basis (Q.24b)   | ❑   | ❑  |
| - decision making by individual employees (Q.24c)        | ❑   | ❑  |
| - decision making by formal groups (Q.24d)               | ❑   | ❑  |

71. **If you ticked any "yes" in Q. 70 (others go to Q. 72):**
    **Why do you expect to introduce DP in your organisation?**

72. **If you ticked any "no" in Q. 70 (others go to Q. 73):**
    **Why do you expect NOT to introduce DP in your organisation?**
    **E. Final Questions**

73. **In what region is your workplace situated?**

74. **What is your job title?**

74.

75. **Fill out:**
    - male ❑
    - female ❑

76. **If you would like to receive a summary of the main findings of this survey, please fill out the following**

    ❑ yes, I would like to receive a summary of the main findings of the survey

    Your name:

    name company:

    address:

    ❑ no, I do not like to receive a summary of the main findings of the survey

77. **These were our questions. If you have any remarks on this survey or on the European Union aspect of it, please use this space to write them down.**

*Thank you for your co-operation!*

# Appendix 3

## Supplementary tables and figures

Figure 5A.1: Patterns of motives in the ten countries - % of respondents practising direct participation

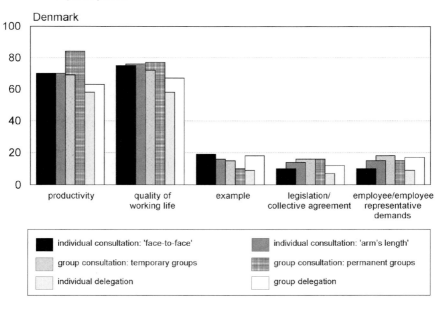

Figure 5A.1: Patterns of motives in the ten countries - % of respondents practising
direct participation

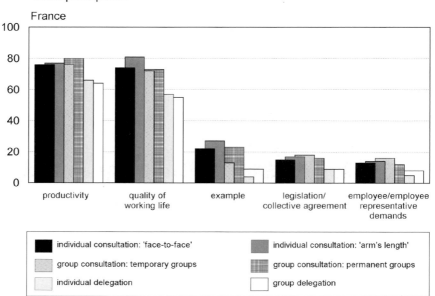

Figure 5A.1: Patterns of motives in the ten countries - % of respondents practising
direct participation

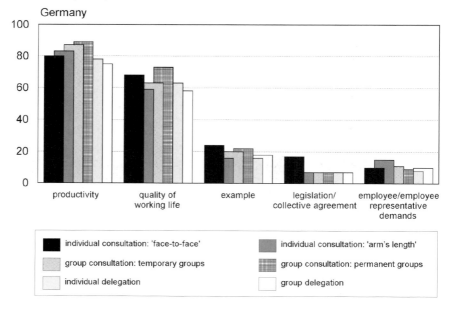

Figure 5A.1: Patterns of motives in the ten countries - % of respondents practising direct participation

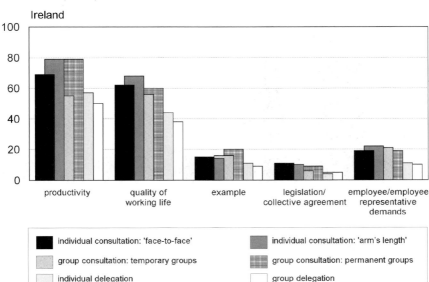

Figure 5A.1: Patterns of motives in the ten countries - % of respondents practising direct participation

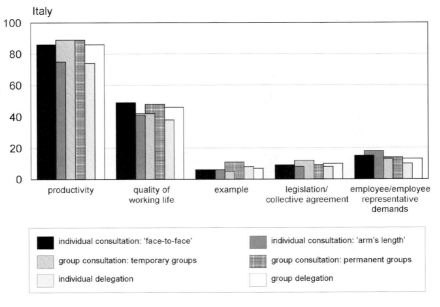

Figure 5A.1: Patterns of motives in the ten countries - % of respondents practising direct participation

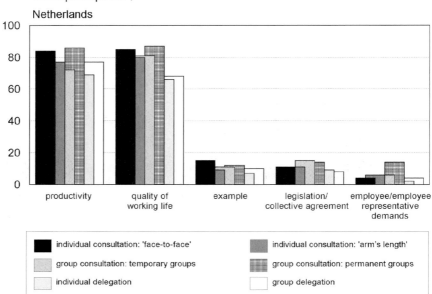

Figure 5A.1: Patterns of motives in the ten countries - % of respondents practising direct participation

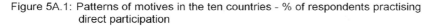

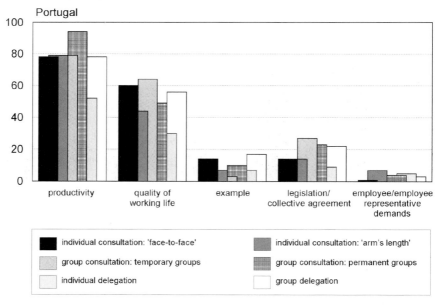

Figure 5A.1: Patterns of motives in the ten countries - % of respondents practising direct participation

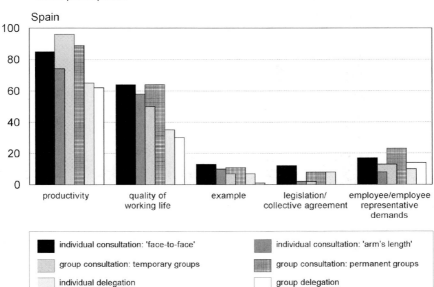

Spain

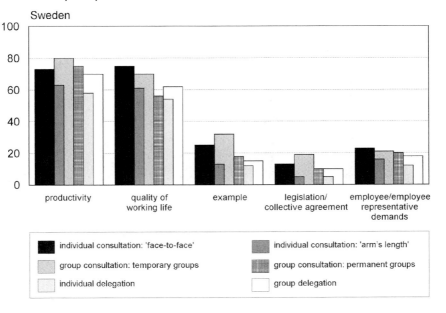

Figure 5A.1: Patterns of motives in the ten countries - % of respondents practising direct participation

Sweden

Figure 5A.1: Patterns of motives in the ten countries - % of respondents practising direct participation

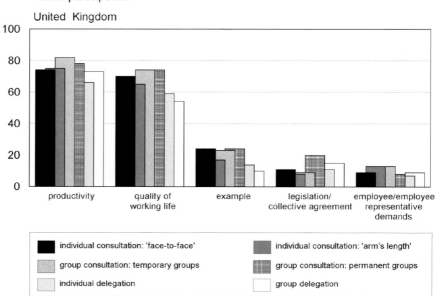

## Table 9A.23  Statement: Investment in vocational training

|  | very significant | significant | not significant |
|---|---|---|---|
| ten-country average | 18 | 50 | 33 |
| Denmark | 9 | 41 | 50 |
| France | 14 | 48 | 37 |
| Germany | 23 | 57 | 21 |
| Ireland | 8 | 52 | 39 |
| Italy | 21 | 43 | 36 |
| Netherlands | 9 | 50 | 41 |
| Portugal | 23 | 37 | 40 |
| Spain | 24 | 68 | 8 |
| Sweden | 12 | 46 | 43 |
| UK | 15 | 42 | 43 |

## Table 9A.24  Statement: Social skill training needed

|  | very significant | significant | not significant |
|---|---|---|---|
| ten-country average | 29 | 53 | 18 |
| Denmark | 25 | 49 | 26 |
| France | 37 | 51 | 12 |
| Germany | 35 | 56 | 9 |
| Ireland | 20 | 58 | 21 |
| Italy | 23 | 52 | 25 |
| Netherlands | 16 | 59 | 25 |
| Portugal | 36 | 49 | 15 |
| Spain | 37 | 47 | 16 |
| Sweden | 31 | 54 | 15 |
| UK | 19 | 50 | 31 |

**Table 9A.25  Qualification requirements by sector**

| sector | very high qualification | very low qualification |
|---|---|---|
| mining | 18 | 13 |
| transport. warehousing and communications | 16 | 6 |
| manufacturing industry | 18 | 6 |
| process industry | 22 | 4 |
| banking and insurances | 20 | 0 |
| professional services | 39 | 10 |
| public utilities | 23 | 7 |
| public administration | 24 | 2 |
| construction and installation | 20 | 2 |
| education | 62 | 3 |
| wholesale | 22 | 3 |
| health and social welfare | 32 | 3 |
| retail trade | 15 | 12 |
| culture and recreation/leisure | 17 | 7 |
| catering, hotels | 8 | 4 |

**Table 9A.26  Skill-oriented workplaces by sector**

| sector | % |
|---|---|
| mining | 3 |
| transport. warehousing and communications | 7 |
| manufacturing industry | 10 |
| process industry | 6 |
| banking and insurances | 21 |
| professional services | 11 |
| public utilities | 7 |
| public administration | 8 |
| construction and installation | 2 |
| education | 20 |
| wholesale | 7 |
| health and social welfare | 6 |
| retail trade | 7 |
| culture and recreation/leisure | 0 |
| catering, hotels | 1 |

### Table 9A.27  Qualification requirements by size

| size of largest occ. group | very high qualification | very low qualification |
|---|---|---|
| 10-14 | 30 | 4 |
| 15-19 | 28 | 5 |
| 20-49 | 28 | 3 |
| 50-99 | 18 | 6 |
| 100-199 | 21 | 8 |
| 200-499 | 22 | 5 |
| 500-999 | 25 | 3 |
| 1000 + | 19 | 4 |

### Table 9A.28  Skill-oriented workplaces by size

| size of largest occ. group | % |
|---|---|
| 10-14 | 8 |
| 15-19 | 3 |
| 20-49 | 7 |
| 50-99 | 8 |
| 100-199 | 11 |
| 200-499 | 13 |
| 500-999 | 11 |
| 1000 + | 19 |

### Table 9A.29  Qualification requirements: % of women in the largest occupational group

| | very high qualification | very low qualification |
|---|---|---|
| >10% | 21 | 4 |
| 10-25% | 30 | 5 |
| 25-50% | 24 | 8 |
| 50-75% | 22 | 7 |
| 75-100% | 23 | 5 |

### Table 9A.30  Skill-oriented workplaces :
### % of women in the largest occupational group

| percentage of women in the largest occupational group | % |
|---|---|
| >10% | 9 |
| 10-25% | 8 |
| 25-50% | 8 |
| 50-75% | 9 |
| 75-100% | 9 |

### Table 9A.31  Qualification requirements (industry): % of women in the largest occupational group

| percentage of women in the largest occupational group | very high qualification | very low qualification |
|---|---|---|
| >10% | 21 | 4 |
| 10-25% | 30 | 5 |
| 25-50% | 24 | 8 |
| 50-75% | 22 | 7 |
| 75-100% | 23 | 5 |

### Table 9A.32  Skill-oriented workplaces (manufacturing): % of women in the largest occupational group

| percentage of women in the largest occupational group | % |
|---|---|
| >10% | 10 |
| 10-25% | 8 |
| 25-50% | 11 |
| 50-75% | 9 |
| 75-100% | 6 |

### Table 9A.33  Qualification requirements (banking/insurances): % of women in the largest occupational     group

| percentage of women in the largest occupational group | very high qualification | very low qualification |
|---|---|---|
| >10% | 40 | 0 |
| 10-25% | 42 | 0 |
| 25-50% | 17 | 1 |
| 50-75% | 16 | 1 |
| 75-100% | 8 | 0 |

### Table 9A.34 Skill-oriented workplaces(banking/insurances): % of women in the largest occupational group

| percentage of women in the largest occupational group | % |
|---|---|
| >10% | * |
| 10-25% | 19 |
| 25-50% | 13 |
| 50-75% | 11 |
| 75-100% | 4 |

European Foundation for the Improvement of Living and Working Conditions

**New forms of work organisation. Can Europe realise its potential?:**
**Results of a survey of direct employee participation in Europe**

Luxembourg: Office for Official Publications of the European Communities

1997 – 252 pp. – 16 x 23,4 cm

ISBN 92-828-1888-8

Price (excluding VAT) in Luxembourg: ECU 30